WOMEN
IN CHAINS

WOMEN
IN CHAINS

A Sourcebook
— *on the* —
Agunah

edited by
Jack Nusan Porter

JASON ARONSON INC.
Northvale, New Jersey
London

Acknowledgments for permission to reprint previously published material appear on pp. 253–255.

This book was set in 10 pt. Times Roman by AeroType, Inc. in Amherst, New Hampshire.

Library of Congress Cataloging-in-Publication Data

Women in chains: A sourcebook on the agunah / compiled by Jack Nusan Porter.
    p. cm.
   Includes bibliographical references and index.
   ISBN 1-56821-440-5
   1. Agunahs. 2. Women in Judaism. I. Porter, Jack Nusan.
  LAW (GENERAL Agunah 1995)
  296.4'44 – dc20   95-9843

Manufactured in the United States of America. Jason Aronson Inc. offers books and cassettes. For information and catalog write to Jason Aronson Inc., 230 Livingston Street, Northvale, New Jersey 07647.

To "Dvorah" and her children and family
and to her sister-*agunot* everywhere
and their families

Contents

Introduction
The *Agunah*—
A Personal Perspective:
Notes on a Sourcebook for
the "Chained Wife"

Jack Nusan Porter

The concept of the *agunah* is a very personal one for me. In the 1960s, my parents and I went through a traumatic and harrowing experience with a neighbor of ours in the Orthodox Jewish community of Milwaukee. Even the greatest rabbis there at the time, Reb Jacob Twerski and Rabbi David Shapiro, stood by helplessly. This experience was so powerful that, like a death in the family, it has taken me over thirty years to bear witness. This book is the end result of that trauma.

It is the story of Dvorah (a pseudonym), her husband, Yakov, and their three beautiful children. She nearly died in a car accident because of the stress of her divorce and the fact that her husband was blackmailing her over custody of their children. For you see, she was an *agunah*, a "chained wife"—a woman unable to marry since her husband would not give her a *get*, a religious divorce. The *agunah* has become one of the most controversial issues in Orthodox Jewish life, and also a poignant one because there are sometimes no "enemies" here. The law itself "chains" the wife. The rabbis themselves, like Reb Twerski and Rabbi Shapiro, condemned Dvorah's husband, the community ostracized him, even my own father Irving (Srulik) Porter, a saintly man whom even the husband respected, could do nothing. We stood by helplessly. We were as "chained" as Dvorah. In fact, we did not even label her an *agunah* back in the 1960s though we knew that something was terribly wrong.

Eventually the blackmail worked: Dvorah's husband took the children to Israel and gave her a *get*. Today, she lives apart from her husband and rarely sees him, although there is some communication and cooperation between them. Time, surprisingly, does heal all wounds. The children have grown up, married, and now have wives and children of their own. Dvorah tells me they turned out all right and were not traumatized. They lead relatively normal lives today, but I am sure they have been affected in some manner by this ordeal as have Dvorah's sister, brother, and parents. I have dedicated this book to my dear friend Dvorah, who has recently remarried and is living happily in the Midwest. In fact, she knows about this sourcebook and has given her *heksher*, her stamp of approval, to it. Thank you, Dvorah.

I have compiled this book in the hope that it will bring solace to women in similar predicaments, showing them that there is hope and that there are organizations to help them. In many ways, the plight of the *agunah* is similar to the plight of abused wives. Indeed, often *agunot* are abused women as are their children. Dvorah and her kids were definitely abused. This embarrassing issue of abuse, kidnapping, and blackmail is finally getting the hearing it deserves.

Life for the *agunah* is a constant state of limbo and even danger from such abuse. Both were common during Dvorah's travail. I still remember the fights in the apartment upstairs and her husband's abuse of their children even in *shul*. The reaction of the men in the temple: please take it outside. It was "disturbing" their prayers.

As noted by Amy Shire in an article in *Jewish Currents* (July–August, 1993, pp. 27–28), the status of the *agunah* is the Jewish equivalent of living in chains: a woman who by Orthodox Jewish law has not been given a Jewish divorce (*get*) by her husband is not free to marry or have "legitimate" children. She is reduced to living in a netherworld where moving forward with her life is impossible. However, this "sin" is caused not by her own actions but by those of a husband who refuses to free her and change her status. (In some cases, a husband may be missing in battle or simply may have disappeared; however, while this may have been true in the past, most *agunot* are of the "chained" variety, "chained" by a very alive husband.)

According to the *Encyclopaedia Judaica* (2:429), the problem of the *agunah* is one of the most complex in halachic discussions and is treated in great detail in the literature. According to the *Responsa Ashrei* (51:2), finding a way for permitting an *agunah* to remarry is deemed a great *mitzvah*. However, the real fear (and barrier) is the danger of legalizing a possibly adulterous union. What is really needed is a new *takkanah*, a new ruling by the *Gedolim*, the Council of Rabbis, but I doubt if we will see this in our lifetime.

Jewish divorce law is unequal in the rights it gives men and women. Not only must the man give a *get* to a woman in order to free her from marriage (but not vice versa), but also any children he may conceive out of wedlock (with an unmarried woman) are considered legitimate, whereas any children conceived by the wife with another man are considered *mamzerim* (bastards). In other words, if an estranged wife chooses to ignore Jewish law and decides to remarry, she is considered an adulteress, whereas the same behavior on the part of the man carries no such stigma! If, however, the second marriage was annulled due to errors in the *ketubah*, the witnessing to it, or the wedding, then the children of her second husband may be legitimate. In short, this is a most complex problem, requiring an astute Orthodox rabbi. (See the sources section in the back of the book for help.)

Since the mid-1980s several groups have been formed to help *agunot* and to mobilize the Jewish community. One of the most important of these groups is called G.E.T. (Getting Equitable Treatment), an organization based in Brooklyn (POB 300 131, 1012 Avenue I, Brooklyn, NY 11230–0003). Another is Agunah, Inc., a Brooklyn-based organization led by Rivka Haut. Agunah, Inc. was established in 1987 to seek societal and halachic solutions to *get* problems.

There are literally thousands of *agunot*. Some say there are over 1,000 in North America and from 5,000 to 16,000 in Israel, with 10,000 cases currently within the Israeli *beit din* (religious court) system, regardless of their status. Thus, we are talking about large numbers of "chained women." However, these figures count *all* women who are waiting for divorce, but not all women who wait for a divorce should be considered *agunot*. If one is more conservative and counts only those women who have *recalcitrant* husbands, there may be only 100 *agunot* in North America and about 1,000 in Israel. In nearly all cases, the husband eventually grants the divorce, and the woman is set free. According to Orthodox rabbis I have talked to, about 5 percent of all Orthodox marriages end in the *agunah* stage. But there are *agunah* groups who disagree and feel that there are thousands of *agunot*, many of whom are silently suffering. Divorce in general, whether religious or secular, is at times a long, painful, and expensive process. The problem of the *get* only adds to the misery. One should not minimize the number but neither should one exaggerate the figures. Even one *agunah* is one too many.

This sourcebook is a compilation of the best articles I could find from the popular press, from scholarly histories, and from literary sources. I hope I am not blamed for what I left out. I have tried to keep the issue as simple as possible because it can become so complex that it may turn off the reader. I have tried to include all points of view. There are both pros and cons in this book, conservative and orthodox viewpoints, as well as a wide range of solutions. They include new legislation, prenuptial agreements, changes in the *ketubah*, grassroot efforts, and community outreach to rabbis and social agencies. (I have also included a glossary to explain the theological concepts used.)

Unless there is a *takkanah*, an authoritative legislative religious decree enacted by duly constituted rabbinic authorities, it is unlikely that the problem will disappear. The last *takkanah*, however, by Rabbeinu Gershom, took place in the year 1000 c.e. It outlawed bigamy. As we approach the second millennium, perhaps a miracle will occur, and a second *takkanah* will appear.

Still, while we wait, there is much to do to lessen the pain of *agunot* and their families and to make life more bearable for them. In short, to give them hope.

This sourcebook describes various solutions to the *agunah* problem. One approach is a prenuptial agreement that would be binding on the husband. The RCA, the Rabbinical Council of America, an organization of 1,000 Orthodox rabbis, unanimously approved a resolution in June 1993 requiring the use of prenuptial agreements in all marriage ceremonies. The resolution also calls for synagogues to ostracize recalcitrant spouses if they do not abide by a rabbinic decision granting a *get* to the wife.

Other approaches include picketing the husband's place of work or his home, shunning him, giving him no honors, maybe even beating him up or imprisoning him.

US/Israel Women to Women, a group that is monitoring the status of *agunot* in Israel, reported that a proposed "Fundamental Human Rights Law" included in a draft constitution for the State of Israel specifies that "nothing in this basic law will in any way affect matters of prohibition and permission in marriage and divorce"—i.e., that religious law predominates. A letter from the Israel Women's Network evaluating whether the law is worth supporting despite its omissions regarding the rights of *agunot*, concluded it is not: "Since inequality in marriage and divorce is the most severe discrimination faced by Israeli women [and since this is not addressed by the human rights bill] . . . it is better to have no law than to have a bad law."

March 4, 1993 marked the launching of the International Year of the *Agunah*, 1993–1994, and US/Israel Women to Women joined with the International Coalition for *Agunah* Rights (ICAR) in Israel to advocate a resolution to the problem of women kept legally and socially imprisoned by a process that they do not and cannot control by themselves, according to Jewish law.

Though the problem of *agunot* is far more common in Israel, where civil marriage ceremonies are not an option, than in the United States, Orthodox women everywhere are affected by this aspect of Jewish law. Thus, the outcome of organizing efforts in Israel in this regard will have ramifications for Jewish women everywhere. (See Amy Shire, op. cit., and Viva Hammer, *Na'amat Women*, March–April 1993; Janet Goller, *Jewish Currents*, November 1989; and *Jewish Currents*, June 1990.)

Yet despite all these actions, one is often *nizrach* (helpless) in these situations. Dvorah finally received her *get* by a painful decision. She gave up custody of her children to her husband until they were adults. Often, a large cash settlement is also necessary. The *agunot* await a solution, and their patience is running out. Often, only the death of a spouse ends the problem.

The *agunah* seems to be one of the "in" issues of the mid-1990s. Why this fascination? There are many reasons, some positive, some negative. First, it shows a deep fissure in the apparently seamless web of Orthodox Jewish life, thus giving people who already dislike Orthodox Jews an additional argument. Second, it is a poignant issue, Here we have intelligent, committed, sophisticated Jewish women who are utterly helpless, "bound and chained," yet why do they remain "chained"? They could leave the faith at any time. Why don't they do so? Why do they remain observant Orthodox Jews? The problem of the *agunah* tests their faith like no other. Third, it is ironic that the great *rabbonim* can give *poskim* (decisions) on virtually every subject on earth, yet seem paralyzed by the plight of the *agunah*. Even the great Rav Moshe Feinstein, blessed be his memory, refused to write a *takkanah* to end the stalemate. Why? It's a question that will be answered in this book. What makes modern-day liberals so fascinated by this topic is the tension between ancient traditions and how they still "chain and bind" contemporary actors.

No wonder, the *agunah* has caught the imagination of writers, novelists, poets, and playwrights through the years—people like Nobel Prize winners S. Y. (Shai) Agnon and Isaac Bashevis Singer, as well as Chaim Grade, Rochelle Majer Krich, Marcus Lehman, and others.

My thoughts of Dvorah and our utter helplessness were brought home to me when my sister, Bella Porter-Smith, recommended a book to read: Rochelle Majer Krich's *Till Death Do Us Part* (Avon Books, 1992). I read the book from start to finish on a plane ride to Los Angeles in the summer of 1992. I couldn't put it down. It was not only an exciting and fast-paced murder mystery, it was also halachically accurate. The author had to be an observant woman to know all the intricacies of the laws concerning *mikveh*, *tahara*, and *kiddushin*.

I hope this sourcebook will spark your imagination as well, but mostly I hope to engage and enrage you, dear reader.

*   *   *   *   *

Part I of this sourcebook begins with several popular contemporary articles about the problem here in the United States. New York is the center of Orthodox Jewry and the national media; therefore there are contemporary essays from the *Village Voice* by Lucette Lagnado (then a reporter for the *Voice* but now the editor of *The Forward*) and from *New York Magazine* by Peter Hellman.

Part II deals with *agunot* in Israel, with reports from the *Washington Post* by Glenn Frankel, *Women's League Outlook* by Sharon Shenhav, and *The Jerusalem Report* by Netty C. Gross.

Part III is an overview of historical and halachic issues in both Israel and America. Irwin H. Haut gives us a majestic sweep of divorce in Jewish law; Moshe Meiselman gives us a short but brilliant history of *agunot* research and activism; and Moshe Chigier presents a more in-depth overview of problems facing the *agunah* in Israeli rabbinical courts.

Meiselman's essay is very important in understanding the history of intervention from Lewis Epstein to Saul Lieberman to Eliezer Berkovits, Edward Gershfield, Ze'ev Falk, Irwin Haut, Meyer S. Feldblum, and Emanuel Rackman. Some approached the issue from a modern Orthodox perspective, others as Orthodox rabbis but within Conservative Judaism. Meiselman is himself a widely read scholar in Orthodox circles and should be read in conjunction with another important work by a Jewish theologian, Blu Greenberg's *On Women and Judaism: A View from Tradition*, and her very important section called "Jewish Attitudes Toward Divorce."

Part IV contains literary sources from classic writers such as Isaac Bashevis Singer and S. Y. Agnon as well as a modern interpretation by Los Angeles mystery writer Rochelle Majer Krich. S. Y. Agnon's story "Agunot" is very mystical and difficult. In fact, Agnon's own name (it originally was Czaczkes) is a variation of *agunah*, for he felt he himself was "chained" like an *agunah*. I. B. Singer's short story "Taibele and Her Demon" is also mystical but more fun-loving.

Debates, both pro and con, are common and lead to enlightenment. Part V contains debates and confrontations. *The Jewish Homemaker*, a popular kosher food guide, asks whether the "system is working" with regard to the granting of a *get* to *agunot*. Activists in Agunah, Inc. of New York City (Susan Aranoff, Rivka Haut, and Susan Alter) say no, it is not working, while Rabbi Leib Landesman, the *rosh beit din*, head of the religious court in Monsey, New York, takes a different view and says it is working despite the claims of "crisis."

Another confrontation is over the New York "Get" bill, this time between Chaim Zwiebel and Marvin Jacob. One possible solution to the problem, the so-called Silver Bill, was introduced by Speaker of the New York State

Assembly Sheldon Silver and enacted in July 1992. The first "get" bill was not very good. It was used only if the man was the plaintiff, not the woman, and it said that the man could not get a civil divorce unless he had already given a religious *get*. This bill proved ineffective. A second "*get*" bill, the Equitable Distribution Law, provided that upon dissolution of a marriage the court shall consider the existence of a "barrier to remarriage" (such as being an *agunah*) in determining the disposition of marital property. In other words, if a man will not give his wife a *get*, the courts can take that into consideration and reward the wife much more in damages and marital property than usual. For example, instead of a fifty-fifty split, the courts can award the wife 100 percent of all assets unless the husband gives a *get*. When he gives the *get*, he will get his 50 percent back. This bill had a few more "teeth" in it. However, it is being used by rabbis against women. Rabbis and *battei dinim* are telling women that if they go to secular courts and apply the "Silver Bill," they will not be allowed to settle the case in religious courts, a mendacious abuse of power and threat—but it has worked. Thus, some pro-*agunah* groups like Agunah, Inc. are ambivalent about the bill.

Agudath Israel, in the article by Chaim Dovid Zwiebel, disagrees with both bills. Marvin Jacob, on the other hand, says Agudath Israel "misperceives" the bill, that while it may perhaps be a form of "pressure," it is not really "duress" or "coercion." To coerce a husband to give a *get* is illegal halachically, but to pressure him until he "decides" to come around and give the *get* is acceptable. Again, these arguments are complex and controversial, but such is *pilpul*.

Part VI contains articles from an Orthodox perspective by Rabbi Shlomo Riskin and from a Conservative point of view by Rabbi Sidney Schwarz. Reform and Reconstructionism are not considered since they reject the idea of male dominance in divorce and domestic issues, and women in their congregations do not hold to a traditional halachic interpretation of *agunah*, or as Blu Greenberg notes in her book *On Women and Judaism*:

> Several solutions have been formulated in modern times. Reform Judaism understood the Halacha to be indefensible in terms of the ethical and social categories central to Reform, so it simply dropped *gittin* and said civil divorce will do. If one is concerned more for equality than for tradition, that solution meets the test. If, however, one's commitment is to both more equality and greater Jewish observance in every sphere of life, then that is no solution at all. . . .
>
> Reconstructionism has formulated a solution that lies somewhere between the two ends of the spectrum—or, more correctly, at the two ends of the spectrum. The Reconstructionist rabbinate uses the traditional *get* and all of the attendant procedures. When a previously divorced woman wants to

remarry but has been unable to secure a *get* from her former husband, the Reconstructionist *bet din* simply gave her a *shtar piturin*, a document that declares her free to remarry, even though she has no *get*, nor has her marriage been annulled.

In short, Reform and Reconstructionist women are thus "not chained" eternally and neither are most Conservative women for that matter. The only reason why Conservative Judaism is concerned with this issue is that at its core, Conservative Judaism is "orthodox," and its rabbis are often Orthodox. In other words, there is a consensus and a desire to preserve its legitimacy vis-à-vis the Jewish tradition. This requires that every action be defensible along halachic lines.

According to Greenberg, Conservative Judaism has gone through three stages of emendation in an attempt to eliminate abuse yet remain faithful to tradition. First, under Rabbi Saul Lieberman in 1954, there was the Lieberman *ketubah* with an appendage, a *t'nai* (a conditional clause) added stating that if a marriage ends in civil divorce, either party can invoke the authority of the *bet din* to determine the Jewish course of action, or a *get*. The Lieberman clause was rejected by most Orthodox rabbis as being halachically invalid because of its indeterminate and vague nature, since the amount of damages (*knas*) was not spelled out.

The second stage came with Eliezer Berkovits's *t'nai* in 1968, which differed from the Lieberman solution in that it attached conditions to the act of marriage itself. Berkovits based his *t'nai*, his conditional clause, on procedures to anull a marriage by rabbinic authorities if certain conditions were not met. This proposal was rejected by the Orthodox *rabbonim* on the grounds that marriage is an unconditional commitment and conditional marriages and divorces are rendered invalid by consummation of the marriage.

The third stage, used widely today in Conservative circles according to Blu Greenberg, is a broader application of *havka'at kiddushin* (the power of rabbis to annul marriages *ab initio*—from *Bava Batra* 48b, *Gittin* 33a, and *Kiddushin* 3a). It is based on the talmudic principle that all who marry within the Jewish community do so with the implied consent of and under the conditions laid down by the rabbis (from the phrase at the *chuppah* "according to laws of Moses and Israel—"*k'das Moshe v'yisroel*"). Thus, a man's act of marrying a woman is validated by the rabbi's sanction of that act, not only because of *halachah*. This, too, naturally has been rejected by Orthodox authorities.

Still, both Conservative and Orthodox rabbis admit that the *agunah* issue cries out for solution. It truly tests the mettle, as Rabbi Schwarz writes, of Conservative Judaism's claim that it can remain halachic even as it allows for change. Other examples of such change are a woman's right to become a rabbi and attitudes toward homosexuality and lesbianism.

The sourcebook concludes with Part VII, a section on solutions: prenuptial agreements, legislative acts, grassroots efforts, jail time, peer pressure, ostracism, excommunication, and community coercion. Since in our secular society such pressure relies on communal will, it is sporadic. The man simply moves to a new community where no one knows him. Time goes by and people forget. Still, education of judges, lawyers, and rabbis is essential. Since the rise of Agunah, Inc., G.E.T., and other organizations helping *agunot*, there has been a definite decrease in *agunot* chained forever and an increase in *agunot* gaining their freedom. Activism definitely works, yet change in Orthodox circles moves at a snail's pace.

Steven Feldman gives a good overview of such solutions, and that is why his article, although written over a decade ago, is still valid today. Little has changed. Honey Rackman in a *Moment* essay, continues the saga. We conclude with a column by Francine Klagsbrun that highlights the Year of the *Agunah*. Her plea is simple: we must put the *agunah* and related problems on our personal and communal agendas, and if we do we can indeed save these "chained women."

$$* \quad * \quad * \quad * \quad *$$

When I started this work, I thought that the material was so complex that I was either totally naive or chutzpadik to do this sourcebook—or perhaps both. Luckily, I have relied on a whole group of experts and consultants to help me, very few of whom I have actually met face-to-face. Mostly, our contacts have been by phone, but I feel I have known them for years. The first group I contacted, through the good offices of Dr. Rifkeh Danzig and Dr. Saul Wachs, was G.E.T. in Brooklyn, New York. Stanley Goodman, Dr. Norman Tokayer, and the entire staff, especially Ruth Englard, were very helpful. Attorneys Irwin Haut and Marvin Jacob are the two premier legal experts on the *agunah* in America. I wish to thank both of them for not only clarifying this complicated issue but also allowing their work to be published in this sourcebook. Though I have not met them, Rivka Haut, Naomi Klass, and Blu Greenberg should also be thanked for their long-time devotion to this problem. Haut and Greenberg have almost reached the level of "theologians" in their interpretation of *halachah*.

In terms of reference, what would we do without librarians and researchers? I must thank Jason Sanders, a Brandeis University graduate student in Near Eastern and Jewish Studies, for being my research assistant and uncovering so many worthwhile sources, both as articles for this sourcebook and items for the bibliography. I would never have found them on my own. Thank you, Jason. At Brandeis as well, I thank Professor Sylvia Barack Fishman for helping me to clarify and expand my knowledge of American-Jewish literature dealing with *agunot* and women's rights. Thank you, Sylvia.

I'd also like to thank Zalmen Alpert, reference librarian of the Mendel Gottesman Library of Yeshiva University, for many interesting leads, especially to Rabbis Leib Landesman and Herschel Kurzrock. Marvin Tuchman and his staff at Hebrew College of Brookline, Massachusetts, and Charlotte Keys, reference librarian at Brandeis University, should also be mentioned. Samuel Gross of Sepher-Hermon Press, a scholar as well as a publisher, helped me clarify some terms in the glossary.

My sister, Bella Porter-Smith, of Minneapolis, first introduced me to Rochelle Majer Krich's mystery novel *Till Death Do Us Part*. This sparked my interest and rekindled my own trauma regarding an *agunah*, and I contacted Rochelle Majer Krich in Los Angeles. We've had several poignant telephone conversations, and she's been most supportive of this book. I thank her for allowing me to reprint a section from this important mystery.

Nearly two decades ago, I wrote a very unhalachic analysis of sex and Judaism (see For Further Reading), which my brother Shlomo told me raised a few eyebrows in yeshivah circles, especially at the Ner Israel Yeshiva of Baltimore, with its executive director, Rabbi Herman Neuberger. Shlomo, I'm afraid I've done it again. Forgive me for treading on rabbinical ground once more, and forgive any mistakes I've made. My intentions were honorable even though I know nothing of *halachah*.

My beloved mother, Faygeh Porter-Arenzon, and my late father, Reb Yisroel Porter (Puchtik), both devout and respected Jews, laid the foundation for my interest in all things Jewish, and I must also thank my sister, Bella Porter-Smith, and her husband, Rabbi Mitch Smith, and their kids for their love and moral support, and also my late stepfather, Juda Arenzon, and his family.

Lastly, I thank "Dvorah." Her three sons, her parents, her sister, and brother, and the rest of her family have had to suffer and endure her status as an *agunah* for many years. (I have, by the way, reconnected with her husband, Yakov, after thirty years. As an *agun*, he too has a point of view that should be heard.) I dedicate this book to "Dvorah" with love from me and my entire family and to *agunot* everywhere. May they break their chains of bondage speedily and in our day.

I

Essays in the Popular Press: The American Situation

1
Of Human Bondage

Lucette Lagnado

A man takes a wife and possesses her. If she fails to please him, and she is obnoxious to him, he shall write her a bill of divorcement, hand it to her, and send her away from his house.

—Deuteronomy 24:1

Her apartment is dark and quiet, on a side street in Flatbush. It's a neighborhood of large families, where the men wear yarmulkes and the women walk with numerous children in tow. Mrs. A., however, lives alone, in a small apartment remarkable for its emptiness, its spotlessness, and the sense it conveys of absolute loneliness.

Mrs. A. is a deeply religious woman who wears long, modest dresses in accordance with Orthodox Jewish tradition. Although estranged from her husband for four years, she continues to wear a *sheitel*, the wig that covers her shorn hair, as is required of all married women. She was married for "over 30" years and has "several" children—precisely how many, she will not say.

Mrs. A. won't be more specific because she is terrified. She dreads being part of an article that might reflect badly on her beloved *rebbes*. She fears what her husband might do to her, and as we talk, she keeps looking around the apartment, as if expecting him to enter at any minute and start breaking the furniture, smashing the windows, and threatening to kill her. Most of all, Mrs. A. fears that, if her identity becomes known, her community will ostracize her even more than its members already have. Hers is a world that does not have much use for a woman alone.

"I had my rebellion at an old age," she says with a slight smile. "It took a tremendous effort to pack up and leave, but that is what I did." Until then,

3

"my husband knew he could take advantage of me." With several children to support, and no professional skills, Mrs. A. clung to a bad marriage, even as she plotted the means of escape. She began to teach—one of the few jobs acceptable for a woman from her sheltered world. One day in 1988, Mrs. A. maintains, her husband threatened to kill her. Leaving all her belongings behind, she made her move.

Since then, she has been locked in a battle to win a civil divorce. Her husband, a lawyer, is representing himself in the case. He spends his days badgering her attorney with motions and countermotions. Skilled in the art of manipulating judges, he has obtained one adjournment after another. But even more important to Mrs. A. than any civil divorce is the *get*. A key requirement under Orthodox, and even Conservative Judaic law, the *get* is a rabbinical dissolution of the marriage vows. The Bible stipulates that it can only be granted with the consent of the husband: he must freely offer his wife a bill of divorcement, and literally place it in her hand.

Mr. A. has adamantly refused to grant his wife a *get*. Without it, she is still considered married. The Bible states that she may not remarry. She is not even allowed to date, lest she be branded as an adulteress. And if she does remarry, the children from that union are regarded as *mamzerim*, bastards who are only allowed to marry other illegitimate children.

Mrs. A. is in limbo, trapped and befuddled by her faith. She has become an *agunah*. The word in Hebrew means "a woman in chains." It once referred to slaves in the galley of a ship whose arms and legs were bound together. The *agunot* of today are a new class of galley slaves—women shackled to dead marriages, powerless to get on with their lives. "We tend to be a hidden group," says Mrs. A. "I would not call it a stigma, exactly, but people do not know what to do with us. We are not widows—we do not have the respectability of widows. We are not married. And we are not divorced. It is like living in a no-man's-land."

Mrs. A.'s plight may seem like something out of the Old Testament, or even the 19th-century shtetls of Eastern Europe. In fact, it is a modern problem, affecting thousands of Jewish women all over America—and for that matter, the world. As Jews have become more assimilated, their divorce rate is soaring, and not even the observant are immune to this trend. Nearly one out of three Jewish marriages ends in divorce, and the rate is close to one out of five among the Orthodox—far higher than it was even a decade ago. No one knows how many Jewish women are refused divorces. In Israel, records indicate that there are 10,000 *agunot*. No one knows for sure how many Jewish American women are living in human bondage. [In 1991] several Jewish women's groups asked the United Jewish Appeal to keep records on divorced couples who obtained a *get*. So far, the data have not been made available.

In olden days, the typical *agunah* was someone whose husband had gone off to war and never returned. More recently, after the Holocaust, there were tens of thousands of such women. Although certain their spouses had perished in Auschwitz or Treblinka, they had no proof. They, too, were in limbo until a rabbi could resolve their dilemma by declaring them widows.

There have always been problems with recalcitrant husbands, but in the shtetls of Eastern Europe such men were dealt with ruthlessly. The local rabbis would denounce them from the pulpit, ban them from centers of worship, demand that the community boycott their business, declare them to be pariahs, and, when necessary, stone them out of town.

But times have changed. The shtetls of Eastern Europe are long gone, and rabbinical authority has ebbed. Nowhere in the world, not even in Israel, can they force a man to give his wife a *get*. And the old strategies of coercion have broken down. Stoning is out of favor, and even excommunication has lost its sting. In a neighborhood like Borough Park, a Jew banished from one congregation will be welcomed in the shul around the corner. In communities where observant men are scarce, rabbis may be reluctant to banish any male, since Jewish law requires 10 men for a minyan, without which a service cannot be held.

That same law grants men total control over the process of divorce. Indeed, if a wife refuses to accept a *get*, her husband can request a court of 100 rabbis to issue the divorce. Or he can forgo the *get* and remarry without running the risk that his children will be considered bastards, thanks to a remnant of the Old Testament law that men may have more than one wife. Needless to say, none of these options apply to women. And until recently, not even the civil courts were willing to help break an *agunah's* chains. Judges were reluctant to involve themselves in the granting of a *get*, because of concerns about maintaining the separation between church and state.

The one venue open to these women has been the *Beth Din*, a rabbinical court comprised of three pious men. Once upon a time, these rabbis could compel a husband to appear before them, but these days, such orders are often disregarded. "In the old days, if the rabbi called, you came. Even if you were an apostate, you came, not like nowadays," says Rabbi Herschel Kurzrock. He presides over a *Beth Din* run by the Rabbinical Alliance of America that's helped *agunot* obtain divorces for the past 15 years. The Kurzrock Court is said to be one of the few sympathetic to women, but he defends his fellow rabbis against charges that they don't do enough. "The level of respect for a rabbi is not what it used to be," Kurzrock laments.

One *agunah* sees the situation differently: "There are no great rabbis nowadays. They are not strong enough. They are afraid of their own shadows." She longs for the days when rabbis imposed corporal punishment on a man who refused to give a *get*. "According to Jewish law, the rabbis could give a man like my husband *machas*. They would beat him up themselves. They would beat him and beat him and beat him until he agreed to give the *get*."

The decline of rabbinical authority has driven these women to unorthodox extremes. A secret order of enforcers has sprung up to make unwilling husbands an offer they can't refuse. They are called "Hasidic terrorists," and they are the Orthodox equivalent of John Gotti's capos. The word among the *agunot* is that one such Brooklyn gang is especially effective. They've been known to kidnap a recalcitrant spouse, spirit him off to a cemetery, pummel him next to a grave, and tell him: "This is where you'll end up if you don't give your wife a *get*."

The rabbis themselves are not opposed to the use of extreme measures in the case of a difficult spouse. One sage recalls how one husband was lured to a hotel room, where a group of rabbis decided to take care of him themselves. They prepared a pot of hot water and threatened to plunge his head into it. The plot was foiled when the husband managed to escape. Such stories are a cross between Isaac Bashevis Singer and Franz Kafka. It is as if the veil over centuries of tradition had lifted, revealing the dark side of the Jewish soul.

Consider the *zayde* (grandfather) from Montreal, wracked by guilt over having arranged a match for his granddaughter with a man who left her. He tried in vain to secure her a *get*, but the husband had run off to New York. The *zayde* paid a detective to stake out famous Kosher eateries until he finally located the runaway spouse. The detective tailed him to a small Williamsburg study hall. The *zayde* arrived, bringing with him a suitcase filled with $250,000 in cash, and a scribe who could write a *get*. "I am an old man," he pleaded. "If you sign now, the money is yours. If you don't sign, I will die, and my sons will see that you never get a penny." The *zayde* got the *get*.

Attorney Dennis Rapps has his own favorite tale: a man walks into his office, saying he'd married a Holocaust survivor who failed to tell him she had contracted tuberculosis in the death camps. Now, the couple is separated, but he does not want to give his wife a *get* unless she turns over money she received in war reparations from the Germans. Will Rapps represent him? Will he take on an *agunah* in a courtroom? Can he get him the money? "I gave him one minute to get out of my office," Rapps recalls.

"The men are perverting the religion," says Rapps, an *agunot* law activist. "They are taking advantage of the fact that these women choose to uphold the letter of the law." According to Rapps, the laws governing marriage were never meant to victimize women. Indeed, compared to

Catholicism, divorce was no more complicated than revoking a contract. But now, the *get* has become a powerful negotiating tool during a divorce. The mere threat of withholding it gives a man a tremendous advantage. He can make all sorts of demands. He can force his wife to waive alimony and child support. He can insist on custody of the children. And if a woman's family is wealthy, he can shake them down.

Yehudah Schwartz went to work for *The Jewish Press* in 1962. The young rabbi started at the bottom, operating the old linotype machines. He was well-spoken, charming, and dapper, and he caught the eye of the publisher's daughter, Naomi Klass. The two made a lovely couple, everyone agreed, and Yehudah and Naomi were married in 1966. After a lengthy sojourn in Israel, they eventually settled in Brooklyn, in a stunning house in Manhattan Beach that had been purchased by *The Jewish Press*. Meanwhile Rabbi Schwartz's career in journalism had skyrocketed. He was now a columnist at *The Jewish Press* and managing editor of the 100,000–circulation weekly. The little linotypist from Brooklyn was raking in about $300,000 a year.

But even as Yehudah's role at the paper grew greater, his relationship with his father-in-law grew worse. The two clashed regularly over the younger man's grand vision for *The Jewish Press*. He wanted to build a skyscraper on the site of the newspaper office, which is lodged in a squat warehouse along the Gowanus Canal. Yehudah's difficulties at the office presaged his problems at home. Although he refers to those early years as "blissful," his wife doesn't quite agree. She had him evicted from the house in 1988. His Lincoln Continental, property of *The Jewish Press*, was towed away at Sholom Klass's request. In her divorce papers, Naomi painted a picture of a spouse who regularly abused her. Judge William Rigler apparently agreed: he granted her a divorce on the grounds of cruel and inhuman treatment.

According to the judge's memorandum. Yehudah Schwartz would taunt his wife in front of their children, calling her "a whore," "a witch," and "a Hungarian gypsy." When a male friend of the family – a doctor – moved into the house after his wife had died, Yehudah accused Naomi of having an affair with him. At one point, he apparently became convinced that the spirit of the doctor's late wife had entered Naomi's body. Yehudah began to follow her around the house, blowing his shofar, a ceremonial ram's horn that makes a trumpetlike bleat. "He would say the noise would drive the evil spirit (Dybbuk) from her body," Judge Rigler wrote. In her depression, Naomi gained 100 pounds.

The case of *Schwartz v. Schwartz* has rocked the Orthodox community, with every sensational development bannered on the pages of *The Jewish Press*. That's because Yehudah Schwartz has refused to grant his wife a *get*, and Rabbi Klass has not been shy about using his paper to showcase his daughter's plight. This ultraconservative weekly has become a militant crusader on behalf of the *agunot*. Its pages regularly criticize the rabbis, the civil courts, and the recalcitrant husbands, demanding reform.

Rabbi Klass declined to be interviewed, but his attorney says he has been motivated both out of love for his daughter and fear of losing control of his newspaper to a man he despises. For at the heart of Yehudah Schwartz's refusal to grant a *get* is his request for "equitable distribution of marital assets." The newspaper's attorney says Schwartz has asked for 12 shares of *The Jewish Press* or anywhere from $750,000 to $4 million. (*The Jewish Press* contends the shares are worth $500 each.) Lately, according to the newspaper's attorney, Yehudah has been asking for a cool million. That's the price of a *get* for the publisher's daughter.

Yehudah Schwartz likes to compare his running battle with *The Jewish Press* to that of David fighting Goliath. He denies that he victimized his wife, and strongly suggests she was guilty of adultery. "How can she be an *agunah*? We are still married." Naomi declined to comment.

For an underdog, Yehudah has chosen his legal counsel very well. He is being represented by Anthony Genovesi, the powerful state assembly member who doubles as a Court Street lawyer. Genovesi did not mince words: "In this particular case, he is the victim, not her. You have a man in his fifties—he ran the damn paper. They want to run him into the ground." As for Yehudah's attempt to seize a chunk of the nation's leading Jewish weekly, Genovesi advised: "Do not think of this as a piece of *The Jewish Press*. Suppose she owned shares of General Motors."

Suppose she owned nothing at all. Suppose she was Joan Birn of the Bronx, with nothing except the spunk to cast herself as a political prisoner.

"My husband had a terrific deal," Joan recalls. "I cooked his meals, I washed his clothes, I took care of his children, and whenever he felt frustrated, he'd hit me." In the 10 years of her marriage, Joan's husband, Joe, lost one job after another; one business venture after another failed, from his photography to his taxicab. She supported the family by working as a computer programmer. Her job in Manhattan was a welcome escape from the violence at home, where the beatings had become unrelenting. The pattern was always the same: he never punched her in the face, where neighbors would see the marks, but struck her instead on the arms, where they were concealed by her long sleeves.

As is often the case in abusive households, the violence intensified, and Joan became frightened for her children. The first time he lashed out at their two young daughters, Joan took her two girls and walked out, leaving him everything else, including their apartment, where he lives to this day. Her husband continues to shadow her. He has taken to accosting her every

Saturday after services, and insists on walking with her and the children. He takes the view that they are still married, that she belongs to him.

Joan's husband denies having abused her either physically or emotionally. He expresses shock that she deserted him; complains of how difficult it is for him to live without his daughters; and notes that, as recently as last Passover, he offered to pay for his wife's stay at a Catskills hotel if she attended a seder with him. As for the divorce, he says he was upset over his wife's choice of a rabbinical court: if she had gone to another of his choosing, he might have been more inclined to grant her a *get*.

Joan is now divorced in the eyes of New York State—but she remains an *agunah*. Only 33 when she separated, Joan has not had a date in the five intervening years.

"It's a terrible, lonely life," she says. "As a religious person, I wonder: 'What have I ever done to deserve this punishment?' " Joan is still enraged when she recalls the reaction of the rabbis as she contemplated leaving her husband. They cautioned her against it, even as she described in graphic detail the abuse she had endured. In their minds, the primary goal was keeping the marriage intact: better she should continue to be abused than become an *agunah*.

After the separation they weren't much better. Joan recalls making one appeal after another to the rabbinical court. She describes endless arguments with her rabbi to take a tougher stand toward her husband, who was still welcome at their synagogue. In her frustration, she formed a Free Joan Birn Committee, complete with flyers distributed throughout the neighborhood. As a result, she succeeded in getting her husband banned from synagogues throughout the Bronx.

That was Joan Birn's first act of rebellion. Now she is contemplating something even more defiant: "At some point, I may even go out and try to date," she confides. And when she says it, Joan sounds as if she were about to commit a crime.

Shocking as it may seem, the anguish of a woman like Joan Birn may be a price the rabbis are willing to pay in favor of a greater goal: keeping divorce rates low in the Jewish community. The *agunot* serve a useful purpose to the rabbinical establishment: A woman is encouraged to stay in a nightmarish marriage because she does not want to end up as a woman in chains. "The rabbis are afraid of change," observes Aviva Hammer, a Jewish feminist lawyer from Australia. "They think, 'if we give these women divorces like it's nothing, what is going to happen to our society?' "

But in fact, the horror of her situation can propel an *agunah* to leave the faith. For Deborah Eiferman, a retired professor of sociology at Brooklyn College, such a defection is a tragedy. "They leave the fold, they remarry without the *get*, and we have lost her. We have lost her children. We have lost her children's children. It is a diminution of the Jewish community."

Moved by tales of the *agunot*, Eiferman has become an activist on their behalf. Ten years ago, she founded Get Equitable Treatment, or GET, the first group to grapple with the problems of Jewish divorce. It does everything from counseling distraught women to running boat rides for *agunot*. Eiferman's group is considered moderate in its tactics. GET believes in quiet, behind-the-scenes negotiations. But the growing number of *agunot* and their willingness to organize have spurred more confrontational groups. Prominent among them is AGUNAH, which was started by Brooklyn City Council Member Susan Alter. Its members have marched through Borough Park and Flatbush, carrying signs with the names of recalcitrant husbands; they have picketed synagogues that allowed such men into their sanctuaries, and rallied outside their workplaces. They have even written to major Jewish groups demanding that rabbinical courts known to be unfair to women have their funds cut off.

The rabbis have reacted with indignation. Is it not a heresy to argue that a biblical solution is possible? Case in point: Last month, AGUNAH held a major symposium on the problem of the women in chains. They invited over 500 rabbis: only 19 showed up. AGUNAH is so threatening to the patriarchal order that these women are being accused of "rabbi bashing." The power of these men is such that neither Alter nor her board members would agree to be interviewed for this piece. They fear that exposing the situation will make it harder for them to foster reform.

Little by little, the genteel world of Orthodox womanhood is waking up. Women are forming the Jewish equivalent of consciousness-raising groups, and issuing challenges to rabbinical authority. It is as radical and seditious a movement as the Orthodox community has ever produced. Twenty years after Gloria Steinem founded *Ms.* magazine, feminism has come to Borough Park.

"The Jewish law will never change," says Elaine Rudnick Sheps, a prominent divorce lawyer who has represented numerous *agunot*. Dennis Rapps, the *Jewish Press* attorney, agrees: the solution to the plight of the *agunah* lies not in the Bible but in the courtroom. Sheps and Rapps are part of the growing army of lawyers who are taking *get* cases to court. There is no other way, they argue, to force a man to give a *get*.

The past few months have seen two extraordinary breakthroughs that could liberate the women in chains. In the *Jewish Press* case, Rapps went into court and made the refusal of Yehudah Schwartz to give a *get* the central issue. That refusal, he argued, was enough to scuttle Yehudah's claim on the paper's assets. On March 11, Judge Rigler handed down a decision that was viewed as a major victory for *agunot*. Rigler noted how Jewish law "gives tremendous power to a husband in a divorce proceeding." He observed how, "without the husband's consent, the wife will not be free to remarry." He wrote that "the disparity of power has not gone unnoticed." And he concluded that a man's failure to give a *get* may be a factor when a judge presides over the division of the marital assets.

According to the advocates, the implications of Rigler's decision are enormous. A judge has now said that, regardless of religious procedures, a recalcitrant husband can be penalized where it hurts the most: in his wallet. "It's the first time that a court is giving legal significance to a husband's refusal to give a *get*," says Sheps.

The flamboyant 68-year-old attorney may have won an even greater victory recently when she took as her client a 24-year-old Orthodox woman named Raizie Golding. Raizie was not an *agunah*: she had given up a fortune for her *get*.

They call themselves Uncle Moishy and the Mitzvah Men, and they're wildly popular both with Orthodox Jewish children and their parents. Uncle Moishy records and tapes are sold in most Judaica stores, and by any estimation they're on top of the Jewish Hit Parade. Each cassette is a kind of morality play, teaching children how to be good boys and girls. An especially catch tune has Uncle Moishy telling a child of the need to observe the Sabbath. Religion is more important than money, and he must be observant, even if it means forgoing a fortune in extra pay.

The man behind the Uncle Moishy tapes is David Golding, a young music producer from Manhattan whose recent divorce is a page out of a Jewish *immorality* play. David and Raizie Golding had been married slightly over a year when the marriage fell apart. The Orthodox community was astonished. They had seemed such a dazzling couple. He was young and successful, yet very religious; Raizie, his chosen, was a great beauty, with a head on her shoulders: She was an excellent accountant. When the couple decided to divorce, David Golding informed Raizie that if she wanted her *get*, she would have to renounce any claims to his money. (She was offered half the value of the house.) He demanded she sign a document in the presence of several rabbis—his and hers—relinquishing her claim. Raizie recalls appealing to the rabbis, but no one seemed ready to take her side.

Panic-stricken at the notion of being an *agunah* at 24, Raizie says she meekly agreed. "Basically, I had a gun pointed to my head, and if I wanted my freedom, I had to sign. I didn't have weeks to think about it. It was a case of 'sign the paper or else.' " Raizie has bitter memories of how the rabbis behaved toward her, saying they simply sided with the party who had the most money. "Sure, there are rabbis who are sincere and well-meaning. But others are not so straight. They are swayed by money. And then there are rabbis from the old school who are used to the man having the extra power." Either way, the woman loses.

Raizie decided to fight the power. She contacted Elaine Sheps, who agreed to take her case. Although the marriage had been brief, Raizie claimed she'd helped the Uncle Moishy empire by coming up with ideas and titles for songs, and was consequently entitled to some of its proceeds. In the discovery process, Raizie and her lawyer learned that the Uncle Moishy fortune was greater than either of them had believed. Sheps claims there are hidden accounts overseas. "At the time she signed the agreement, she had no idea he had so much income," says Sheps.

"Fortune? What fortune?" says Richard Kurtz, David Golding's former attorney. "What are we dealing with here, the Beatles? Only the extreme Orthodox listen to this music. You are talking about a small business. You are talking about a one-year marriage. She contributed *nothing* to the business."

A few weeks ago, Raizie won a stunning victory, when the Court of Appeals upheld a prior decision voiding the agreement, saying she had signed it under duress. The papers relinquishing all claims to Uncle Moishy were deemed null and void. The case of *Golding v. Golding* is not wrapped up yet. The court is still reviewing how much she is entitled to receive from the Mitzvah Men.

Rabbi Kurzrock, like many of his colleagues, insists that, even in the face of social crisis, the word of God cannot be tampered with. "The Law is the Law," he says, pounding his fist on the table, "There are people who abuse the law, but you cannot make up a new law."

But the *agunot*, and the women who support their cause, are not so sure. They believe that, even within the confines of Orthodoxy, rabbis have the power to free them from bondage. Is it the fault of the religion that they choose not to do so? Or is it the fault of the rabbis themselves? The women have a ready answer: The problem is not biblical, but sexist. "The beauty of the Torah is that it's a living, flexible document," observes Deborah Eiferman. "Down through the ages, it has been interpreted and reinterpreted, explained and commented upon. My feeling is the problem lies with the men who are doing the interpreting. I think we have to make rabbinical scholars sensitive to the needs of women."

There are hints of progress, whispers of reform among the rabbis. Several of them now endorse the notion of a prenuptial agreement that would guarantee a woman her *get* in the event of a divorce. Among the sponsors of such a solution is the eminent rabbi and legal scholar David Bleich of Yeshiva University's Cardozo Law School. Bleich has fashioned a document he thinks is religiously acceptable. Unfortunately, he can't get enough of his rabbinical colleagues to agree: "I can't get them together in one room. The problem is that we do not have one authoritative body with the power to issue fiats."

In Riverdale, activist Rabbi Avi Weiss says he no longer performs a marriage unless there is such a prenuptial agreement. "I will not perform a wedding unless bride and groom sign the agreement that says that if, G-d forbid, there is a civil divorce, there will have to be a *get*," says Rabbi Weiss, "I had my own daughter, Ilana, sign such an agreement when she got married." Weiss is proud of the fact that he has stood at his synagogue door to block the way of a recalcitrant husband. "I am the rabbi of one of the most open synagogues in the world. But this is one person I will never permit in my shul. America is an open society, but there is much more we can do to cast these men as pariahs."

Some Orthodox leaders are even urging rabbinical courts to utilize their authority to dissolve a marriage. That way, there will be no more *agunot*. "There has always been tremendous room for creativity. One does not like to use the word *change* because it is a divine text—you would be playing the role of God," says Rabbi Emanuel Rackman, chancellor of Israel's Bar-Ilan University. Rackman has been pushing annulment as a way out of the conundrum. Although his colleagues once derided his approach, Rackman thinks the time for his idea has come. After years of insisting nothing could be done, the rabbis are suddenly discovering solutions. The activism of the *agunot* may leave them no choice.

"Look, I am not a crusader," Raizie insists. "I am not a person who makes waves," says this young woman, who married a man whose hands she had never held. "But this situation is so unbelievably unfair. The scales are so unevenly balanced that I had to act. After being a victim, there comes a point when you feel you have to set matters straight."

2
Playing Hard to *Get*

Peter Hellman

According to Jewish tradition, the piercing blast of the ram's horn is generally heard in the synagogue—and then only on the most solemn holidays. But as his marriage of 21 years was falling apart, Yehudah Schwartz found a new use for the shofar. He chased his wife, Naomi, around their expensive Manhattan Beach home, she says, blowing the shofar in her ear as loudly as he could.

According to Naomi Schwartz's court testimony, her husband was trying to scare a malevolent spirit, or dybbuk, out of her body. But it wasn't just any dybbuk. Half of Naomi was inhabited by her own spirit, her husband told her, while the other half had been invaded by the dybbuk of Gail Mauer, a close family friend who died in 1985. Whatever else they did, the shofar blasts signaled the start of a divorce battle so messy and so highly public that it seemed better suited to Palm Beach than to Brooklyn's Orthodox Jewish community.

The struggle has been played out for more than a year in the pages of *The Jewish Press*, the nation's "largest independent Anglo-Jewish weekly newspaper," with a circulation of more than 100,000. Readers haven't expected impartiality. The newspaper's founder and publisher is Naomi Schwartz's father, Rabbi Sholom Klass, 77. Until Klass fired him, in December 1988, Yehudah Schwartz had been the paper's managing editor.

Schwartz may no longer work at *The Jewish Press*, but he still has an interest in the paper. At stake in the divorced couple's incomplete property settlement is the disposition of a 24 percent share in the weekly, which Klass gave Naomi in 1983. (Her sister also owns 24 percent. Klass and his wife own 52 percent.) Because New York is an "equitable distribution" state, Yehudah Schwartz may be entitled to half of Naomi's shares. That would no doubt irk his ex-father-in-law, who hasn't exactly hidden his feelings about Schwartz.

"Yehudah Schwartz never held an executive position prior to his marriage to the daughter of the Publisher of *The Jewish Press*," said an "Editor's Note" last January. "With his marriage to the daughter of the Publisher, he was given certain managerial responsibilities with the unusually high salary of more than $3,000 per week, plus personal expenses, the use of a car and residence. . . . At some point, Yehudah Schwartz began to conduct himself in a disruptive manner in his interaction with other employees as well as with the Publisher, in which he acted in a grossly insubordinate and disrespectful manner, which included verbal abuse, tirades, threats and efforts at intimidation. On a number of occasions, he declared himself to be in control of *The Jewish Press*, expressing his intent to oust the Publisher." (Yehudah has consistently denied these and other allegations, and neither he nor Naomi Schwartz would comment on issues surrounding their divorce.)

Fueling Klass's anger was his former son-in-law's protracted refusal to give Naomi Schwartz a Jewish bill of divorce called a *get*. Since Jewish law does not recognize civil divorce, a wife without a *get* remains married until the death of her husband. The source of the *get* procedure is in the book of Deuteronomy, which instructs that a man whose wife "fails to please him" shall give her a bill of divorce. The *get* is normally written in the presence of both husband and wife by a scribe using a quill and black ink. It is handed directly from husband to wife. He must give it of his own free will, and that's generally how she must receive it. Both parties are then free to remarry.

The *get*, however, goes only one way. A wife can't give one to her husband. And if he refuses to give her a *get*, she may neither remarry nor even date within the Orthodox world. In this dread state, trapped in a dead marriage, she is known as an *Agunah*, a Hebrew word meaning "a woman in chains." (The word once referred to slaves in the galley of a ship whose arms and legs were bound together.) Only her husband can release her. Naomi Schwartz was one of these *Agunot* for a mere ten months after being awarded a civil divorce. For other women, the months turn into years, the years into decades. By Jewish law, any child an *Agunah* dares to bear—even with a civil divorce in hand—will be a *mamzer*, or bastard.

Orthodox women can usually be counted on to uphold their religious traditions, but not when it comes to a *get* unjustly withheld. Increasingly, the plight of *Agunot* has moved Jewish women to organize. The writer Blu Greenberg tells of going to a protest one bitterly cold February day on behalf of a Brooklyn woman whose husband was withholding the *get*. Later, the woman got her *get*, but only after her husband had dragged her for a block as she held on to the open door of his car, breaking her leg. She got her *get* after giving him $15,000 and agreeing not to file assault charges. "I don't consider myself a radical person," Greenberg says. "I affirm *halacha* [Jewish law]. But enough is enough. Abuse by a recalcitrant husband is such a waste of time, energy, life, productivity. It's beneath the dignity of *halacha*."

The *get* has survived for millennia as the tool for divorce because it was always easier to use than to misuse. An observant Jew dared not ignore the summons to the *Beth Din* (rabbinical court) to arbitrate a *get* dispute. The power of community opinion normally compelled him to obey the decision of the rabbis. If he ignored an order to give his wife a *get*, he could be flogged until he changed his mind. (To paraphrase Maimonides, the great Jewish authority of the Middle Ages, he could be beaten until he said, "I really want to.") But these days, peer pressure is weaker, as is the power of the *Beth Din*. Civil matrimonial courts make the rulings, and killer divorce lawyers are held in more awe than white-bearded sages. Often, the only way a woman can wangle a *get* is to offer her husband a tidy sum, but sometimes even cash can't buy a *get*. One woman in Boston, for example, had been granted a divorce in civil court, and her ex-husband had remarried and converted to Catholicism. Delivering a *get* to his ex-wife became irrelevant to him, and unless the marriage can be annulled, the ex-wife will remain an *Agunah* until she dies.

Last year, reverberations from the Schwartz divorce battle seemed to reach Albany, where the legislature enacted the so-called *get* law. Now, when a judge distributes property in a divorce proceeding, the law authorizes him to take into account any "barrier to remarriage" put up by either party. But just as the war between the Schwartzes finally subsides, a new battle is being fought over the *get* law apparently spawned by their divorce.

Dark, dynamic, and quick-tongued, Yehudah Schwartz soon caught Naomi Klass's eye when he was hired as a Linotype operator at *The Jewish Press* in 1962. Naomi worked at the paper as an editor and writer then—as she does now. She had one child from her first marriage, and he had had three children with his first wife. Naomi and Yehudah were wed in 1966. In 1971, the couple moved to Israel, where Yehudah worked for *The Jewish Press* getting advertising and coordinating columns. The Schwartzes soon had three children of their own.

Yehudah made it clear that he was the king of his Jerusalem castle, but that didn't mean Naomi was queen. He didn't like her to invite her friends over, not even family members who were visiting the country. "Don't I have the right to be comfortable in my own home?" he would ask, according to Naomi's testimony.

"It didn't occur to me then," she added, "that I also had the right to be comfortable in my own home." Yehudah didn't welcome his wife's opinions any more than he welcomed her friends. He once explained to her why she had no right to express her views. Suppose she were invited to observe brain surgery, Yehudah said. She'd be expected to watch quietly. But what if she were to say to the neurosurgeon, "Maybe you should make the incision one inch to the left"? She'd be thrown out of the operating room for her impertinence.

To voice an opinion on a particular subject, concluded Yehudah Schwartz in this lecture to his wife, "first you have to be an expert. You're only an expert on chicken soup." In time, as Yehudah would learn, Naomi came to be an expert on more than chicken soup. Well before her own *Agunah* problem, she had sympathized with the plight of an Israeli woman whose violent husband had refused for sixteen years to give her a *get*. Even with the marriage long dead, the rabbinical court was still counseling her to try to patch things up.

"The platitudes she heard were more than she could bear," Naomi once said. Standing before the court, the woman told the chief rabbi that just as Hitler had killed countless Jewish children by putting them in the crematoria, countless more Jewish children would never be born because women like her were forced to remain *Agunot*. When the chief rabbi heard this, according to Naomi, "he began to tremble."

A friend wrote to Naomi with a tale of her travails in trying to get a *get* from her ex-husband. It read, Naomi told a friend, "like a survivor's manual from Auschwitz." Her husband agreed to give her the *get* only after he was forced to spend several months in an Israeli prison. "The other inmates beat him up," says a source who knows Naomi. "They respect 'manly' crimes like robbery or murder, but not making a woman into an *Agunah*."

Even while she demonstrated on behalf of *Agunot* in Israel, her marriage was still happy, Naomi told friends—so long as she remained submissive to Yehudah. "I loved him," Naomi once said. "I adored him."

The family returned to Brooklyn in the early eighties, and Yehudah Schwartz took over as managing editor of *The Jewish Press*. But, as Sholom Klass would later testify, the two men didn't get along: "Never in my life, even when I was poor and struggling, does anyone scream at me the way Yehudah does." Klass ordered Schwartz to start reporting to Jerry Greenwald, another *Jewish Press* executive (who is married to Naomi's sister), which enraged Schwartz.

The couple's home in Manhattan Beach, bought by *The Jewish Press*, was near Naomi's parents and her sister's family. But Naomi testified that Yehudah did not welcome their visits, even on the Sabbath. Naomi's friends were similarly rebuffed. If Yehudah answered the phone when they called, he was often nasty. Even if Naomi was home, he'd say she wasn't.

In Israel, Naomi had accepted her husband's wishes as law. Now her years of acquiescence were over. The end of the marriage may have been in sight when, after the death of their friend Gail Mauer in 1985, the Schwartzes took in her two children to live with them. Their father, Dr. Ivan Mauer, also moved in with the Schwartzes in the spring of 1986.

It wasn't long before the house resounded with the blasts of Yehudah Schwartz's ram's horn. According to Naomi's testimony, he accused her of having an affair with Mauer. In the presence of the children, she said, he recited biblical passages on adultery and the dire penalties for the crime. He called Naomi a "whore," a "witch," and a "Hungarian Gypsy."

Mauer moved out of the Schwartz home in 1988. According to Dennis Rapps, a lawyer for the paper, *The Jewish Press* owned the house, and Yehudah Schwartz was ordered by the court to move out that same year. *The Jewish Press*—which claims it owned the Lincoln Continental he drove (Schwartz says he paid for part of it)—had the car towed away. In 1989, Naomi Schwartz sued for civil divorce. She also asked her husband for a *get*.

Despite the strife at home, her children professed surprise when she sued for divorce after 23 years of marriage, Naomi testified. She searched for a biblical story to explain the situation. "I hate to compare myself to a donkey," she said, "but I felt like Balaam's donkey, whose master was asked by the king of Moab to go place a curse on the Israelites. Along the way, the donkey stops. It won't go forward, no matter how much Balaam beats it. Finally, it turns to Balaam and speaks. 'Why are you beating the one who has served you so long and so well?' it asks.

"I was like that donkey," said Naomi. "It was such a shock to my family when I finally spoke up."

Naomi Schwartz was awarded a civil divorce by Judge William Rigler in a Brooklyn courtroom in July 1991. Yehudah Schwartz "tried to explain away all the claims made by plaintiff," wrote Judge Rigler. "However, this court did not find his evidence to be credible." The grounds were cruel and inhuman treatment. Only then did Rigler turn to the "economic aspects"—and the question of equitable distribution. Before he would give Naomi a *get*, according to Rapps, Yehudah Schwartz said he felt he was entitled to half of his wife's share in *The Jewish Press*, or $1 million, under the equitable-distribution laws. (Schwartz denies Rapps's claim.)

"It's an abuse of Jewish law to put a price on a *get*," says Rapps, who is also a longtime activist on behalf of *Agunot*. "But that's what's happening more and more. A *get* has become a commodity with a price on it like any other."

A husband who refuses to give his wife a *get* may be required by Jewish law to appear before a rabbinical court. In 1990 and 1991, Yehudah Schwartz ignored three summonses to appear before a rabbinical court under the auspices of the Rabbinical Alliance of America—a tribunal known for its sympathy to the plight of *Agunot*. Schwartz soon tried to move the proceedings to Israel, asking a rabbinical court in Jerusalem to order the couple to attempt "reconciliation." Since Naomi had already been awarded a civil divorce, reconciliation seemed unlikely.

In Israel—where there are no civil marriages or divorces, only religious ones—the decisions of rabbinical courts can be enforced by state police. Naomi Schwartz found that out in early November 1991, just as she was boarding a flight back to New York after a vacation in Tel Aviv. Suddenly Israeli police took her in hand.

She was forbidden to leave the country they told her, until she appeared before the rabbinical court on November 20. After learning that the *get* debate was already before the rabbinical court back in Manhattan (and that Yehudah Schwartz wasn't cooperating), the Jerusalem court threw out his case.

Naomi was allowed to go home to New York—and catch up with her luggage and her 21-year-old daughter, who had gone ahead the morning she'd been detained.

In 1988, Raizie, 24, an Orthodox woman from Brooklyn, married David Golding, well known in the Orthodox world as a producer of children's religious music by the group Uncle Moishy and His Mitzvah Men. But there were marital problems, according to Raizie Golding, and after just one year of marriage, she asked for a *get*. Before her husband would agree, she says, he demanded that she "give him everything he wanted." In several documents written in Hebrew, she signed away her economic rights. Arriving in a rabbi's study where she thought her husband would at last hand her the *get*, she was confronted with yet another document to sign. She resisted four and a half hours of negotiation. But at another meeting, the following day, she succumbed. "The threat of being denied a *get*," the Manhattan Supreme Court later wrote, "was particularly terrifying to plaintiff, whose sister had suffered the consequences of having been unable to obtain a Jewish divorce."

Deciding she'd gotten a raw deal, Raizie Golding sued for divorce in Manhattan Supreme Court. David Golding countered that the contract she'd signed prevented her from enforcing her economic rights. Judge Elliott Wilk disagreed, ruling that Raizie's signing of the contract had been coerced. The decision was upheld by the appellate division, and the pre-*get* contract was labeled "nothing other than a document born of and subsisting in inequity." A civil divorce trial will soon begin in Judge Wilk's courtroom. (Raizie Golding's lawyer is 68-year-old Elaine Rudnick Sheps. A Juilliard-trained concert pianist, Sheps decided to become a matrimonial lawyer at the age of 37 after her own divorce was handled badly.)

In the aftermath of the Golding ruling against *get* "extortion," Naomi Schwartz asked Judge Rigler to deny her ex-husband equitable distribution of joint assets because he refused to give her a *get* without—she claimed—being paid off. Rigler wouldn't go that far, but, invoking the Golding precedent, he did note the "power differential" that favored the husband who can withhold a *get*. He also agreed to take into account the fact that "one spouse's actions in relation to a *get* may be subject to review in the equitable distribution portion of a matrimonial action."

With the *get* controversy showering sparks everywhere, Sheldon Silver, an Orthodox state assemblyman from the Lower East Side, pushed ahead with a bill he had introduced in Albany in 1984 to address the problem. Treading lightly on the line between church and state, Silver's bill authorized judges, "where appropriate," to consider the effect of a "barrier to remarriage" when determining equitable distribution and maintenance. Without mentioning *get* extortion, the bill seemed to be aimed directly at men who would not grant *gittin* to their wives.

Silver's bill breezed through the Legislature last June and was quickly signed into law by Governor Mario Cuomo. "Over the years, the lives of perhaps thousands of individuals will be directly and positively impacted by this new law," wrote *The Jewish Press*. But rumbles of dissatisfaction were being heard from other factions of the Orthodox community—notably Agudath Israel of America, an Orthodox group representing more than 100,000 American Jews. "This law creates very fascinating and frightening questions of *halacha*," says David Zwiebel, a lawyer for the group. "A husband must give the *get* of his free will. The question of monetary pressure on him constitutes a revocation of free will." Agudath Israel asked two distinguished Israeli rabbis last July to rule on whether the new law was kosher, and they ruled against it. "A cloud may be put over many *gittin* given in New York while this law remains in force," says Zwiebel.

Another opponent of the *get* law, Professor Yehuda Silver of Touro College, near Times Square, says, "As an American, I am insulted by this intrusion of government upon religion. I don't want judges with the family values of Sol Wachtler making decisions that touch on Jewish divorces." The *get*-law, in fact, keeps the courts well clear of religious proceedings, indirectly encouraging the divorcing couple to settle the *get* issue in front of a rabbinical court before a civil court considers the distribution of joint property. Nevertheless, Agudath Israel and other Orthodox groups are determined to have the new *get* law amended or repealed.

Using his paper, Sholom Klass, a shy, slender man with blue eyes and a wispy white beard, has fought back fiercely. There was an attack on "certain rabbis who can't read English" who have declared the *get* law invalid: "When it comes to deciding on a law of a foreign government," one correspondent wrote, one must not "hear it from a translator"—a slap at the two Israeli rabbis who have ruled against the *get* law.

One apparent result of the law's passage is that last October, Yehudah Schwartz finally gave Naomi a *get*—in Jerusalem. Days later, she was back in Judge Rigler's Brooklyn courtroom, where, almost two years after the case had begun, testimony on the property issue was still being presented. As Naomi left for lunch that day, she was heard to say, "When I got my *get*, I suddenly knew how the hostages felt when they were released from Lebanon."

While his daughter's divorce battle may be nearly over, Sholom Klass continues to fight Yehudah Schwartz. In a suit filed by *The Jewish Press*, Klass has demanded the return of an array of property—ranging from "a bed night table" from the Manhattan Beach house to $406,021.80 in loans that have allegedly not been repaid. Yehudah Schwartz has denied all of the claims made by *The Jewish Press* and has filed his own multi-million-dollar countersuit alleging, among other things, that he was tricked into dropping his demand for "a long-term employment contract with a profit-sharing plan." He also claims that he was fired, evicted from his home, and libeled by *The Jewish Press* solely because Klass wanted him to give Naomi a *get*.

Though his daughter now has her *get*, the *Agunah* problem still consumes Klass. He compares the plight of these women to that of Jewish maidens who were kidnapped and sold into slavery in ancient times. "Our Torah required any means to redeem them from captivity," explains Klass. Each week, the newspaper carries "Chained," a listing of men who have ignored three summonses to a *Beth Din* to arbitrate the giving of a *get*. Their peers then place the men in "minor excommunication." While they are in this state, other Jews may not enter their homes, eat with them, or pray with them. "Chained"—edited, appropriately enough, by Naomi Schwartz—currently includes the names of several men and one woman, a reminder that while a husband must give a *get* of his own free will, his wife can choose not to receive it. Like a man, she may refuse out of spite or greed or both.

Like her father, Naomi Schwartz continues to campaign on behalf of *Agunot*. Listening to several such women tell their stories at a symposium on the problem in Queens last month, Schwartz wrote in *The Jewish Press*, "I found myself in tears. . . . I was crying for them and for all of us." For five years, one of those *Agunot* has been divorced—at least in the eyes of a civil court—from a violent husband. Though he refuses to give her a *get*, he does stand outside the Bronx synagogue where she worships to stare at her. Another *Agunah* at the symposium also told of fleeing her violent husband, who now lives in Europe with his second wife and child. Claiming that as a Sephardic Jew he is permitted to have more than one wife, he refuses to give her a *get*. When Rabbi Leib Landesman of the Monsey *Beth Din*, in Rockland County, referred to the *Agunah* problem as "grossly exaggerated" and called it "one big cholent" (a precooked stew traditionally eaten on the Sabbath), Naomi Schwartz wrote, "I felt my blood boiling."

Although the *get* issue still inflames her, Naomi Schwartz's husband no longer does. "I wish [Yehudah] the best of luck," she has said. In a brief telephone interview, Yehudah Schwartz said that he can't talk now about his divorce except to dismiss the current *get* controversy as "a plot of the feminist movement. This new law," he predicted, "will go down the tubes."

Next week, Naomi Schwartz will remarry. The groom-to-be is Dr. Ivan Mauer. So far, Yehudah Schwartz and his shofar have been silent.

II

Essays in the Popular
Press: The Israeli
Situation

3
The Rabbinical Ties That Bind

Glenn Frankel

Jerusalem—It took 17 years, one murder and a half-dozen rapes before Aliza Shmueli convinced a rabbinical court that her husband was a violent and dangerous man. Finally, after Shlomo Shmueli was given a life sentence for killing a business partner, the rabbis forced him to give his wife what she had been seeking all those years: a divorce.

Her case was extreme, but not unprecedented. Ruth Yalomi had to wait 24 years until a rabbinical court coerced a divorce for her from a husband who regularly beat her up during the one year she lived with him. Iris Levy waited 16 years. Daniella Valenci had to wait 12 years until her husband relented—after the rabbis finally threatened to send him to prison if he didn't.

All of these women were victims not only of their spouses, but also of Israel's peculiar legal system, which places total authority in marriage and divorce for Jews in the hands of the country's Orthodox rabbis. The rabbis' power in these matters is absolute, their methods at times appear whimsical, and their rulings can be deeply humiliating for women who find little sympathy in the all-male world of the rabbinate.

The rabbis base their rulings on traditional Jewish law, which dates back some 2,000 years. In its time, the law was considered unusually progressive because it required the mutual consent of husband and wife for divorce. But in modern times, that requirement has become a chain around the necks of thousands of Israeli women who without their husbands' approval cannot dissolve their marriages.

Under the law, a husband who separates from his wife can live with another woman and even have children without attaching any stigma to himself or to them. In certain cases, he is even allowed to commit bigamy. But a wife who begins a second relationship is branded as an adulteress and can lose custody of her children; and any new children born from that relationship are *mamzerim* — bastards — who can marry only other *mamzerim*.

One woman had to appeal to the Israeli Supreme Court to overturn a rabbinical court order forbidding her from allowing another man to enter her house. The woman had been separated from her husband for three years, but he refused to give her a divorce and he himself was living with another woman. Nonetheless, the rabbis ruled that his estranged wife was "living in sin" and corrupting their children by seeing another man.

The high court, which can overrule the rabbis on questions of alimony and child custody but not on divorce itself, issued a permanent injunction against the rabbinical court, ruling that the question of whether the mother was dating another man was none of the rabbis' business.

In the old days, the rabbis could order a husband to be shunned or even beaten to compel him to grant a divorce. The pressure that rabbinical leaders in the insular world of the ghetto could apply on a recalcitrant community member was usually sufficient. Even today, the courts can obtain an arrest warrant and order a defiant husband imprisoned until he consents. But the rabbis have only used such a sanction about 30 times in the past 40 years.

By contrast, they have granted at least 91 husbands the right to commit legal bigamy over the past five years, according to women's rights groups. One rabbinical court in Beersheba even allowed a 60-year-old man to take a second wife after his first produced three daughters but no son.

To avoid the limbo of separation without divorce, many women pay off their husbands with cash or property. "It's nothing less than blackmail," says Sharon Shenhav, a lawyer who has handled divorce cases for the past decade.

She recalled the case of a woman from Iran whose husband vanished for eight years, then reappeared one day and demanded half the value of the apartment she had bought and paid for to grant her a divorce. The woman was 34 and felt desperate to get the divorce and find a new husband before her childbearing years ended.

"She finally paid him off with $12,000 she raised from family friends," says Shenhav. "I was so angry I had to step out of the case."

Others who either can't or won't pay wait years for the rabbinical courts to act against their husbands. They are called *agunot*—chained women—and women's groups and lawyers estimate there are somewhere between 8,000 and 10,000 of them in Israel.

For decades the rabbis' monopoly over marriage and divorce has gone largely unchallenged. But during Israel's recent coalition crisis, the small, ultraorthodox parties overplayed their hand and wound up with little influence in the new government. That has led secular Israelis to consider anew the many ways in which the rabbis impinge on their lives. Many are pressing for reform in this most private yet public of arenas.

Despite Israel's image as a sexually liberated and egalitarian society, the days of Golda Meir are long gone and women's rights are a low priority. Only seven of the 120 members of the new Knesset are women, down from 10 during the previous session. There are no women cabinet ministers this time around—the one who served in the last cabinet was unceremoniously deposed by the usually progressive Labor Party—nor even any deputy ministers.

But critics contend nothing challenges female dignity as much as a trip to the divorce court.

In Jerusalem, the rabbis preside over a collection of dingy offices and unheated waiting rooms in a run-down four-story building on the main Jaffa Road. All of the judges and officers of the court, and most of the lawyers, are men. Women at best are guests, and sometimes they are treated as intruders.

On a recent morning, clerks and secretaries barked orders at bewildered petitioners while rabbis and lawyers scurried from room to room. The computer age was just a rumor—most files were handwritten and stored in piles around the clerk's office. In one drafty cubicle, a young rabbinical student painstakingly wrote out on parchment each bill of divorcement, as the Talmud requires.

The courts often start late and recess early. If three judges cannot be collected to constitute a court, a day's worth of cases is simply postponed.

Ariel Rosen-Zvi, a senior lecturer at Tel Aviv University's law school, described the courts as haphazard, sloppy, and inefficient in a study he did two years ago for Naamat, the women's branch of the Histadrut national labor federation. He found that because there are no written guidelines for judicial procedure, judges often hand down oral rulings without relying on evidence or even explaining their decisions.

"There is no feeling that there is an authority actually in charge of the proceedings," wrote Rosen-Zvi. "Rather, the feeling seems to be that whoever shouts most loudly will be heard and that ultimately 'might is right.' "

"The courts are absolutely intolerable," says Alice Shalvi, a veteran activist who heads the Israel Women's Network. "There are no regular working hours, no privacy, and things get lost all the time. The system is left completely to the whim of the judges."

The rabbis defend their system as more informal and humane than Israel's civil courts. "This is the only court in the world where a woman can come without a lawyer and without a lot of money and get justice," contends Rabbi Avraham Amaliah, national director of the courts.

Rabbi Ezra Basri is a noted religious scholar who has spent 18 years on the Jerusalem court, and he is considered by some women activists to be among the court's more sympathetic members. He acknowledges that the system is overworked and sometimes unfair to both parties. But he insists that there is no judicial bias against women and contends they themselves are often more to blame than their husbands.

"The problem is with a woman who just decides she does not love her husband anymore and wants a divorce and he still loves her," he says. "There are certainly not 7,000 *agunot*—I am doubtful there are even 70. A lot of the problem is financial. Women say they want this and they want that—things they are not entitled to according to the law."

Such comments evoke a bitter laugh from Aliza Shmueli. She is a slim, working-class woman in her early forties who lives in a small, ground-floor Jerusalem flat that is well kept and radiates an air of quiet dignity. She has an easy smile that freezes into a scowl when she begins to recount the 17 painful years it took for her to convince the rabbis that her husband Shlomo was a liar and a brutalizer.

Aliza Shmueli first left her husband after he regularly beat her and abused their two children. The rabbis persuaded her to go back after extracting a pledge from him that he would grant her a divorce if he hit her again. He broke his word, she says, and the rabbis broke theirs—they did not compel him to divorce her.

"My second home was the rabbinate—I was there every month," she recalls. "Every time he would go to court, he would cry, 'I love my wife, I love my children,' and the rabbis would always believe him. They never listened to me."

Shlomo Shmueli even got away with murder, killing an Arab business associate at the Shmueli apartment and dumping the body somewhere outside Jerusalem. He threatened his wife and children with death if they ever told what they knew, and for a while they kept silent. Finally, when he was arrested for raping teen-agers from a nearby public school, Aliza Shmueli gathered her courage and went to the police.

Even then, he refused to give her a divorce. He was brought to the divorce court in handcuffs, which the police removed at the order of the judges. But once freed, he struck his wife across the face while the rabbis watched in horror. Still, they refused to act against him until Aliza Shmueli obtained a lawyer, Sharon Shenhav, from Naamat. She persuaded the rabbis to order the husband to be placed in solitary confinement until he relented. He did so almost immediately.

"If the rabbis had pressured him at the very beginning, maybe there would have been no murder and no rapes," says Aliza Shmueli. "It's not that they are stupid, but they are very biased toward men. A woman comes into the court and you can see she's been beaten up, but they tell her to wait another month and then another. For me they are like terrorists."

There is another bitter irony in the fact that, despite all that has happened, Aliza Shmueli is still not free financially. Under the terms of the divorce agreement, she is required to pay her husband half the value of her flat if and when he is ever released.

Shenhav, herself a religious Jew who moved here from Washington a decade ago, says the problem is not with Jewish law, which she insists can be reasonably flexible. "It's the rabbis who sit in the religious establishment today and who refuse to be creative," she says. "They have all the tools they need but they aren't using them."

Shenhav contends the rabbis are so entrenched politically that the Knesset will never overturn the rabbinical courts system. The only hope, she believes, is in reforms such as requiring a prenuptial agreement written into the Jewish marriage contract that could make divorce less difficult.

Women cannot be ordained as orthodox rabbis, but Shenhav would like to see them sitting on the committee that chooses rabbinical judges. She would also like a new set of criteria adopted that would ensure that judges have a broadly based educational and legal background and some experience in modern family issues.

Other critics contend the only answer is to set up a second, parallel system of civil family courts that plaintiffs can turn to.

"The bottom line is that as long as religion is a political issue in this country, we won't get any real reform in marriage and divorce," says Alice Shalvi. "Even a number of rabbis have told me that until there is competition from civil marriage and divorce, there will be no real reform. After all, they have a monopoly."

4

The *Agunah*: An Ancient Problem in Modern Dress

Sharon Shenhav

Ruth, a beautiful, dark-haired Jerusalemite in her early 40s is a modern day *agunah*. Abandoned by her husband, Yossi, 14 years ago, Ruth cannot remarry because Yossi has refused to give her a religious divorce known as a *get*. Chained to a fictitious marriage, she has been denied a basic human right—the right of every individual to marry and build a family.

The story of Ruth is typical of the painful situation faced by thousands of Jewish women today, victims of an ancient problem in modern dress, that of the *agunah*. A poignant figure in Jewish history and the subject of much talmudic discussion and rabbinic concern, the *agunah* in ancient times was a woman whose husband had disappeared, leaving no witnesses to testify to his death. Therefore looked upon as an "anchored" or "chained" (*agunah* in Hebrew) woman, she could not remarry unless, or until, her husband was found or witnesses to his death testified.

In the modern world of telecommunications, satellites, and Interpol, husbands rarely disappear off the face of the earth. The modern-day *agunah* often knows her husband's whereabouts. Unfortunately, this knowledge does not free her from a failed marriage as long as the husband refuses to give a *get*. Jewish law provides that a divorce can take place only when there is mutual consent of the parties, evidenced by the husband delivering the *get* and the wife's acceptance of the document. Until the act occurs, there is no divorce.

Let us look at Ruth's story and try to understand her pain. Yossi had been attracted to her when she was just a beautiful junior-high school student. He approached Ruth's parents about marriage when both families were still living in Iran. Ruth's family, which was making *aliyah*, refused to consider Yossi's offer since they wanted their children to raise their own families in Israel. Six months after their arrival in Israel, Yossi, on a visit, promised to make a home in Israel if Ruth's parents would consent to the marriage. However, despite Yossi's good looks and sophistication, 15-year-old Ruth was not interested in marriage.

Unbeknownst to Ruth, Yossi told her parents that Ruth and he had been intimate, a blatant lie, and that he planned to spread her loss of virginity among their friends and relatives. He also claimed that he would be willing to marry Ruth without demanding a dowry. Without verifying Yossi's story with Ruth, her parents, afraid that the story would damage her chances at finding a husband and impressed with Yossi's successful business in Iran, agreed to set a date for the wedding. In 1972, Ruth and Yossi were married in Jerusalem.

After the wedding, Yossi took Ruth to Iran to meet his family and supposedly to sell his business and property. Instead, Ruth found herself married to a man who was physically and verbally abusive and who had no intention of returning to Israel. Settled in Teheran, Yossi's "successful" business kept their standard of living at the poverty level.

Ashamed of the situation, Ruth kept her suffering to herself, convinced that Yossi's abuse was a result of her inability to create a good home. She bore two children, kept house, and tried to make the marriage work.

After seven years, Yossi agreed to move to Israel. Ruth was ecstatic, certain that the move would improve their family life. She would be reunited with her beloved parents and siblings. However, three months after their move to Israel, Yossi returned to Iran, leaving Ruth and the children. In letters, Yossi made threats on her life and on the lives of her parents. He had no intention of returning to Israel nor would he send money for Ruth's or their children's support.

Desperate, Ruth found a job as a bank clerk. By exercising extreme frugality and with her family's help, she was able to purchase a modest apartment. Despite the difficulties, Ruth managed to support herself and her children. Still young and attractive, abandoned by her husband, she applied to the Rabbinic Court in Jerusalem for a divorce. The Israeli rabbis wrote to rabbis in Iran, asking them to find Yossi and to obtain his consent to a *get*. Their efforts were to no avail; Yossi refused.

Ruth, true to her tradition, would not date as long as she was still Yossi's wife. She returned repeatedly to the Rabbinic Court (*bet din*), begging the rabbis to find a way to release her from her nonexistent marriage. She was told by the rabbis that nothing could be done until Yossi agreed to give the *get*.

Finally, in 1986 Yossi returned to Israel. Ruth rushed to the Rabbinic Court, confident that at last she would receive a *get* and be able to start a new life. When Yossi was brought to the Rabbinic Court, he claimed he still loved his wife and wanted a reconciliation (*shalom bayit*). When questioned by the rabbis, Ruth emphatically refused to consider a reconciliation, asking only for the *get* and her freedom. Yossi said he would consider the matter. The rabbis suggested that the couple negotiate a divorce agreement and ordered Yossi to pay child support.

Since 1986, Ruth has spent hundreds of hours at the Rabbinic Court, pleading, begging, crying, and demanding justice and freedom. Yossi has said he will never give her a *get*. Occasionally, he has relented on the condition that Ruth compensate him, the "compensation" requiring financial payments ranging from $12,000 to the most recent extortionary demand of $80,000. Unable to buy her way out of her marriage, Ruth remains a modern *agunah*.

How did this painful, unjust situation develop? In most countries where Jews live today, civil divorce is available, although it does not end a Jewish marriage according to *halakhah*. The Reform rabbinate does not require a *get* in order to perform a marriage for a Jew who has been previously married. The Conservative Movement, in following *halakhah*, requires a *get* for the religious dissolution of a marriage. However, Conservative rabbis have been willing to annul the marriage (*havkaat kiddushin*) in cases of recalcitrance or disappearance. All Jewish betrothals are done with the consent of the rabbis. There are talmudic cases in which the rabbis remove the consent, thereby annuling the betrothal. Based on that principle, Conservative rabbis today annul marriages.[1] Retroactive annulment is used in cases where there was fraud or deception at the time of the marriage ceremony. If Ruth were living in America, she would be able to present her case to the Joint *Bet Din* of the Conservative Movement. If the marriage were annuled, she would be able to be remarried by a Conservative rabbi.

However, Ruth lives in Israel where exclusive jurisdiction over marriage and divorce among Jews is in the Rabbinic Courts, and only Orthodox rabbis sit as religious court judges. Orthodox rabbis generally do not apply retroactive annulment as a solution.

As the number of modern-day *agunot* has risen to the estimated level of 10,000 in Israel and over 15,000 in the United States, Jewish women have decided to take action. Frustrated by the failure of religious scholars, rabbis, and male leaders, Jewish women's organizations have formed an

International Coalition for *Agunah* Rights (ICAR). Women's League for Conservative Judaism as well as the Orthodox women of Emunah have joined with secular women of WIZO, Na'amat, Hadassah, Women to Women, and the Israel Women's Network. This is not an issue important only to Orthodox and Israeli women. Every divorced woman without a *get* is a potential *agunah*.

ICAR has formed two committees in Israel. The Law Committee, devoted to finding civil legislative solutions, has approved draft legislation that would impose civil sanctions on recalcitrant husbands. These sanctions include the inability to be a government employee and the denial of a driver's license, passport, or credit card. Other proposals make the refusal to grant a *get* a criminal offense. Most of these proposed bills have been sitting in the Knesset for over three years, raising doubts over their eventual passage.

Civil legislation has been introduced in several countries, including Australia, New Zealand, Canada, and the U.S. The New York "*get* law" was passed by the State Legislature in 1983. Typical of similar legislation in other countries, it states that a final judgment of divorce cannot be entered in the civil court until all barriers to remarriage have been removed—that is, a *get* has been given. Yet, despite the legislation, the problem of *agunot* has still not been resolved in New York: Husbands simply do not ask for a civil divorce.

For generations rabbis have found halakhic solutions to free *agunot*. The ICAR Halakhic Committee consists of Orthodox and Conservative rabbis, religious court judges (*dayanim*), lawyers, talmudic scholars, professors, representatives of women's organizations, and *agunot*. After studying various halakhic solutions used in the past, the Committee presented the following recommendations to the Chief Rabbis in Jerusalem who promised to set up a special rabbinic committee.

Pre-nuptial Agreement

The concept of a pre-nuptial agreement has always been acceptable in Jewish law. The *ketubah*, which contains promises and obligations, is in fact a pre-nuptial agreement as it is always signed prior to the wedding ceremony. The Halakhic Committee's recommendation is the addition of a paragraph promising that the husband will pay the wife maintenance of $100 a day during any period when they might be living apart. The groom would sign this prior to the ceremony. Such an agreement would be merely a recognition of the obligation of the Jewish husband to support his wife. By specifying the amount, the husband obligates himself to a particular sum of money. The wife would be able to enforce payment of this obligation by attaching his salary, bank account, real property, etc., until he consented to the *get*. If the wife should refuse to accept the *get*, the husband's obligation under the pre-nuptial agreement would end.

Compulsory *Get*

The compulsory *get* was used in the Middle Ages. Israeli law provides that if the Rabbinic Court issues a compulsory *get* order and the husband refuses the *get*, the case can be turned over to the Attorney General, who will take the case to the district court with the request that the recalcitrant husband be imprisoned until he gives the *get*. While the compulsory *get* is a legitimate halakhic solution, it is rarely used in Israel. Despite the thousands of *agunot* who are waiting to be freed, the rabbis have given compulsory *get* orders in less than one or two cases a year.

Obligatory *Get*

In those cases where, for halakhic reasons, a compulsory *get* order cannot be given, an obligatory *get* order could be issued by the Rabbinic Court. The Halakhic Committee recommended that if the *get* has not been given within 30 days, the court should order the husband to pay his wife maintenance or alimony up to 95 percent of his monthly income in addition to the amount of compensation that is written in the *ketubah*.

Annulment

The Committee suggested that the Chief Rabbis restore annulment as practiced by the Conservative Movement in their *bet din* in the U.S. This solution would free the *agunah* who could show fraud or deceit at the time of the marriage ceremony. Furthermore, if the husband became mentally ill and legally incompetent, an annulment would free the *agunah* from marriage to a man incapable of giving a *get*. An annulment granted by the rabbis would also free the woman whose husband had disappeared.

Conditional *Get*

This solution was used at the time of King David when every soldier gave his wife a *get*, conditional on his not returning from war. The conditional *get* has been recommended by many scholars as a viable solution to the problem of modern *agunot*. The conditional *get* would be given at the time of the marriage ceremony and would include conditions for separation.

Despite all the thought and study devoted to the recommendations of the ICAR Halakhic Committee, there is still a long way to go to free modern *agunot* and to eliminate the injustice that is being perpetrated in the name of Jewish law.

Note

1. See OUTLOOK, Summer, 1991, "When a Jewish Marriage Is Over," by Rabbi Mayer Rabinowitz, for a discussion of the Joint *Bet Din* of the Conservative Movement.

5

A Horror Story—Ours

Netty C. Gross

At 19, Ariella found herself in a Jewish marriage as written by Stephen King. Part I of that tale was the 3½ years she spent with her husband. Part II was the 6½ years she spent in a cruel and peculiar form of limbo created by Jewish law while she waited for him to grant a *get*—a religious bill of divorce.

It would be comforting to regard Ariella's ordeal as a purely personal horror story. It isn't. The cast includes the rabbinic establishment who let her husband keep her hostage, then blackmail her. And it includes the many other women in her position—*agunot*, "anchored" women, as Hebrew calls them, chained to husbands who refuse to hand them their walking papers. There are reportedly several thousand such women in Israel, where religious courts have exclusive jurisdiction over divorce. That's besides an unknown number of *agunot* abroad, women who might be able to re-marry under civil law but who accept halakhah and so the need for a religious divorce.

Ariella, an Orthodox American immigrant, was married off to a scion of a prominent Jerusalem rabbinic family, an advanced Talmud student, the eldest of 9 children. Within weeks of the marriage, he began regularly locking her in the bathroom for hours at a time. He progressed to throwing things at her. Sometimes he insisted she have intercourse with him 10 times a night. After the birth of her third child, she opened her oven's gas jets full blast because it was the only thing she could think of doing that fit in with her rabbinical marriage counselor's sage advice: "Try not to provoke him." Fortunately, she survived that tactic.

When at last Ariella moved out, her husband ignored a court order to provide child support—yet exercised his halakhic right to leave her "anchored" to him.

From a lone line in Deuteronomy—"he writes her a bill of divorcement and puts it in her hand"—the laws of divorce as codified in the Talmud grew. The key point: Dissolution of a marriage is effected by the husband granting a *get* of his own free will. (If a wife refuses to accept a *get*—a far rarer phenomenon—a halakhic safety valve exists: The rabbis can grant the husband permission to take a second wife.)

"Free will" is a flexible concept. If a wife so much as declared that the sight of her spouse disgusted her, Maimonides permitted beating a recalcitrant husband until he "freely" declared he wanted to untie the knot. The Israeli rabbinate, though, has fastened onto the pure sense of "free will" with ferocity. A husband who refuses to grant a *get* will either be encouraged to go home and be nice to his wife; admonished to grant her a *get* because it is a *mitzvah*; or be given a "forced divorce" decree. That last option means jailing the man until he agrees to grant the *get*, but it's rarely used. In practice, you have to be estranged for at least seven years, then show that your husband is gay, impotent, or violent—and even then, the court may not act.

Applying pressure more often or more creatively—for instance, by imposing financial penalties—could produce an "unwilling *get*," that is, an invalid divorce and a woman still really married, or so the rabbis argue. And that, in turn, could lead unintentionally to an adulterous union with another man. The rabbinate claims to be protecting our purity.

Another myopic illusion. At a recent Knesset subcommittee hearing, one *agunah* rose and announced she was pregnant with another man's child. Only the rabbinate's representative let out a "gevalt." Others present applauded.

In fact, the more the *agunah* values the halakhic system, the more she is hurt by it. Many *agunot* tragically waste crucial fertile years waiting for a divorce; lucky ones are left with a year or two to scramble for a man, a relationship and a baby. Orthodox rabbis who ordinarily seem to care a great deal about Jewish women having children are curiously unconcerned with these particular women's atrophied reproductive organs.

Last year Ariella's husband surfaced and indicated he would grant a divorce—if she paid $40,000 in cash.

Ariella was persuaded by her attorney to accept. Some such men make an offer just once. With her mother as intermediary, she received the money as a 14-year loan from a sympathetic American Jew.

The rabbinic court judges, who supervised the counting of the greenbacks, were unconcerned that blackmail also created a halakhic defect in the divorce. (According to the Talmudic law of torts, the rabbis could have legally seized the extorted money.)

Do we sell our 12-year-old daughters, sacrifice animals, or indenture people—all of which the Torah permitted? No. As Orthodox author Blu Greenberg writes, "When there is a rabbinic will, there is a halakhic way." Until a rabbinic will is found on this issue, every Jewish woman is a potential *agunah*.

III

Scholarly Essays

6

"The Altar Weeps": Divorce in Jewish Law

Irwin H. Haut

Introduction

In the cycle of life, there are moments of extreme joy and of profound sadness, both of which come into play in connection with marriage and divorce. In this chapter we shall explore Jewish law as it relates to divorce — including the equality of the spouses in initiating divorce proceedings, the particulars of the divorce process itself, modern dilemmas confronting the Jewish community in divorce law, and finally some possible solutions to those dilemmas.

Under Jewish law, a marriage validly entered into can be ended *only* by the death of one of the parties or by a document known as a *get*.[1] The writing, transmission, and acceptance of the *get* are all governed by specific rules. Moreover, *only* the husband has the right to give the *get* to his wife; if he refuses to do so, his wife is unable to remarry. She is then called an *agunah*, or "anchored woman" — that is, one who cannot free herself from the marital bonds. Various approaches have been suggested for the resolution of this problem, including that of a legislative enactment, or *takkanah*, that would permit the wife to sue for divorce.[2] And indeed, some ancient Semitic traditions, evidence of which is reflected in the records of the

45

Jewish community of Elephantine, did permit the wife to initiate divorce proceedings.[3]

The basic rules relating to marriage and divorce are enunciated in the Torah, the five books of Moses. Prior to the performance of a marriage ceremony, the parties enter into an agreement, known as the *ketubbah*,[4] which provides that in the event of divorce or the death of the husband, the husband or his estate is obligated to pay the wife[5] a sum of money somewhat similar to today's alimony.

The biblical rules relating to divorce are set forth in Deuteronomy 24:1, as follows: "A man takes a wife and possesses her. She fails to please him because he finds something obnoxious [literally, a matter involving nakedness—*ervat davar*] about her, and he writes her a bill of divorcement, hands it to her, and sends her away from his house."

Over the centuries, through their explanations of these phrases, the rabbis erected an elaborate legal system, often exhibiting great compassion for the husband and wife. For instance, although bound by the explicit provisions in the Torah giving the husband the right to divorce his wife, they sought both to avoid divorce and to limit the power of the husband.

The rules relating to divorce under Jewish law are elaborated upon at great length in the Mishnah Gittin and in the Talmuds of Babylonia and Palestine, Tractates Gittin, which contain the comments and rulings of the early rabbis. Later, they were codified in various codes of Jewish law— written by Maimonides in the *Mishneh Torah* in the twelfth century; Jacob ben Asher in the thirteenth century; and Joseph Caro in the Shulhan Arukh in the sixteenth century.

Both Talmuds contain sayings reflecting the sanctity of marriage and the distaste of the rabbis for divorce, best exemplified by the statement of Rabbi Eleazar, that "one who divorces his first wife, even the very altar sheds tears because of him."[6] It is understandable, then, that the rabbis insisted that prior to any divorce proceedings the parties should attempt to resolve their differences and be reconciled with each other in mutual love and respect. As pointed out by a leading writer in the field,

> The reconciliation of persons about to be divorced, or who had already been divorced, afforded a fair field for the application of . . . ethical precepts. Besides the legal safeguards against unreasonable and ill-advised divorces, moral suasion was a potent factor, and it was the duty of the judges or Rabbis to exercise their influence in checking the unrestrained passions that often prompted men to divorce their wives without cause.[7]

The monetary payment required by the *ketubbah* agreement was instituted by the rabbis to discourage hasty divorces. They reasoned that the fact that the husband is required to make a substantial payment acts as a check on an ill-advised decision to divorce his wife.[8] The detailed procedures established in connection with the writing and transmission of the *get* also were designed to dissuade the husband from acting precipitously.[9] Thus, although the rabbis accepted the Divine ordinance written in the Torah permitting divorce, they did so with reluctance.

The attitudes of the rabbis differed as to the grounds for divorce, with the school of Shammai holding that divorce is appropriate *only* in a case of adultery, by the wife, while the school of Hillel maintained that some fault, however minimal, had to obtain. A third view was that of Rabbi Akiba, who lived a hundred years after them, that divorce is permitted even in the complete absence of fault on the part of the wife. Their disagreement centered on the proper interpretation of the term *ervat davar*. Shammai, the strict constructionist, took this phrase in its literal sense, of involving physical nakedness,[10] whereas both Hillel and Rabbi Akiba understood the term figuratively.[11]

Formal Requirements

Get is the Aramaic term for a legal document. (*Shetar* is the more commonly used Hebrew term.) The *get* is written in Hebrew and contains twelve lines, which is the numerical value of the Hebrew letters *gimel* (three) and *tet* (nine) spelling that term.[12]

The formal requirements for the writing of the *get* include the following:[13]

1. The *get* must be dated. According to custom, it is dated from the year of creation of the world according to the Jewish calendar (thus, 1990 = 5750). If the date is erroneous or if it was omitted, the *get* is not valid.
2. The *get* must be handwritten and include the exact names, including all nicknames of the particular individuals involved in the divorce.
3. The husband must specifically request of the scribe preparing the document that the *get* be written for his wife.
4. The place of residence of the parties must be included specifically.
5. Since the *get* certifies divorce and establishes the end of the marital relationship, it must contain words of complete separation. It must therefore explicitly state that the wife is permitted to remarry at will whomever she chooses. Then the *get* must be signed by two competent witnesses.
6. Finally, a *get* must be physically delivered by the husband (or his agent) to his wife (or her agent), or delivered to a place, such as her residence,

that is under her actual and physical control. This rule assures that the wife has actual or presumptive notice of its contents and, thus, of the change in her marital status. At the time of delivery, the husband must inform the wife that a *get* is being delivered. Under Jewish law, either the husband or the wife may appoint an agent to give or to accept a *get*.

Procedure

The *get* procedure, including the formalities of preparing the *get*, are so complex that the Talmud declares: "Rabbi Yehudah said in the name of Shmu'el: those [Rabbis] who are not well versed in the intricacies of marriage and divorce may not participate in divorce proceedings."[14]

Technically under Jewish law, appeal to the Jewish court, the *bet din*, in connection with the preparation and transmission of a *get* is unnecessary, since a *get* properly prepared, even by learned laymen, is valid. The complexities involved have led over time to the custom that the *get* be prepared and transmitted under the supervision of a rabbi learned in the law of divorce. Recourse to a full *bet din* is necessary to compel either spouse to participate in divorce proceedings.

Briefly, the proceedings are as follows:[15]

1. The parties appear before a rabbi learned in the law, a scribe, and two witnesses.
2. The husband orders the scribe to write the *get* for his wife, which the scribe proceeds to do, using a quill pen.
3. The husband declares that he is giving the *get* of his own free will, and a similar declaration is made by the wife concerning its receipt.
4. The *get* is then signed by the two witnesses.
5. The parties are again questioned as to whether they are giving and accepting the *get* voluntarily. The husband must state that he will never in the future cast any aspersion on the validity of the *get*.
6. The husband takes the *get* and drops it directly into his wife's cupped hands, stating: "This is your *get* and you are divorced from me, and are permitted to marry any man."
7. She then places the *get* under her arm and symbolically leaves by turning and moving several steps away.
8. The divorcée then returns, and the *get* is taken from her by the officiating rabbi, who tears the *get* crosswise.
9. Finally, the divorced woman is given a receipt (*petur*) to prove her divorced status.

The Search for Equality

The Talmudic Period (220–500 C.E.)

Although it is a fundamental principle of Jewish divorce law that only the husband is empowered to give a *get*, from early times the wife did have some rights in the matter. The husband's rights to divorce his wife against her will were limited by the Torah in two instances, in which it was explicitly declared that divorce was prohibited (though if she consented, of course, the divorce could proceed).[16]

First, Deuteronomy 22:28–29 states that in the case of the rape of an unmarried woman, the rapist must marry her, if she so chooses, and he is prohibited from ever divorcing her. Second, Deuteronomy 22:13–19 states that a newly married groom who falsely accuses his bride of having committed adultery after their formal betrothal (*erusin*) may never divorce her. As previously noted, there also existed a difference of opinion as to whether fault on the part of the wife was a prerequisite to the husband's right to divorce her. Later, the right of the husband to divorce his wife was curtailed under talmudic law if she was insane or else so mentally incompetent that she could not care for herself.[17]

In fact, according to the Talmud a wife could demand that her husband give her a *get* in the following cases:[18]

1. if the husband became afflicted with a loathsome disease after marriage, or if the existence of the disease was unknown to her prior to the marriage;
2. if the husband was impotent or sterile;
3. if the husband refused to provide her with necessities, or refused to engage in sexual relations with her;
4. if she was subject to physical or verbal abuse by the husband, or to misconduct, as, for example, if he forced her to violate a religious precept;
5. if her husband was engaged in some malodorous occupation, such as gathering dog dung, smelting copper, or tanning hides;
6. if the husband sought to leave the place where the couple resided and move to another country and she refused to go with him;
7. if the husband became an apostate.

In these cases, if the *get* was not forthcoming from the husband, the wife would petition the court (*bet din*), which would then compel the husband to give a *get*, even applying physical coercion if necessary.

Technically, in these circumstances it is not the *bet din* that is granting the *get*, or terminating the marriage, because unlike the situation in Western societies,[19] the giving of the *get* is a personal act between a husband and wife, with the courts and state (in Israel today) playing no role. The aid of the *bet din* is sometimes invoked to force one of the parties—usually the husband—to participate in divorce proceedings. Nevertheless, the role of the *bet din* is that of aiding the enforcement of rights that already exist. It is the husband, and he alone, who gives a *get*, rather than any *bet din*, or, in Israel today, the state.

There is obviously a tension between the halakhic rule that the giving of the *get* must result from the husband's free choice and the notion that the court can force the husband to give a *get*. This tension was resolved in talmudic times by the exotic logic that compulsion is applied until the husband objectively states his consent.[20] At a later period this apparant contradiction was rationalized by Maimonides, who asserted that the husband really wants to follow the decree of the *bet din* which has ordered him to give a *get*,[21] but he is being prevented from doing so by evil inclination, which spurs him to rebelliousness. By applying force, reasoned Maimonides, the court is doing no more than helping the husband to overcome his evil inclination, thereby permitting the husband's goodwill to emerge so that he complies with the court's directive and gives his wife a *get*. Admittedly, this is a legal fiction, designed to reconcile the rigorous requirements of Jewish divorce law with justice for the wife.

Not every court is authorized to use such compulsion, however. Problems have arisen in this area of law, precisely because it is *only* a Jewish *bet din* that can so pressure a man, and then *only* when authorized by Jewish law. Thus, if a particular *get* was not required under Jewish law, it is void, even if given under the compulsion of a *bet din*.

Where, however, a *bet din* has ordered a husband to give a *get* that is required under Jewish law, and a Gentile court, or even Jews or Gentiles acting individually, then performed the act of forcing the husband to give the *get*, the divorce is generally held to be valid because the Gentile court, or the individual Gentiles or Jews, were properly enforcing the directives of the *bet din*.

The Geonic Period (600–1200 C.E.)

For solutions in this troubled area of law, one need only review developments in the law during the period of the ascendancy of the Geonim. There existed two ancient and respected legal traditions in Jewish law affording protection to women in connection with divorce. The first of these, dating back to the Jewish community in Elephantine in Egypt and extending through the early medieval period, gave protection by means of an explicit provision in the *ketubbah* granting the wife the right to demand and obtain a *get*.[22] This approach is supported by respectable historical precedents.

After the conclusion of the Babylonian Talmud in approximately 500 C.E., there followed a period of legal efflorescence in the academies of Babylonia under the leadership and direction of their titular heads, called Geonim. This period lasted until the thirteenth century. The Geonim were particularly active in the area of divorce law; their compassion for women embroiled in unhappy marriages is manifested by their rulings. As the direct successors of the talmudic rabbis, they wrote, as it were, on a blank slate. Their jurisprudential genius is clearly manifested by their rulings in this as in other areas of law, *none of which have been ever duplicated* and many of which were later rejected outright by European authorities. Their spectacular achievements in this area of law consisted in the fact that for the first and unfortunately last time in Jewish jurisprudence, almost complete equality was effected between men and women as regards the rules relating to *get*.

Under the Geonic legislation, which lasted approximately five hundred years, it was enacted that a wife, if she desired a divorce, could petition the court for a *get*.[23] As stated by Sherira Gaon, in the tenth century:

When the Rabbanan Savorai [predecessors of the Geonim—successors of the Amoraim, 500–698 C.E.] saw that Jewish women go and attach themselves to the Gentiles, in an attempt to force their husbands to give a *get*, and sometimes the latter give *gittin* [pl. of *get*] under duress and grave questions arose as to whether they are properly being forced to give a *get* or improperly, and dreadful consequences ensue, it was enacted by [earlier Geonim] . . . that the husband is forced to give a *get* where the wife seeks a *get* . . . and we follow this *takanah* [legislative enactment] more than three hundred years later, and you do the same.[24]

In such circumstances, the court would direct the husband to give a *get*, applying compulsion if necessary.[25] Under this approach, the right of the husband to divorce his wife against her will remained inviolate; yet the wife was given a corresponding right to demand a *get*, even against the will of her husband. The wife's rights were thus equalized with the husband's except that it was still necessary for her to apply to the court to compel the giving of the *get* if the husband refused to do so voluntarily. Of course, the husband was under no such disability, since he could direct the preparation of the *get* and transmit it, at his will, as under talmudic law. This practice might be seen as the earliest form of "no-fault" divorce.

Maimonides, although rejecting the Geonic approach in the matter,[26] demonstrated his own lenient approach by ruling as follows: "If she says [she is rebelling] 'because he is repulsive to me, and I am unwilling voluntarily to engage in sexual relationships with him,' we force him to divorce her immediately, for she is not as a slave that she should be forced to have intercourse with one who is hateful to her."[27]

It is indeed unfortunate that the attitudes of both the Geonim and Maimonides in the matter were resoundingly rejected in Spain, France, and elsewhere,[28] owing to the force of the personality and scholarship of Rabbenu Tam, a French authority. Rabbenu Tam ruled that compulsion was *never* again to be exercised, *except* in those cases specifically provided for in the Talmud.

The pressure to interject a measure of equality into divorce law did exist on the European continent. However, it took a different direction under the leadership of Rabbenu Gershom of Mainz, who legislated in the tenth and eleventh centuries that a woman could not be divorced against her will,[29] thus somewhat improving the position of women in countries subject to that decree. As stated by Rabbenu Asher: "When he [Rabbenu Gershom] saw how the generation was abusive of Jewish daughters, insofar as divorcing them under compulsion, *he enacted that the rights of women be equal to those of men*, and just as a man divorces only from his own will, so too a woman might henceforth be divorced only willingly."[30] Although this enactment was a far cry from the liberal rights accorded women by the Geonim, and even under the approach of Maimonides, it was nevertheless a step in the right direction, which unfortunately has not been followed up by appropriate enactments to this day.

Modern Dilemmas and Solutions

The development of the institution of civil divorce in various European states gave rise to problems in Jewish divorce law, the reverberations of which are still being felt.[31] As long as divorce was subject to the authority of the church in Europe, Jewish residents generally retained autonomy over divorce, which was governed and controlled by Jewish courts. With the growth of civil divorce, however, Jewish law had to come to grips with a situation where a Jewish couple seeking divorce would be required to apply to the secular authorities for the civil termination of their marriage, and *then* to end their marriage under Jewish law by means of the *get* process. This duplication of effort was necessary because the state did not recognize a *get* as effecting the legal termination of the marriage, and conversely, Jewish law did not consider the civil divorce valid. Thus has arisen the problem, particularly pressing in Western societies, of the husband or wife refusing to permit the termination of the marriage under Jewish law by agreeing to give or accept a *get*, though a civil divorce has already been pronounced.

The "recalcitrant spouse" is a concern to both the Orthodox and Conservative branches of Judaism, which adhere to the requirement that a *get* is necessary to end a marriage. It poses a less direct and immediate problem in those branches of Judaism that consider civil divorce sufficient for Jewish law, though even here problems can emerge later on. For instance, under Jewish law, any children of a second marriage are deemed illegitimate (*mamzerim*) unless any first marriage of either of the spouses was ended by a *get*. The disabilities of such illegitimacy under Jewish law are considerable. Under Deuteronomy 23:3, an illegitimate person is prohibited from entering into a marital union with another Jew unless he or she is also illegitimate. While this may seem esoteric to many readers, in fact more than one-third of the world's Jews now live in Israel and another substantial proportion in other countries where traditional Jewish law holds sway. Given modern mobility, one cannot know with whom one's children will fall in love. Therefore the lack of a *get*, in an era with a high divorce rate, can cause problems for tens of thousands of children of second marriages.

It is therefore crucial for contemporary Jews to realize that regardless of whether they, or their ancestors, followed the liberal or the more traditional branches of Judaism, they can be affected by the reach of Jewish law. There are certain procedures available to the husband that in many circumstances enable him to evade the application of the enactment of Rabbenu Gershom that a wife has the right to refuse a *get*.[32] No such procedures are available to the wife, however, with the result that it is usually women who suffer most from recalcitrant spouses. Unable to remarry under Jewish law, and unable to obtain *gittin* from their husbands, these women remain "anchored" indefinitely unless they are willing to violate Jewish law.

The preceding survey, of course, relates only to the historical situation that continues today within the Diaspora, in which Jewish courts lack autonomy. In modern Israel, autonomy of Jewish courts exists once again over marriage and divorce. Nonetheless, the day-to-day situation is not much different from that in the Diaspora. The Israeli courts, although empowered to apply compulsion to force a recalcitrant husband to give a *get*, rarely do so, under the residual influence of the views of Rabbenu Tam.[33] Moreover, Israel does not provide an option of civil divorce for those who do not wish to observe halakhah.

Extensive abuses can be found today, both in Israel and in the Diaspora, including documented instances of extortion by one spouse or the other (usually the husband). In these instances, a *get* may be refused unless and until certain demands—often involving child custody or support provisions—are met or acceded to. Therefore, one finds numerous cases of women whose religious convictions have prevented them from ever re-marrying.

Men and women from within the traditional Jewish community have been greatly troubled by the difficulties faced by *agunot* who have struggled to obtain a *get*. Within the last decade, a number of grassroots organizations have been organized whose purpose is to alleviate the pain and suffering of these women. For example, the GET (Getting Equitable Treatment) organization was formed to facilitate the giving of a *get*. The Kayama organization is dedicated to educating the Jewish public on the necessity of transmitting and receiving a *get* and helping women obtain one.

The pressing nature of these problems has in the last few years become the focus of activist Orthodox Jewish feminists, who support various approaches to resolution of this problem. Agunah is one such women's group, which applies pressure to recalcitrant husbands by holding public demonstrations at their homes or places of business. It also acts as a pressure group to galvanize public opinion to motivate the Orthodox rabbinate to resolve this festering problem, seriously and in an organized fashion. Agunah's immediate goal is to provide concrete social service assistance and encouragement to individuals involved; its long-range goals are to serve as a catalyst for debate and to seek societal solutions from the organized rabbinate, a swift resolution of this problem being the ultimate wish.

Jewish courts have also attempted to keep pace with the growing dimensions of the problem by intensifying efforts at reconciliation of the spouses. Some Jewish courts will not issue a *get* unless the parties have first undergone a specified period of marital counseling, hoping that such counseling will remove or lessen the discord and obviate the desire for a *get*. However, this approach, though worthwhile before the fact, is useless if the marriage has already been dissolved civilly.

. . . [T]he Conservative movement, through its respected leader, the learned late Professor Saul Lieberman, has attempted to prevent the problem of the *agunah* through an amendment to the *ketubbah*.[34] In 1954, the Conference on Jewish Law, a joint body created by the Jewish Theological Seminary of America and the Rabbinical Assembly of America (both institutions of the Conservative branch of American Judaism), formulated the following addition to, or modification of, the traditional *ketubbah*:

> And, in solemn assent to their mutual responsibilities and love, the bride-groom and bride have declared: as evidence of our desire to enable each other

to live in accordance with the Jewish Law of Marriage throughout our lifetime, we, the bride and bridegroom, attach our signature to this Ketubah, and hereby agree to recognize the Beth Din of the Rabbinical Assembly and the Jewish Theological Seminary of America, or its duly appointed representatives, as having authority to counsel us in the light of Jewish tradition which requires husband and wife to give each other complete love and devotion, and to summon either party at the request of the other, in order to enable the party so requesting to live in accordance with the standards of the Jewish Law of Marriage throughout his or her lifetime. We authorize the Beth Din to impose such terms of compensation as it may see fit for failure to respond to its summons or to carry out its decision.[35]

Under this agreement, where a marriage has been civilly dissolved, and either spouse refuses to participate in *get* procedures, the other one may summon the recalcitrant spouse to appear before the *bet din* of the Jewish Theological Seminary for the purpose of counseling to enable the writing of a *get*. This approach has received civil judicial approval by the New York Court of Appeals in the case of *Avitzur* v. *Avitzur*.[36] That court, in a divided four-to-three decision, held that the clause was enforceable and that the parties could be directed by the courts to appear before the *bet din* for counseling for that purpose. The Court of Appeals did not, however, decide the ultimate issue of whether it would enforce an order of the *bet din* directing the parties to engage in *get* procedures.

There have also been attempts in Orthodox circles to implement a prenuptial agreement, under which the parties agree, under the threat of monetary sanctions, to participate in *get* proceedings upon the civil termination of their marriage.[37]

Another recent approach has been to resolve this problem directly through the civil legislative process. In two jurisdictions, New York and Canada,[38] legislation has been enacted that gives women equivalent rights to men. In New York, a plaintiff in a divorce proceeding may not obtain a civil divorce without complying with *get* procedures, if the marriage was celebrated in accordance with Jewish law. This rule, however, while sometimes helpful where the husband seeks the civil divorce, is generally ineffective because usually it is the wife who is the plaintiff in civil divorce proceedings.

The Canadian legislature has gone one step further. It has enacted a law in which *neither* party to a civil divorce proceeding may obtain any relief from the court unless he or she complies fully with the *get* procedures. This is a wholesome development and, if implemented elsewhere, would be most helpful in resolving this problem outside of Israel.

The *only* viable and complete solution under Jewish law for the pressing problem of the recalcitrant spouse is that of the reenactment of the type of legislation utilized by the Geonim. That solution involves the enactment of a *takkanah*, limited in scope, through which *the refusal by one spouse or the other to participate in get proceedings, after the civil termination of their marriage, would result in the retroactive annulment of that marriage.*[39]

It is to the speedy resolution of this pressing problem that this chapter is hopefully dedicated.

Notes

1. I. H. Haut, *Divorce in Jewish Law and Life* (New York: Sepher-Hermon Press, 1983), ch. 4. On divorce generally, see *Encyclopaedia Judaica*, vol. 6, "Divorce" (Keter Publishing House Ltd., Jerusalem, 1973), p. 122; D. W. Amram, *The Jewish Law of Divorce According to Bible and Talmud*, 2d ed. (New York: Hermon Press, 1968); *Jews and Divorce*, ed. J. Fried, (New York: Ktav Publishing House, 1968); S. Daiches, "Divorce in Jewish Law," in *Studies in Jewish Jurisprudence*, vol. 2 (New York: Hermon Press, 1974; reprinted from *Publications of the Society of Jewish Jurisprudence* 1, [1929]) p. 215.

2. Haut, supra, n. 1, ch. 3; I. H. Haut, "A Problem in Jewish Divorce Law: An Analysis and Some Suggestions," *Tradition* 16 (1977):29.

3. See generally, E. Lipinski, "The Wife's Right to Divorce in the Light of an Ancient Near Eastern Tradition," *Jewish Law Annual* 4 (1981):9; S. Riskin, *Women and Jewish Divorce* (Hoboken, N.J.: Ktav Publishing House, Ltd., 1989); M. Friedman, "Divorce Upon the Wife's Demand as Reflected in Manuscripts from the Cairo Geniza," *Jewish Law Annual* 4, supra, p. 103.

4. Haut, supra, n. 1, ch. 2; *Encyclopaedia Judaica*, vol. 10, "Ketubbah," p. 926.

5. See M. Chigier, *Husband and Wife in Israeli Law* (Jerusalem: Harry Fischel Institute for Research in Talmud and Jurisprudence, 1985) p. 159, n. 15, and by the same author, "The Widow's Rights in Jewish and Israeli Law," *Jewish Law Annual* 5 (1985): 44, 48, n. 34.

6. Rabbi Eleazar was a third generation Palestinian Amora, who flourished in the latter half of the third century c.e. His saying is found at B. Gittin 90b.

7. D. W. Amram, supra, n. 1, ch. 7, p. 79, points out that according to an ancient tradition the greatest glory of Aaron, the high priest, was his work in reconciling discontented husbands and wives, inducing them to live in harmony.

8. See B. Ketubbot 11a: "What is the reason for the *Ketubbah*? So that it shall not appear easy to divorce her." For further discussion see Haut, supra, n. 1, p. 7; Amram, supra, n. 1., p. 114; *Encyclopaedia Judaica*, supra, n. 4.

9. Haut, supra, n. 1, pp. 20–21.

10. Shammai was a Tanna who flourished in the second half of the first century b.c.e. and the first half of the first century c.e. Hillel was a Tanna who was a contemporary of Shammai. Their disagreement is found in Mishnah Gittin 9:10. See Amram, supra, n. 1, pp. 32–33:

The school of Shammai interpreted nearly all the Biblical laws strictly and rigorously. They were, to use a term applied to certain interpreters of the Constitution of the United States, Strict Constructionists; they held that a man cannot divorce his wife unless he has found her guilty of sexual immorality. . . . They held that these words (Hebrew, *ervath dabar*; literally, "the nakedness of the matter") signified immorality; and that the old law recognized this as the only legitimate cause for divorce.

11. For further discussion, see B. Gittin 90a.

12. B. Gittin 2a, Tosafot (beginning with the words, *hamayve get*).

13. Haut, supra, n. 1, ch. 6, pp. 27–30.

14. B. Kiddushin 6a.

15. Haut, supra, n. 1, ch. 7, pp. 31–41.

16. Ibid. ch. 4, pp. 18–19.

17. Ibid. p. 20.

18. Ibid. ch. 5, p. 25.

19. For further discussion, see Haut, supra, n. 1, p. 20, and, particularly, n. 18.

20. See generally, Haut, supra, n. 1, ch. 5, pp. 23–24. See Mishnah Erchin 5:6, "and the same rule applies in the case of divorce, we apply coercion, until he [the husband] says I agree [to give the *get*]."

21. See Maimonides, *Mishneh Torah*, "Laws of Divorce" 2:20.

22. See generally, J. J. Rabinowitz, *Jewish Law—Its Influence on the Development of Legal Institutions* (New York: Bloch, 1956), pp. 6–7 and chs. 5–6. Lipinski, supra, n. 3, pp. 20–21, suggests that there existed an ancient semitic tradition of law, manifested in the marriage contracts of the Jewish military colony in Elephantine, dating to the 5th century B.C.E., pursuant to which there was equality between the spouses as regards divorce. See Riskin, supra, n. 3, pp. 29–32, who takes the existence of such tradition in Elephantine as reflecting a continuing tradition to the talmudic period in Palestine, pursuant to which the wife was entitled to initiate divorce proceedings, presumably on the basis of a provision in her *ketubbah* to such effect. In such regard, he cites two discussions in the Palestinian Talmud, which appear to approve of such practice, at Ketubot 5:9. He also points out that such tradition extended to the beginning of the medieval period, as reflected in the findings from the Cairo Genizah. See ibid, ch. 5.

23. See generally, Riskin, supra, n. 3; Haut, supra, n. 1, ch. 9 and, particularly, pp. 51–52; Haut, *Tradition*, supra, n. 2, pp. 36–37.

24. The responsa quoted in the text at this endnote is quoted in full in Haut, supra, n. 1, p. 51, from C. Tykocinski, Tekanot Ha'geonim (New York: Sura, Jerusalem and Yeshiva U., 1960), ch. 1. These "dreadful consequences" consist of the fact that if the wife remarries on the basis of a coerced, and hence, invalid *get*, any children born of that union are deemed illegitimate, with serious disabilities under Jewish law.

25. See Responsa of Rabbenu Asher (Asher ben Yechiel, 1250–1327 C.E.), no. 43, subd. 8, who opposes the subject enactment but acknowledges, nonetheless, that it is properly based on the theory that all who wed do so in accordance with the will of

the Rabbis and that the Geonic Rabbis, therefore, acted within their power in annulling a marriage in which the wife wanted a divorce. For further discussion, see, Riskin, supra, n. 3, ch. 4.

26. Maimonides, *Mishneh Torah*, "Laws of Ishut" 14:14.

27. Id. at 14:8.

28. Haut, supra, n. 1, pp. 51–52; Haut, *Tradition*, supra, n. 2, pp. 37–38.

29. Rabbenu Gershom is also well known for his enactment prohibiting polygamy. It is interesting to note that unlike the prohibition of polygamy, which was not accepted by Oriental communities, the prohibition of divorce against the will of the wife was universally accepted. See B. Schereschewsky, *Family Law in Israel* (Jerusalem: R. Mass, 1974), p. 323; Y. Epstein, Aruch ha'-shulchan (*even ha'ezer*), vol. 6, 119:14; Haut, supra, n. 1, p. 55, n. 31.

30. Responsa, supra, n. 25, no. 42, subd. 1.

31. Haut, supra, n. 1, ch. 10, pp. 59–61.

32. See Haut, supra, n. 1, p. 56 and n. 33, for discussion of circumstances wherein the husband may avoid the application of the subject rule of Rabbenu Gershom, such as where the wife is declared to be "rebellious," by recourse to the *bet din*, or by means of permission obtained from one hundred rabbis.

33. See Haut, supra, n. 1, p. 13; Haut, supra, n. 2, *Tradition*, Appendix.

34. See Haut, supra, n. 1, ch. 11, pp. 63–65.

35. Quoted from A. Leo Levin and Meyer Kramer, *New Provisions in the Ketubah: A Legal Opinion* (New York: Yeshiva University, 1955), p. 2.

36. 58 N.Y.2d 108, 459 N.Y.S.2d 572, 446 N.E.2d 136 (1983). For further discussion of the decision in that case, see Haut, supra, n. 1, pp. 77–80.

37. On prenuptial agreements generally, see Haut, ibid, ch. 15, pp. 98–99.

38. Domestic Relations Law §253, enacted by Laws of 1983, ch. 979, §1, eff. August 8, 1983. For Canadian statute, see R.S., c.3, 27 (2d supp.).

39. Haut, supra, n. 1; Haut, *Tradition*, supra, n. 2. It is unfortunate that in his otherwise fine work of scholarship, Riskin, supra, n. 3, after detailing the brilliant contributions by the Geonim to this area of law, and after fully supporting and justifying their *takkanah*, refrained from advocating reenactment of the like type of *takkanah* called for by this writer. Instead he suggests a prenuptial agreement, which is far less effective. See ibid., p. 140.

Suggestions for Further Reading

Encyclopaedia Judaica (Jerusalem: Keter Publishing House, Ltd., 1973), 6:136–137 ("Divorce").

E. Lipinski, *The Wife's Right to Divorce in the Light of an Ancient Near Eastern Tradition*, vol. 4, *Jewish Law Annual*, p. 9.

I. H. Haut, *Divorce in Jewish Law and Life* (New York: Sepher-Hermon Press, 1983), App. A and Bibliography.

D. W. Amram, *The Jewish Law of Divorce According to Jewish Law and Talmud*, 2d ed. (New York: Hermon Press, 1968), a pioneering work in English by a noted and respected legal scholar, is a good introduction to the subject.

S. Riskin, *Women and Jewish Divorce* (Hoboken, N.J.: Ktav, 1989), is a scholarly book detailing the brilliant contributions by early rabbis, the Geonim, in this area.

7
Jewish Woman in Jewish Law: Solutions to Problems of *Agunah*

Moshe Meiselman

The past century has seen various attempts to solve the problem presented by husbands refusing to grant divorces to their wives when a beth-din determines that one is in order. Unfortunately, the proposed solutions were made by persons not sufficiently versed in the Jewish marriage and divorce laws and thus were rejected by the rabbinate as being inconsistent with halakhic requirements.

On July 29, 1884, secular divorce was introduced in France. A short time subsequent to that date, a Rabbi Michael Weil of Paris declared that upon receipt of a secular divorce a Jewish woman would be automatically divorced from her husband in the eyes of Jewish law. He based this on a series of talmudic statements. Essentially he claimed that the contemporary rabbinate had the power to annul any marriage. Thus, he said, the rabbinate of Paris would annul all marriages terminated in secular courts.

The response of the rabbinic authorities to this proposal was immediate.[1] They asserted that while the power of annulment allows the rabbinate to introduce certain very limited changes in the marriage and divorce ceremonies, Jewish marriage can be terminated only by a Jewish divorce or by the death of one of the parties. Furthermore, the legislative prerogative granted to rabbinic authorities came to an end with the termination of the talmudic period. Among the many reasons the legislative prerogative came to a close is the fact that subsequent to the talmudic period no beth-din was universally accepted by all Jews, and universal acceptance is a sine qua non for legislation.[2] Hence, no legislative prerogative to change the basic marriage and divorce laws was granted to any rabbi or group of rabbis subsequent to the talmudic period; even in that period, no rabbi or group of rabbis was allowed to terminate a marriage other than by a Jewish divorce or on the death of one of the two parties.

This decision was accepted by the entire French rabbinate. Rabbi Weil, however, put forth another proposal. He suggested that all marriages henceforth be made conditional. Thus, during the marriage ceremony the groom would declare: "Behold you are wed to me. However, if the judges of the state shall divorce us and I not give you a Jewish divorce, this marriage will be retroactively invalid." Thus, upon refusal by the husband to grant a Jewish divorce, the marriage would be retroactively dissolved. The couple would never have been married in the eyes of Jewish law and hence no Jewish divorce would be required.

Rabbi Tzaddok HaKohen of Paris turned to Rabbi Isaac Elchanan Spector of Kovno, the leader of the European rabbinate, for his opinion. In a letter dated 4 Sivan 5753 (1893), R. Isaac Elchanan reiterated the initial opposition to annulment. He then proceeded to rule unequivocally against the proposed conditional marriage.

After Rabbi Tzaddok HaKohen passed away in 1906, the movement to make all marriages in France conditional was initiated again by Rabbi Joseph Lehman of Paris. Rabbi Yehudah Lubetsky, also of Paris, wrote a responsum detailing the reasoning behind R. Isaac Elchanan's position and called on the entire European rabbinate for support. When the European rabbinate unanimously opposed the proposed conditional marriage, the matter was dropped. The entire correspondence was subsequently published in Vilna in 1930 under the title *Ain Tnai bi'Nisuin* (There Are No Conditional Marriages). This volume contained responsa from Rabbi Chaim Ozer Grodzenski of Vilna, Rabbi David Friedman of Karlin, Rabbi David Zvi Hoffman of Berlin, Rabbi Shlomoh Breuer of Frankfort, Rabbi Moshe Danishevsky of Slobodka, Rabbi Chaim Soloveichik of Brisk, Rabbi Meir Simhah HaKohen of Dvinsk, Rabbi Yehiel Epstein (the author of the *Arukh ha-Shulhan*), Rabbi Menahem Krakowski, and a host of other rabbinic luminaries.

The opposition to the proposed conditional marriage revolved around the fundamental differences between financial and personal contracts. One can stipulate any condition he wishes in a financial contract, but marriage is a very unique type of contract. The underlying assumption behind a large part of Jewish law is that cohabitation is an unconditional act.

The etiquette required of Jewish marital relations demands that they express a complete, unconditional commitment by each party to the other. This translates into a contractual assumption that a couple that has lived together as man and wife has waived all conditions in their marital contract, and that the marriage cannot henceforth be revoked by a failure of either party to abide by the conditions of the contract. The few exceptions to this rule are so limited and well defined that they cannot be extended to cover the suggested conditional marriage. Since the entire scholarly rabbinic world subscribed to this thesis, the proposal was dropped, and most rabbis felt that the reasoning behind the opposition precluded any such method for solving the divorce problem.

The next proposal came in 1930, from the American Conservative rabbinate. Louis Epstein of Boston suggested that, subsequent to every marriage, the husband appoint his wife as an agent to execute a divorce on his behalf. Thus, if the husband disappeared or refused to grant a divorce, the wife, acting as his agent, would be enabled to execute a divorce on his behalf. The woman would, in effect, divorce herself.

The proposal was made in a book entitled *Hatza'ah Lemaan Takanat Agunot*. Epstein realized that such agency to execute a divorce presented serious problems. The thrust of his book lay in his attempt to demonstrate the halakhic propriety of such agency. In the book he called upon the world rabbinate to evaluate the merits of his idea. In 1935 the Rabbinical Assembly, the rabbinic body of Conservative Judaism, voted to accept Epstein's proposal.

Again, the world rabbinate responded with unanimous disapproval. At a meeting in New York, convened by the Agudat ha-Rabanim, various halakhic presentations were made, demonstrating the impossibility of the appointment of an agent in such manner to execute a divorce. Furthermore, it was pointed out, if a husband subsequently refused to grant his wife a divorce, he could simply dismiss her as his agent, and hence not only was Epstein's proposal halakhically unsound, but also of very little practical benefit.

A more serious objection was presented to the meeting by Rabbi Moshe Soloveichik of New York. His reasoning was similar to that of the earlier rejection of the Paris proposal of conditional marriages. Cohabitation is an unconditional act expressive of unconditional commitment. Thus the appointment of an agent for a divorce is nullified by cohabitation, and just as conditional marriages cannot be utilized, so too conditional divorces cannot be utilized. In his address Rabbi Soloveichik quoted the words of Maimonides:

If he [the husband] was together with his wife after he appointed the scribe to write, or the witnesses to sign, or the agent to deliver the divorce to her, they may not proceed. It is logical to conclude this. A divorce which has already been delivered to her is rendered invalid when they are together, because we assume that they had marital relations [which invalidates all previous divorce proceedings]. Certainly a divorce which has not been written yet is rendered invalid. If the scribe wrote the divorce, the witnesses signed it, and the agent delivered it after they were together, the divorce is invalid.[3]

The effect of this law is to render impossible the initiation of any divorce proceeding at the time of marriage.

As a result of the unanimous protest by the world rabbinate, Epstein's proposal was shelved. The entire world-wide correspondence was published in 1937 in a volume entitled *Le'Dor Aharon*. In 1940, embittered by the rabbinate's rejection of his proposal, Epstein reiterated his suggestion in a book entitled *Le'Shaalat ha-Agunah*. Attempting to defend his position against his critics, he maintained that his method was a valid means of appointing an agent, but he completely ignored the complaint of Rabbi Moshe Soloveichik that marital relations render all previous divorce proceedings invalid. The book did not succeed in changing the minds of the rabbis whom Epstein wished to convince, and his proposal has never been revived.

In 1967 Dr. Eliezer Berkovits of Skokie, Illinois, published a book entitled *T'nai bi'Nisuin Ve'Get* (Conditional Marriages and Divorces) in which he asked the world rabbinate to reopen the question of conditional marriage. The book elicited virtually no response from the Orthodox rabbinate since his proposal was nothing more than a slight modification of the earlier Paris proposals. There was nothing substantially new in his book.

In response to a request from Rabbi Dov Katz, director of courts, Office of Religion of the State of Israel, Rabbi Menachem M. Kasher issued a responsum in *Noam*. After a detailed analysis of Berkovits's book, Rabbi Kasher concludes:

> In short, the author has not proposed anything new . . . to what was proposed in Paris, which proposals were unequivocally rejected by the rabbinic leaders.
>
> I have analyzed the work at length to show that in the essential point which is of practical significance in the proposed conditional marriage, he has clearly not proposed anything significant. He writes only of his doubts, his searching and seeking in the style of "for example, we might consider such and such."
>
> Even if he had advanced a brand-new type of conditional marriage, fundamentally different from the Paris proposal [which in fact he did not do] this would not alter the situation. The rabbinic leaders have rejected all

conditional marriages and have decided that under no circumstances can one terminate a marriage without a divorce. . . .

I am especially shocked that the author is completely oblivious to the fact that thirty years ago all rabbinic leaders of the day issued a decision, which was countersigned by over one thousand rabbis, in which they forbade and imposed a *herem* [decree of excommunication] against anyone who wishes to introduce the delivery of a *get* by means of an agent appointed at the time of the wedding. They included in this *herem* also the proposal of conditional marriage. This fact is well known in America and was printed in the book entitled *Le-Dor Aharon*. Furthermore, Rabbi Yehiel Yaakov Weinberg, who wrote a letter of quasi-approval to Dr. Berkovits's book, has written to me as follows:

"At the time that I wrote my letter, I was unaware of the discussion that had occurred in America. . . . Furthermore I am surprised that the author [i.e., Dr. Berkovits], who certainly knew of the entire correspondence in this matter, dragged me into this controversy. Because of my poor health, I am not capable now of dealing with a matter of such serious implications and I regret ever having written the letter to him."[4]

Dr. Berkovits's proposal was completely rejected by the Orthodox rabbinate. The Conservative rabbinate, faced with the utter impracticality of its own proposal of 1954, voted in 1968 to adopt Dr. Berkovits's proposal.

The various proposed solutions have placed the essence of the problem in sharp focus. In Judaism, marriage is a contract initiated and terminated only by the parties involved. No court was ever given the right to alter the marital status of a specific individual. The rabbis of the talmudic period were granted certain exceptional powers to establish or alter certain rules of the contract under the power of *afki'inhuh rabanan kiddushin minay*,[5] but these were universal rules of contract. The status of a specific person could not be determined by a court on an individual basis. A marriage, once finalized, could be terminated only by divorce or by death. Furthermore, the absolute seriousness of marital relations has ruled out the possibility of conditional marriage and divorce.

The only remedy that seems to be consistent with Jewish law is the one specifically suggested by the Talmud—the use of the secular judicial system. Outside Israel this means the enforcement by the secular courts of the directives of a rabbinic court—a beth-din.

In 1954 Professor Saul Lieberman proposed to the Rabbinical Assembly that the solution to the divorce problem lay in the Ketubah. He proposed the inclusion in the Ketubah of a statement wherein the husband and wife, at the time of marriage, would accept the authority of the religious court of the Rabbinical Assembly: "We authorize the Beth-din to impose such terms of compensation as it may see fit for failure to respond to its summons to carry out its decision." In this proposal, all aspects of conditional marriage and divorce are dropped. It was hoped that a financial penalty enforceable in the civil court would coerce unwilling husbands to grant to their wives religious divorces.

The response of the Orthodox rabbinate to this proposal was negative. There were a number of objections to Lieberman's proposal. The major one was that the contract wherein the husband or wife agreed to pay whatever compensation the beth-din would impose was halakhically questionable. A contract, according to the Halakhah, is required to be more specific. Most Orthodox scholars felt that such an indeterminate commitment as was proposed by the Conservative rabbinate was an *asmakhta* — a contract invalidated by the Halakhah because of its vagueness. Rabbi Norman Lamm of New York presented this view in an article in *Tradition*:

> The essential fault of the Conservative proposal . . . is its extremely indeterminate nature, a vagueness which Jewish law cannot tolerate as the proper basis for legal negotiation.[6]

Rabbi Binyomin Rabinowitz-Teumim of Jerusalem gave the same reason and also objected to this form of constraint to deliver a divorce.[7] Many forms of monetary constraint are valid, but certain forms of monetary constraint invalidate a divorce. The Ramah rules:

> When a man voluntarily accepted monetary sanctions upon himself should he refuse to issue a divorce, it is not considered an improper form of constraint, for he has the option of paying and not divorcing. However, there are some who invalidate the divorce in this manner. Therefore, initially one does not issue a divorce in this manner and our practice is to dismiss the threat of monetary sanctions.[8]

Rabbi Rabinowitz suggested utilizing such a contract but modifying it to avoid the problem of *asmakhta* — indeterminate contract — and adding the provision that financial constraint would only be applied if a competent Jewish court initially declared that the man is required to divorce his wife according to Jewish law. He advanced this as a tentative proposal and requested support from the American rabbinate.

This support was slow in coming for two reasons. First, in order to avoid the problem of *asmakhta*, the contract would have to be more specific and detailed. It was felt that once a contract was drawn up with specific and detailed financial penalties, the parties would be unwilling to sign it. In fact, it seems that this was the very reason for the vague wording of the contract proposed by the Rabbinical Assembly. Hence such specific contracts would not reasonably function toward solving the problem of enforcing a divorce where the husband is unwilling. The failure of the Conservative rabbinate to persuade people to sign their vaguely worded Ketubah subsequently confirmed this judgment.

Secondly, it is not at all clear whether such a contract would be upheld in the civil courts. This was argued very convincingly in a pamphlet by A. Leo Levin and Meyer Kramer, both of the University of Pennsylvania Law School.[9] They summarized their criticism of the proposal in

> the following major propositions: (1) the new *ketubah* in its truncated official English version is not a legally binding contract; (2) properly interpreted, the terms of the *ketubah* do not authorize the *Beth Din* to make an award for failure to give a *get*; (3) under arbitration law, authority of the *Beth Din* to make an award is, in any event, revocable; (4) punitive damages are not recoverable in a court of law and it will be for the court to determine whether the amount of an award constitutes a penalty; (5) in any event, court enforcement of a financial award made in order to compel the granting of a religious divorce would offend against the First and Fourteenth Amendments and would be unconstitutional.[10]

While these objections were made against the contract of the Rabbinical Assembly, the last three would seem to be applicable to any similar contract, including the proposal of Rabbi Rabinowitz.

I am unaware of any cases that have tested the validity of such contracts. Apparently, the agreement has not been used often enough to make it a meaningful solution. The fact that the Rabbinical Assembly accepted Berkovits's proposal in 1968 is the clearest indication that their own proposal had failed.[11]

The best way to effect a solution in the civil courts is not particularly clear. The small number of instances where a beth-din has been unable to extract a *get* has produced only a limited number of cases in the civil courts. Furthermore, great confusion has arisen regarding the details of Jewish divorce and the proper role of secular courts in their execution. Unfortunately, the courts have relied on less than expert advice in determining the halakhic facts.

The first significant case regarding Jewish divorce was *Koeppel* v. *Koeppel* in New York.[12] In the proceedings dissolving their marriage, Maureen and William Koeppel had signed an agreement containing the following provision:

> Upon the successful prosecution of the wife's action for the dissolution of her marriage, the Husband and Wife covenant and agree that he and she will,

whenever called upon and if and whenever the same shall become necessary, appear before a Rabbi or Rabbinate selected and designated by whomever of the parties who shall first demand the same, and execute any and all papers and documents required by and necessary to effectuate a dissolution of their marriage in accordance with the ecclesiastical laws of the Faith and Church of said parties.

When the husband refused to authorize a *get*, the wife sued in civil court. The court ruled that forcing the husband to grant a *get* "would not interfere with his freedom of religion." The judge wrote: "Complying with his agreement would not compel the defendant to practice any religion, not even the Jewish faith to which he still admits adherence. . . . His appearance before the Rabbinate to answer questions and give evidence required by them to make a decision is not a profession of faith." The court seemed to assume that if the beth-din ordered a *get*, the husband would be required to authorize it.

Unfortunately, a case arose in 1973, also in New York, which complicated the issue.[13] Selma and Myron Margulies had agreed to "appear before a Rabbi to be designated for the purpose of a Jewish religious divorce." The court initially ordered Myron Margulies to appear before a beth-din. When he refused to do so, he was fined and jailed for contempt of court. The case was appealed and the decision reversed. The court, in its opinion, stated:

It is argued that the court was without power to direct the defendant to participate in a religious divorce, as such is a matter of one's personal convictions, and is not subject to the Court's interference. We are told further that since a Jewish divorce can only be granted upon the representation that it is sought by the husband of his own free will, any such divorce, if obtained under compulsion by the court, would in any event be a nullity.[14]

The court, unfortunately, misunderstood the role of secular courts in enforcing a beth-din's order to grant a *get*. It also seems that the court misunderstood the entire process of Jewish divorce. Marriage and divorce are contracts in Judaism and require no declaration of dogma. The court, by comparing in its decision the granting of a *get* to Catholic confession, assumed incorrectly that a *get* is a sacrament.

Also in 1973, in *Pal* v. *Pal*, the court ordered the parties to submit to a beth-din. On June 17, 1974 the decision was reversed,[15] and the court, citing *Margulies* v. *Margulies*, ruled that it had no authority to convene a rabbinic court to decide whether or not a *get* was required. There was, however, an important dissenting opinion by Justice Martuscello. He pointed out that the court had erred in *Margulies* v. *Margulies* when it assumed that a divorce under constraint of a secular court is invalid. He further cited *Koeppel* v. *Koeppel* that an order to deliver a *get* is not a violation of constitutional rights.

At this time it is still unclear what direction the courts will take. There is precedent for the courts to refrain completely from forcing a husband to deliver a *get*. On the other hand, there is also precedent for a civil court to require a husband to appear before a beth-din and accede to its demand. However, it is essential that the courts understand the facts. A *get* delivered purely under coercion of a secular court is invalid. However, if the secular court merely coerces the husband into acceding to the beth-din's ruling, the *get* is valid. This is an indisputable fact of Jewish law. Also, it is essential that the courts realize that marriage and divorce in Judaism are contracts and not sacraments. It is certainly questionable whether forcing a person to execute a contract recognized as such only under religious law is constitutional. However, this is the only relevant question.

In the meantime, the standard practice of lawyers is to make the authorization of a *get* part of the property and support settlement. This is generally an effective means for dealing with husbands unwilling to grant, or wives unwilling to receive, a *get*. The legality of this practice was upheld in a recent case in New York, *Rubin* v. *Rubin*.[16] The couple had been divorced in Alabama, and the payment of support and alimony had been made dependent on the wife's appearing before a beth-din and accepting a *get*. The wife refused to accept a *get* and sued the husband for support. The court, in 1973, upheld the validity of the agreement whereby the husband withheld support pending the appearance of his ex-wife before a beth-din to accept a *get*. The implication of the decision was that it is completely legal to attach to the property and support settlement the requirement of giving and receiving a *get*.

A similar situation prevails in Canadian courts. Roberta Morris was divorced in Canada on July 14, 1972. When her husband refused to give her a *get*, she petitioned the court to force him to do so. She claimed that the Ketubah is a valid contract, and that her husband, in her Ketubah, had agreed to act "in accordance with the law of Moses and Israel," which requires a husband to accede to the ruling of a beth-din. Thus the wife demanded that the court enforce her Ketubah and force her husband to give her a *get*. On March 16, 1973, Justice Wilson of Manitoba Queen's Bench ordered the husband to give a *get* to his ex-wife in accord with the demand of the beth-din, adding that where there is no conflict of dogma, the court cannot be said to be entering a religious dispute.[17]

On December 27, 1973, Justice Wilson's decision was reversed by the Manitoba Court of Appeals,[18] Chief Justice Freedman dissenting. In his opinion, which concurred with Justice Wilson's, he claimed that the Ketubah is a valid contract, and hence the husband was contractually obligated to deliver a *get* to his wife.

Unfortunately, the justices who disagreed with Chief Justice Freedman misunderstood certain essential aspects of Jewish law. Some of them equated the Ketubah with a marriage vow, with its vague commitments to honor, love, and cherish the mate. This is incorrect. The Ketubah is not merely a marriage vow. Every party to a Jewish marriage, of necessity, must voluntarily accept upon himself all the detailed provisions of the Ketubah. Each of these obligations has detailed legal specifications and hence is not to be considered merely a vague promise.

Some of the judges wrongly assumed that Jewish law forbids the initiation of divorce proceedings by a woman, and therefore held that Roberta Morris, by initiating divorce proceedings in a Canadian court, had violated the tenets of Judaism. This is false. There are no religious directives whatsoever regarding divorce proceedings in a secular court. Moreover, a woman may petition a beth-din for a divorce. If the beth-din accepts her petition and orders the divorce, the husband must authorize the preparation of a *get* and deliver it to her. The beth-din can force him to carry out its directives if he refuses to do so voluntarily.

The case was appealed to the Supreme Court of Canada. The court's agreement to hear the case apparently indicated that it attached significance to both sides of the dispute, but the case was dropped because the plaintiff could not afford the additional legal costs attendant to a Supreme Court appeal. Thus in Canada, as in the United States, the issue remains unresolved.

Fortunately, cases where husbands refuse to grant divorces when required by Jewish law are few and far between, and a beth-din very often has sufficient power, by using social pressure, to secure compliance with its decision. Nonetheless, even if only a very few cases need to be resolved in the civil courts, we must do everything in our power to solve this problem. It is incumbent on the observant Jewish community to devise halakhically valid means of enforcing the orders of a beth-din through the civil courts.

Notes

1. The source material for the rabbinic rejection of annulment and conditional marriage is contained in R. Yehudah Lubetsky, *Ain Tnai be'Nisuin* (Vilna, 1930). In addition, the entire matter is discussed thoroughly in Abraham Chaim Freiman, *Seder Kiddushin ve'Nisuin* (Jerusalem: Mosad Harav Kook, 1945); R. Elyakim

Elinson, "Siruv Latet Get," *Sinai* 69, nos. 3–4 (1971): 135 ff.; R. Nisan Zaks "Kiddushin Al Tnai," *Noam* 1 (1958): 52 ff.

2. See Maimonides, introduction to *Yad Hazakah.* See in this connection *Shaalot u-Teshuvot ha-Rosh* 43:8.

3. Maimonides, *Hil. Gerushin* 9:25.

4. R. Menachem M. Kasher, "Be'Inyan Tnai bi'Nisuin," *Noam* 11 (1968): 346.

5. *Yeb.* 90b, 110a; *Git.* 33a, 73a; *B. B.* 48b; *Ket.* 3a.

6. "Recent Additions to the *Ketubah*," *Tradition* 2, no. 1 (Fall 1959): 93–119.

7. "Self-Imposed Constraint in Divorce," *Noam* 1 (1958): 287–312.

8. *Rama* to *Even ha-Ezer* 134:4.

9. A. Leo Levin and Meyer Kramer, *New Provisions in the Ketubah* (New York: Yeshiva University, 1955). Another article, "Civil Enforceability of Religious Antenupital Agreements," which appeared in 23 *University of Chicago Law Review,* p. 122, also demonstrates the legal tenuousness of the Rabbinical Assembly agreement.

10. Levin and Kramer, op. cit., p. 3.

11. *Proceedings of the Rabbinical Assembly* 32 (1968): 229–41.

12. 138 N.Y.S. 2d 366.

13. 344 N.Y.S. 2d 482.

14. Ibid.

15. 356 N.Y.S. 2d 672.

16. 348 N.Y.S. 2d 61.

17. 36 D.L.R. (3d) 447.

18. 42 D.L.R. 3d 550.

8
Ruminations over the Agunah Problem

Moshe Chigier

The problem of the *Agunah*[1] has absorbed the minds of many great Talmudic scholars during the ages. This was most probably due to the fact that of all prohibited marriages in Jewish Law, the marriage of a married woman (*eshet ish*) is most strongly guarded against and most scrupulously avoided. This is not because the punishment for transgressing it is the heaviest. On the contrary, of all the prohibited marriages punished by a Rabbinical Court, the punishment for marrying a married woman is the lightest.[2] The reason, most probably, is because this transgression does affect not only the transgressors but also the fruit of their sin—the offspring.

Furthermore, while the transgressors go nowadays unpunished, since capital punishment is no more practiced,[3] the punishment of the offspring, namely their being prohibited to marry within the Jewish community, is strongly upheld and insisted upon to the present day. Prohibition does not only apply to the first generation but also to all the issue throughout all generations that may follow. A child whose father or mother is a *mamzer(et)* inherits all disadvantages and disqualifications of the one parent notwithstanding that the other parent is a *kosher* Jew of Jewess in every respect.[4] Although the prohibition of *mamzerut* belongs to the lighter category of prohibited marriages, whose offspring are normally not considered *mamzerim*, the offspring of a *mamzer(et)* are excepted.[5]

True, incestuous marriages also bastardize their offspring.[6] But these cases are rare since the prohibition is usually supported and strengthened by the rules of nature: the instinct of a normally healthy person makes such union repulsive and repugnant. This is not the case with the married woman. On the contrary, quite often when the sexual instinct is not satisfied within the marriage relation, it insists on having intimate relations with another male or female. In addition, the married woman has to fight a stronger temptation than those mentioned above, since she has a good cover to her disgraceful action, her husband providing the excuse and protection in case of pregnancy.[7]

One may thus be justified in saying that the great difficulty the Rabbis experience in solving the *Agunah* problem to her satisfaction is not only because of the gravity of the sin of *eshet ish*, but also—and perhaps mainly—because of the serious consequences which may result from giving her an ill-founded permission to remarry, namely that the offspring may be *mamzerim*.

It is not, as some think, that the Rabbis are inconsiderate of the tragedy of the woman who seeks rehabilitation by remarrying and starting a new life. Indeed, they have the greatest sympathy with her and would willingly help her out of her miserable situation. What often prevents them from finding an easy solution to the problem is thir concern about the offspring, who might be declared *mamzerim* in case the permission was ill founded.[8]

The difficulty in solving *Agunah* problems seems to be due to the fact that we have here two impulses equal in strength, each pleading for consideration. The Rabbi who is called upon to release the woman from the bonds of her unhappy marriage sympathizes very strongly with her but, in his mind's eye, he sees also the fate and misery of her offspring. He begins thus to weigh one against the other and sometimes the scale is tipped against her.

It is probably this inner conflict that would explain the seemingly contradictory attitudes towards the *Agunah* problem to be noticed in the *halakhah*. There is no need, as some may think, to say that the different attitudes represent two different schools—the stern Shammai school and the more magnanimous Hillel school.[9] It is not a controversy among the Rabbis, but an inner conflict of emotions within each Rabbi who has to decide an *Agunah* case.

The Rules of Evidence

Thus we find that the Rabbis have permitted many relaxations in the rules of evidence in order to relieve the *Agunah* of her suffering and misery, notwithstanding the seriousness and gravity of the *eshet ish* transgression. The evidence of one witness that the woman's husband was dead is sufficient to grant her permission to remarry, although in other cases, less serious, such evidence is not sufficient. And this single witness need not be a person who would be qualified to testify (with another witness) in other matters. He may be a slave, even a slave-woman (two defects!), or a close relative. Even if he only states that he heard of the death of the husband from another person, also a relative—i.e., heresay evidence of and from a disqualified witness—such evidence is acceptable and the woman gets permission to remarry. Furthermore, a statement by the woman herself made in the presence of a Rabbinical Court that her husband has died would suffice to get that permit. Also, when she only states that someone told her that her husband died, she is believed, and the Court is relieved from inviting that person to testify before them.[10] When two witnesses give contradictory evidence regarding the circumstances of the death (for instance, one says he died a natural death and the other says he was killed), in other cases such evidence would be rejected, but in the case of the *Agunah* the fact that both have testified that the man has died suffices to permit the woman to remarry.[11] It even suffices when a person tells the Court that in passing a certain place he heard a voice saying this or that person is dead, or even when a piece of paper was brought to Court on which it was written that such and such a person died.[12] Such flouting of almost all the rules of evidence can only be explained by saying that the sympathy of the Rabbis for the poor woman was so great and so deep that, in spite of the gravity of *eshet ish*, they found a way to relieve her of her misery.[13]

Rules of Accuracy and Identification

On the other hand, we find in *halakhah* very rigid rules regarding the truth of the statement the witness has made, whatever it was. The Court is prepared to take his word for what he has said. But, if this statement is ambiguous, if he himself is not sure whether he heard it correctly, etc., then the Court would be unable to accept his evidence. Also, if they have a suspicion that what he has said was due to imagination, or that what he had stated was the result of a deduction or an inference which he has made, the woman will not get the permit. The *halakhah* seems to distinguish between the method of giving the evidence and the subject matter of the evidence. Any doubt as to the identity of the person testified to be dead would be fatal to the woman who seeks a permit to remarry. A great deal of time and consideration is given to establish the identity of the person in the case concerned, as well as to the accuracy and precise meaning of the evidence given.[14] Here the seriousness of the matter demanded great care and precaution, notwithstanding the sympathy the Rabbis felt for the poor woman, because they realized how fatal any slight error as to the identity of the dead person might be to the offspring of such a marriage.

The Types of *Agunah*

By definition,[15] there are three types of *Agunah*:

1. A woman whose husband refuses to grant her the *Get*,[16] defying the order of the Rabbinical Court
2. A woman whose husband is mentally ill and is incapable of performing the procedure of the divorce
3. A woman whose husband has gone and whose whereabouts are unknown

The great difficulty in dealing with these *Agunot* is caused by the *halakhic* demand that only the husband[17] may give the *Get* with a further condition that it should be given of his free will and with his full consent.

Of all these types, the first one is the most aggravating and agonizing to the woman as well as to all concerned. A wife whose husband has fallen ill may sometimes bear her sorrow heroically, knowing that there is no one to blame, and may hope for a change for the better. Also, the wife whose husband has disappeared may sometimes not condemn him forthwith. She may condone his disappearance by finding a possible excuse for it. He might have fallen ill or in bad times, and circumstances may prevent him from informing her of his whereabouts. She may thus bear no malice to him but await patiently his arrival or some information from him.

Entirely different is the case of the woman whose husband, just out of acrimony or jealousy, sadism or sheer cruelty and, sometimes, even cupidity, refuses to grant her the *Get* thus torturing her and making her suffer, often where the fault is his own. Here she becomes infuriated and often gives vent to her rage by protesting and demanding strongly that the Rabbinical Court should act to free her from her husband's tyranny and cruelty. In such cases the judges also feel very unhappy. They fully sympathize with the poor woman and would most willingly help her. They very much regret their incompetence to provide her with the succor she fully deserves. They further feel the degradation of their position as a Court of Justice in being unable to execute their own decision.

Small wonder then that, with the establishment of the Jewish State of Israel, came the public demand to rectify this situation and provide legal means to terminate it. But finding the remedy was not an easy task. The legislator could and indeed would enact that the husband should be forced to comply with the order of the Court on pain of suffering imprisonment. But before that, it would have to be considered whether such a *Get* would be valid from the *halakhic* point of view, since it would be, as it seems, in violation of the principle that the *Get* must be given freely.

A Forced Will

However, this problem was as old as the Law itself. The early Sages themselves realized already that to leave the wife at the mercy of a husband, depending in all cases upon his goodwill and discretion, could lead to grief and anguish, which the sense of justice and the feeling of mercy, so strongly emphasized and stressed in Jewish law and ethics, would unequivocally oppose. Accordingly, they declared that although the husband's will is necessary for the validity of the *Get*, it does not necessarily need to be an absolutely free will without the application of any force to induce him to agree to the granting of the *Get*.[18]

Consequently, we have the following Mishnaic Law: ". . . so also regarding a divorce we force him until he says 'I want to' (give the *Get*)."[19] A further elaboration is given in another Mishnah. "A *Get* given under compulsion is valid if it is ordered by an Israelite Court, but if by a Gentile court, it is invalid. But if the gentiles beat a man and say to him 'Do what the Israelites bid you,' it is valid."[20] Later on a proviso was made to it. The order must be according to the law; if the order of the Israelite Court was not in accordance with the law, the *Get* is invalid.[21]

This condition refers to the laws which state the cases when compulsion against the recalcitrant husband is permitted. The first list of cases is found in the Mishnah.[22] The Amoraim added another list[23] and, in course of time, some further cases have been added. As could be expected, the later lists were not unanimously accepted.[24] True to the nature of Jewish Law codification,[25] the codes recorded both opinions, leaving the matters in dispute to the discretion of the judging court.[26] If this had remained the position, the court could consider each case on its merits and by a process of deduction could decide whether an order of compulsion was lawful in the particular case, although it was not explicitly mentioned in the earlier lists. The list would thus remain open to be added to in the course of time, taking in consideration any new conditions of life.[27] But, regrettably, this is not the case in present times. The later *Poskim* have stated that compulsion would be lawful only in the cases distinctly stated by the Talmud; where the word "compelled" was omitted, no physical compulsion would be permissible and only moral pressure or persuasion may be applied.[28] As a result, the list is now closed.

The Rabbinical Courts Jurisdiction
(Marriage and Divorce) Law 1953[29]

Since the *halakhah* allows compulsion in certain instances it was felt by the religious members of the Knesset[30] that in the above law the Rabbinical Courts should be empowered to issue an order of compulsion against a recalcitrant party. As a result the following paragraph was incorporated.

> "6. Where a Rabbinical Court, by final judgment, has ordered that a husband be compelled to grant his wife the Bill of Divorce or that a wife be compelled to accept a Bill of Divorce from her husband, a district Court may upon expiration of six months from the day of making the order, on the application of the Attorney General, compel compliance with the order by imprisonment."

The Law has thus prescribed the following steps:

1. Only when the Rabbinical Court has issued an order distinctly stating that the husband should be compelled to grant a *Get* would compulsion become possible.
2. Only the Attorney General can apply to the district (Civil) Court for an Order of Imprisonment.
3. Only the Civil Court has jurisdiction to issue such an order.
4. Only after six months have elapsed from the date the Rabbinical Order was issued is the Attorney General to petition the Civil Court.

It is quite obvious that this procedure is cumbersome and uninviting either for the Rabbinical Court to institute or for the party concerned to pursue. One can understand why the Rabbinical Court must make it explicit that the husband should be compelled, for otherwise the civil court may apply force in cases in which the *halakhah* does not permit it. One may also accept the attitude of the legislator in not granting jurisdiction to the Rabbinical Court to issue an order for imprisonment, because this would mean granting them punitive powers. But the interim of six months seems to be quite an unnecessary postponement, especially in the case where the husband refuses point blank to comply with the Rabbinical decision. In fact, the Rabbinical Court would already have tried all kinds of persuasion and even threats, and would have given the husband time enough to consider and reconsider the matter, providing him with many opportunities to comply with the judgment. Only after all other means have failed would it have decided to issue an order of compulsion.[31] So what is the reason for a further delay of six months?

The exclusive authority granted to the Attorney General to lodge the petition to the District Court is also incomprehensible. Why could not the wife lodge the application? Why this double censorship on the order of the Rabbinical Court? Is the censorship of the District Court insufficient? Moreover the law, as it seems, has given the Attorney General absolute discretion in lodging the petition. Being an Executive Official he is not obliged to give reasons for his decision either to lodge or not to lodge the petition. Recourse to the High Court of Justice is only possible on the grounds of gross injustice, or willful negligence or another complaint of that nature. It is very unlikely that the Court would be prepared to listen to such arguments unless it could be proved positively beyond all doubt.[32] The woman who seeks relief by divorce has to overcome a very strong barrier in the Rabbinical Court. It may take a long time, sometimes several years, before the Court decides on divorce. Then she has to lift up the heavy bolt to open the door to obtain a special Order of Compulsion with which she could enter the Palace of Justice to get an Order of Imprisonment from the Civil District Court. Is such a difficult and protracted procedure[33] insufficient to assure that justice will be done? The extra impediment of having to pass another scrutiny by the Attorney General prolongs the time[34] and curbs her hopes of obtaining succor, with the result that she often abandons the only remedy provided by the legislator.

Moreover, the Rabbinical Court is discouraged by this extra censorship on their decision. Why should they strain their brains and enter into very complicated problems in order to pass a judgment which may not achieve the desired result? They feel the snub of the legislator, as if mistrusting their sincerity and impartiality.

Some have suggested that the reason for having the Attorney General's intervention was because it was feared that the Rabbinical Court might issue a Compulsion Order to couples whose prohibited marriage is indeed valid but must according to the *halakhah* be broken up by a divorce, as for instance when a Cohen marries a divorcee.[35] But if this was the reason, the Legislator would have provided a much easier means for preventing its occurrence. As a rule the Rabbinical Court issues the Compulsion Order only by the special application of the party concerned. It is a very remote possibility that the party seeking a divorce would rely only on the fact that the marriage was contrary to Jewish Law. Furthermore, as no such marriages could take place in Israel it can only occur in the case of Israeli citizens or residents who married abroad.

Ultimately it is the District Court which has to issue the order for imprisonment. Is not its censorship enough to guarantee that no miscarriage of justice will be done? Furthermore, the party affected has access to the High Court of Justice to lodge an appeal against the Rabbinical Court as well as against the District Court. Does one need further precautions over and above that?

One might have justified such extra precautions in 1953 when this law was enacted. At that time the High Court of Justice derived its authority from the Palestine Order in Council[36] and the mandatory Courts Ordinance.[37] There was no mention there of any authority to set aside a decision of a religious court. Petitions to the High Court of Justice of a party affected by a decision of a Rabbinical Court were not directed against the Rabbinical Court but against the Chief Execution Officer, ordering him to stay the execution.[38] Possibly the Legislator thought this remedy to be insufficient to prevent what he considered injustice. But in 1957 the Knesset enacted the Courts Law, where it empowered the High Court of Justice to issue a Mandamus or a Prohibition Order against a religious Court, ordering it to desist from considering a certain case or from passing judgment contrary to natural justice.[39] The affected party has thus several ways of preventing what he thinks is an unjust judgment of the Rabbinical Court.

General Trend of Curtailing the Jurisdiction of the Rabbinical Court

One cannot help but assume that the Attorney General's intervention is another illustration of the general trend to curtail the powers of the religious courts generally and of the Rabbinical Court in particular. This can be noticed in legislation but it is more obvious in the interpretations of the law, given by the High Court of Justice. They seem either to have been unaware or to have taken no notice of the fact that the less authority given to the Rabbinical Court the more *Agunah* problems would arise. A few illustrations will suffice to substantiate this contention.

Let us consider the following examples.

A Jewish girl living in Israel goes abroad where she marries an English or an American citizen. After some time she leaves him and returns to her home and family in Israel. Here she lodges a petition for divorce in the Rabbinical Court. When the husband receives a summons from the Court he does usually go to see his attorney, expecting him to arrange for another attorney in Israel to represent him at the proceedings and perhaps also to file a defence. He is however much surprised when he is told that he has nothing to worry about because according to the interpretation given to the Rabbinical Courts Jurisdiction Law by the High

Court of Justice, the Rabbinical Court has no jurisdiction if one party is not a citizen or resident of Israel.[40] Moreover, even in the case where the girl is a non-resident of Israel, but her husband is a resident, the High Court of Justice will order the Rabbinical Court not to deal with the petition because the petitioner is a non-resident, even though she may be very anxious to have her case decided by the Rabbinical Court.[41]

A more aggravating example. A couple, both Israeli citizens, go abroad. She returns to Israel determined to stay there even if her husband would remain abroad. She lodges a petition for divorce. Unless the husband, as is hardly likely, comes to Israel specially for the purpose of the case, that petition is doomed to failure *ab initio* in accordance with the interpretation given by the High Court of Justice that the jurisdiction of the Rabbinical Court is limited to the case where both parties are present in Israel.[42] Moreover, even if by luck or by chance the wife becomes aware that her husband is in Israel and hurries to her lawyer and serves a summons upon him, he will probably have nothing to worry about if it cannot be proved that the marriage took place in Israel.[43]

A final example. Suppose that all conditions of the limited jurisdiction have been satisfied and the court has issued an order for divorce. But the husband refuses to comply. The woman applies for an order of compulsion. The court, in considering her petition, comes to the conclusion that imprisonment is not warranted, but is prepared to apply a certain degree of pressure on him by issuing an order of maintenance for the wife over and above the amount which they would have given in a normal maintenance claim. This pressure might have resulted ultimately in granting the *Get*, but if the husband consults his attorney he would be told that he should take no notice of this order of maintenance, because the High Court of Justice has ruled that a maintenance order made *in terrorem*, for the sake of inducing the husband to grant a *Get*, is not valid.[44]

The High Court of Justice, so it seems, did not consider the consequences of curtailing the jurisdiction of the Rabbinical Court. This could lead either to the woman remaining an *Agunah* with very little chance of rehabilitating herself, or to her ignoring the Jewish (as well as the Israeli) law and living unmarried with another man, or perhaps arranging a civil marriage outside of Israel, thus increasing the number of *mamzerim*, who will present serious problems when they come to marry.

Suggested Remedies

Consequently it may be suggested that in order to reduce the number of *Agunot* or *mamzerim*, the legislator as well as the High Court of Justice should change their attitude towards the Rabbinical Courts. They should grant them the maximum authority to deal with matters of marriage and divorce. The above restrictions should be removed. Even as regards foreigners Private International Law would in many cases not object to passing a judgment for divorce. In many cases the local court would confirm the decision and would be prepared to charge the recalcitrant husband with contempt of court. The *Get* given after the husband has been threatened with imprisonment, and even after he was jailed for some time, could be considered a *Kosher Get* also from the halakhic point of view, since it would be based on an order issued by a halakhically competent court, as mentioned above. In any event, legislation to this effect could be sought in the foreign countries whose laws do not provide for such eventualities. It would be no difficult task to convince the authorities that it would be an act of justice and kindness to help the poor woman, provided however that the Israeli authorities, who are expected to care for their religious principles and tradition, would take the lead.[45]

Diffidence of the Rabbinical Courts

It would however be an overstatement to say that the above remedies would solve the *Agunah* problems. It would reduce the dimensions of the problem but it would not solve it, even as regards the recalcitrant husband. Neither is it possible to find a solution to all and every *Agunah* problem. There were and there will be difficult problems which defy any solution, but there can be no excuse for not trying to solve them.

Another cause for the increased number of *Agunah* problems is the diffidence and hesitation the Rabbinical Court displays in issuing compulsion orders. During the years 1953–1977 the Rabbinical Court issued only twelve compulsion orders.[46] There can be no doubt that there were, during that period, many more recalcitrant husbands and that some of them remained adamant to the last, making the wife either an *Agunah* or a *Zona*.[47] Thus some criticism of the diffidence of the Rabbinical Courts in issuing Compulsion Orders may be justified.

The writer is aware that he is treading on dangerous ground. Matters of *halakhah* are matters of conscience. No one can be criticized for acting according to the dictates of his conscience. Rabbis of great fame, great authorities in *halakhah*, have been dealing with the *Agunah* problems and seldom solved them. The author knows that "little learning is a dangerous thing" and does not wish the epigram "fools rush in where angels fear to tread"[48] to be applied to him. Nevertheless, since he has encountered these unfortunate women and considered their problems, it may not be improper to put these thoughts in writing.

Encouragement to do so is provided by the words, quoted below, written by the famous Gaon who was highly revered by orthodox Jewry all over the world, Rabbi J. J. Weinberg (of blessed memory):

> . . . . the position has become worse. New, difficult problems have arisen, problems that did not exist in former generations. Matters have reached such a stage that women obtain a decree of divorce from the civil courts and remarry, thus increasing the number of *mamzerim* among Jewry. The matter has now become widespread, not just a casual occurrence. It is therefore my opinion that we may not remain silent regarding this vile evil. It is an urgent need and a vital necessity to contemplate and consider how to remove this abomination.[49]

One must admit that he does not refer directly to the *Agunah* problem, which already existed in Talmudic times and is dealt with by Responsa literature of all ages. By saying that new problems have arisen which did not exist in former generations, Weinberg surely meant that we have to view these problems in a different light and consider them from a different angle. In former generations the effort of the Rabbi was directed towards saving the *Agunah* from her unfortunate position. He had to consider not only her position but also the position of her future children.[50] Consequently any doubt as to the *Kashrut* of the *Get* where compulsion is used against the husband caused the Rabbi to desist from applying it. The God-fearing woman was resigned to her fate, knowing that otherwise she would disgrace herself before God and before people, and would bring shame and misery to her offspring. The Rabbi could then permit himself to maintain that unless there existed absolute certainty that the *Get* would be *Kosher*, he must not insist that it should be granted.

Could a Rabbi or a Dayan in present times continue to maintain this attitude? Would he go home complacently after refusing a compulsion order and be satisfied that he did a good thing? Could he be sure that as a result of his refusal, the woman will bear her grief in silence? One glimpse of the situation would suffice for giving a categorically negative answer to these questions. On the contrary, his conscience would prick him very sharply. He acted with the aim of avoiding a small doubt as to the *Kashrut* of the *Get*[51] and consequently the *Kashrut* of the children. But as a result the woman would go to live with another man without having obtained a *Get*. By refusing to issue a compulsion order he thus turned a doubtful bastard (*safek mamzer*) into a certain bastard *(mamzer vaday)* – an outcome which would certainly cause the Rabbi to regret the way he handled the case. It may, therefore, be right to remind the Rabbi that when weighing the pros and cons for issuing a compulsion order he should put on the scale also the possible result of his refusing the order. It is this new factor, and this new approach to the *Agunah* problem, that Rabbi Weinberg was referring to in the above quotation.

This new factor appeared comparatively recently. It first appeared in Napoleonic times and has produced a vast literature hence. Many suggestions for remedying the situation have been put forward, some by well-known Talmudic authorities, but so far without result.[52] In Israel the Knesset has taken cognizance of the problem. But most deplorably it did not produce the results expected, due to the causes mentioned above.

Marriage by Free Will Only

At a time when *patria potestas* was universally practiced, when children were considered the personal assets of the father to deal with as he wished, Jewish law declared that marriage can be effected only with the free and full consent both of the man and of the woman.[53] In the Talmud the marriage agreement (*kidushin*) is treated as a consensual obligation. Both parties may make all sorts of stipulations, the fulfillment of which would be required to make the marriage valid.[54]

Accordingly, when a woman stipulates that if a certain thing will happen (or will not happen), the marriage shall be null and void, the validity of the marriage will depend upon fulfillment of the stipulation. Thus if a woman declares at the time the *kidushin* is made that she consents to be married to this man on condition that he will not ill-treat her, or that he will not one day disappear without informing her where he was, or that he will not go to stay with another woman, or on condition that he does not become so incurably ill that he is not able to attend to his affairs, etc. – the marriage would then be conditional, and if any of the above happens she could come to Court for a declaratory judgment that the marriage is null and void. She would then revert to the status of a spinster and be allowed to re-marry.

Presumption of Waiving the Conditions

It would thus be a proper solution to *Agunah* problems of the ill or lost husband to introduce conditional marriages. This might have been the case in the times prior to the Amoraic period. But then a great obstruction was put in the way of contracting conditional marriages.

Rav – one of the leading authorities – made, so to speak, a psychological analysis of such a stipulator, and stated that if the husband did not repeat the stipulation when the marriage was consummated, it may be presumed that he has waived it. In his opinion a man does not wish to live with a woman without marrying her, which might result if the condition is not discharged. Accordingly, the fact that he did not repeat this condition at the time of consummation suggests that he changed his mind and waived the condition.[55] And since the condition to be effective would have to be proved by reliable witnesses, the repetition of the stipulation became practically impossible, and no marriage could therefore henceforth be considered as conditional.

But this presumption is not irrebuttable. Indeed Samuel—an Amora of no lesser authority—has absolutely denied and rejected such a presumption.[56] And although the *halakhah* has accepted the former opinion[57] it did not entirely discard the second. Many great authorities of later times have stated that Rav himself only said that we doubt whether the person was still insisting upon the condition. Consequently the wife could not be permitted to remarry without obtaining a *Get*, even if the condition was not discharged. But should she become betrothed to another man in the interim, the betrothal would be valid just as if she were not a married woman.[58] One may thus maintain that a woman that made a stipulation of the kind mentioned above would be only *safek eshet ish*.

The Presumption in Present Times

The above presumption was surely based upon careful observation of the behavior of the people in society, but such an estimation is only man-made and therefore may not hold good at all times and in all circumstances. Surely Rav did not mean to say that this presumption holds good for all generations no matter what their behavior might be. To say that a presumption of this kind is not susceptible to changes neither of time nor of environment, nor of human conduct, beliefs or opinions, etc., would be sheer naivety and gross misunderstanding.

Could we entertain such a presumption nowadays, observing the conduct of people of present society? Surely, one who suggested in present times, that no person would wish to make the marriage conditional, being worried that it might turn out that he (or she) had lived with the consort unmarried, would be considered to be absolutely unobservant of his environment, sitting on Olympus and seeing nothing of his surroundings.[59]

Marriage Nowadays

In addition there is a further consideration. In former times the betrothal was made a considerable time before the marriage. It was then reasonable to doubt whether the stipulator still insisted on the stipulation if he did not repeat it. But this practice has now been stopped, and it became forbidden to make the betrothal before the marriage.[60] Nowadays the betrothal as well as the marriage is performed at the time the couple stand under the wedding canopy. Afterwards they are left alone to symbolize consummation. Could any doubt enter the mind of a reasonable person that the man who made a stipulation a few minutes before has changed his mind?

Furthermore, we may doubt whether Rav meant to apply this presumption also to a woman stipulator. It is especially doubtful whether Rav meant the presumption to apply to all sorts of conditions.[61] Surely a stipulation made by the woman of the kind mentioned above, which would affect her whole future life and happiness, cannot be assumed to have been waived because of a doubtful presumption.

Presumption That Women Are Not Particular in Choosing Their Consort

The opinion has been expressed in the Talmud that if something very unpleasant has occurred to a married woman subsequent to her marriage, we may annul the marriage by maintaining that had she known what was going to happen she would not have consented to be married. However, this opinion was not accepted by other authorities, because they held the view that a woman was not particular about her consort and was willing to marry almost anyone unconditionally.[62]

Here too we may doubt if this assertion regarding the nature of women applies equally nowadays. Surely this supposition too was based on observation and is not an eternal unchangeable fact. The emancipated woman of the present day with the ability to earn her living and with a strong sense of independence, is entirely different from the women of the time of the Talmud. There can be no doubt that woman nowadays are more selective and take greater care in choosing their consort than did the women of old. Consequently, one may argue that nowadays if the *Agunah* (of any kind) declares that had she known that this would happen, she would not have consented to marry, her declaration should be given effect.

Conclusion

Reflections on the *Agunah* problem lead one to maintain that it is possible, in many instances, to make out a case that the woman is not a *vaday eshet ish*.

In the case of the recalcitrant husband when the Rabbinical Court has decided that the husband has to give the *Get*, there should be little hesitation to issue an order of compulsion, knowing that this can only result in imprisonment, and not in the heavier corporal punishment of whipping. The slight doubt that may perhaps remain should be overcome by considering the result of refusing such an order. Of course, the lay authorities should give the Rabbis assistance by allowing them more freedom to act in matters of marriage and divorce.

In the case of the husband's illness or disappearance, the remedy is more difficult for those already married, but also there one may argue that the woman is not a *vaday eshet ish*. As for the future, conditional marriages should be considered as such, and a condition providing for such eventualities should be worked out by the great Rabbinical authorities for insertion in the *Ketubah* or in an additional document, signed by bride and bridegroom just before they come under the canopy. Here too, there may remain a residue of doubt. But the seriousness of the position strongly demands remedial devices. The inertia so far shown should give way to serious consideration in order to find ways and means to remedy the present intolerable situation.[63]

Notes

1. "The term Agunah is applied to a married woman who is separated from her husband but cannot obtain permission to remarry because her husband is either unwilling to grant her a divorce or because he cannot do so on account of illness or because he is absent and cannot be traced." *Encyclopaedia Judaica*, "Aguna."

2. Of all four forms of capital punishment: stoning, burning, guillotining, and suffocating, the last one meted out for fornication with a married woman is the lightest. *Maimonides, Hilkhot Shoftim* 14:4.

3. The authority to impose capital punishment ceased already in the first century A.D.: *Maimonides, Hilkhot Shoftim* 14:13.

4. *Shulhan Arukh, Even Ha'ezer* 4:1:18.

5. *Maimonides, Ishut* 1:7; *Shulhan Arukh, Even Ha'ezer* 4:13.

6. See *Shulhan Arukh, Even Ha'ezer* 15.

7. The *husband-shield* is so strongly impregnable that even when it is well known to all that he was absent for a very long time—to some authorities even for many years—it is still presumed that he is the father of the child his wife bore in his absence by assuming that he came to visit her one night using supernatural powers (*shem hameforash*). *Tur Even Ha'ezer* 4; *Shulhan Arukh, Even Ha'ezer* 14:14. (Incidentally, this matter provides a clear illustration of how reluctant the Rabbis were to stigmatize a child as a *mamzer*, undoubtedly because of the great misery this would cause.

8. The greatest tragedy is that of the young woman who is yearning for a normal life with a husband and family. The writer, in his capacity as legal adviser, has more than once succeeded in dissuading such a woman from marrying without the permission of the Rabbis by picturing to her the fate of her future children.

9. Only in one case do we have a difference between the two schools (*Yeb.* 122a).

10. *Shulhan Arukh, Even Ha'ezer* 17:3, 4, 5.

11. *Ibid.*, 17:9.

12. *Ibid.*, 17:10.

13. "The reason why the rabbis have relaxed these laws of evidence in this case, is in order that Jewish daughters should not remain *Agunoth.*" Maimonides, *Hilkhot Gerushin* 3:28-29.

14. On section 17 of *Shulhan Arukh, Even Ha'ezer*, which deals with *agunah* problems, we have six thick volumes of the *Otsar Haposkim*, giving a synopsis of the various Responsa on this subject. See Chigier, "Codification of Jewish law," *The Jewish Law Annual* II (1979), 27.

15. See note 1.

16. The Bill of Divorce required by Jewish Law, which must be given by the husband.

17. He may however appoint another person to deputize for him. But, as the procedure is quite complicated, it is made use of only in exceptional circumstances.

18. Philosophically speaking, it seems that an absolute free will is non-existent. All human actions are motivated and are performed with a purpose of gaining or achieving something. Altruistic activities are, at their best, unselfish but not unmotivated. The mother is moved by a strong sentiment of love to tend her child. The philanthropist is induced to be charitable by a strong sense of pity and sympathy for the poor and needy or, as it occurs in some cases, in order to achieve fame and a good name. Even the seemingly passive activity of thinking is conative. When the law demands that an act to have legal validity must be done with a free will, and that, for instance, a sale, or a contract entered into by force, is not valid, it refers only to a strong physical force. Force of circumstances of any kind does not invalidate it. Fear for punishment, either imprisonment or a fine or any other kind of unpleasantness, for not fulfilling an obligation, would not vitiate the act done in the process of fulfillment. All these are the motives for willing to perform the act. They, so to say, force him to will. But the will is there so that one cannot say that it was done without his will. Indeed, Jewish Law — unlike other systems of law — does not invalidate a sale done by the seller in order to save his life (*B.B.* 48b.). To say that a *Get* granted as a result of any kind of pressure, or in order to avoid any kind of punishment, is invalid would indeed be an unreasonable polarization. (See *Tosafot B.B.* 48a, s.v. *Elima*, where it is stated that a forced *Get*, when one is obliged to grant it, is to be treated on the same principle as a forced sale.)

19. *Arak.* 21.

20. *Gitt.* 88b.

21. *Ibid.* See *Maimonides, Hilkhot Gerushin* 2:20 for an explanation of why the *Get* granted after whipping is still considered to have been given willingly. This explanation holds good only when compulsion was lawful.

22. *Ket.* 77a.

23. *Ket.* 77a.

24. See *Shulhan Arukh, Even Ha'ezer* 154 and *Rema* there.

25. See Chigier, *supra* n. 14, at 17ff.

26. For authorities adopting such attitude see Warhaftig in *Shenaton Hamishpat Ha'ivri* 3–4 (1976–7), 160.

27. Generally speaking we may say that the causes for divorce in Jewish Law correspond more or less to those found in many systems of law in modern times, which can be summarized under the following headings: Adultery, cruelty and desertion. But apart from adultery, which is a definite act, admitting of differences of opinion only as to proof, the other two causes are flexibly defined and in many cases it is left to the discretion of the judging court. As a result one may find seemingly contradictory judgments in these cases. So also in Jewish law.

28. *Shulhan Arukh, Even Ha'ezer* 154:21 and *Rema* there. It is rather surprising that these Rabbis considered only the two possibilities: whipping or rebuking, but nothing in between these two polarities such as imprisonment or a fine. For further opinions on this subject see Warhaftig, *supra* n. 26. Particularly harsh is the following opinion of the *Hatam Sofer* regarding the epileptic husband, "since it is the opinion of the *Mordekhai* that compulsion is not to be used against this husband to divorce his wife, and we are in no position to determine who is in the right, if he divorces his wife by compulsion, the *Get* is invalid and she remains an *eshet ish medeoritha* for all purposes, without any doubt whatsoever" (*Even Ha'ezer* Section 116, quoted in *Piske Din Harabaniyim* I. 73–74). Needless to say, this statement deters many Rabbis from even discussing compulsory measures.

29. *Laws of the State of Israel*, vols. 5–8, p. 139.

30. The sponsors of this law were the National-Religious party members, headed by the then-deputy Minister of Religious Affairs Dr. Z. Warhaftig.

31. The procedure adopted by the Court is first to reach a decision that the husband is to divorce his wife. Only when the wife has waited for some time and the husband remains adamant may she apply to the Court to issue an order of compulsion. From what was stated above one may gather that it would take a considerable time before that order would be issued.

32. Only once was an attempt made to appeal to the High Court of Justice against the decision of the Attorney General not to lodge the petition. The Court dismissed it in a few words without giving a proper explanation for the rejection (*15 Pesakim Elyonim* 455).

33. Most likely she would have to await the results of the rabbinical Court of Appeal, since the law demands that the judgment must be final.

34. Professor Z. Falk in discussing this matter mentions a case where three years had passed before the Rabbinical order for compulsion was placed before the District

Court, *Tevi'at Gerushin mitsad ha'ishah bedine yisra'el* (Jerusalem: Institute for Legislative Research and Comparative Law, 1973), 42.

35. See Warhaftig, *supra* n. 26, at 204.

36. R. H. Drayton, *Laws of Palestine* (London: Waterlow & Sons, 1934), sec, 43 at 2579.

37. Drayton, *supra* n. 36, sec. 6 at 399.

38. See Chigier, "Rabbinical Courts in Israel," *Israel Law Review* 2 (1967), 147–171.

39. Section 7 (b) (4), *Laws of the State of Israel*, vol. 11–12, p. 158.

40. See M. Silberg, *Hama'amad Ha'ishi beyisra'el* (Jerusalem: Hebrew University of Jerusalem, 1961), 87.

41. *Ibid.*, at 90. That both parties must be citizens or at least resident was never doubted and is referred to in many Court decisions.

42. Matalon v. Rabbinical Court, 17 P.D. 1640; Reiss v. Rabbinical Court, 27 (1) P.D. 25. See especially Hen v. Rabbinical Court, 31 (3) P.D. 679, where Justice Landau (the present President of the Supreme Court) argues very strongly against the opinion of the majority.

43. See Kahanof v. Rabbinical Court, 29 (1) P.D. 449.

44. 9 P.D. 1541, 1543, 1550.

45. Indeed, we have several cases where the foreign court has adopted the view that a husband should be punished for refusing to give a Jewish *get* to his wife. Brett v. Brett [1969] 1 All E.R. 1007. See further Freeman, *infra*.

46. Warhaftig, *supra* n. 26, at 205.

47. A woman who lives in sin.

48. A. Pope, *Essay on Criticism* (Oxford: The Clarendon Press, 1928), 203, 211.

49. Translated from his Foreword to A. Berkowitz, *Tenai binesu'in uveget* (Jerusalem: Mosad Harav Kook, 5727).

50. See above p. 207f.

51. See above p. 213 for the doubts expressed by the later *Poskim* as to the validity of the *Get*. We may add a further doubt as to whether imprisonment is tantamount to whipping. One may rightly distinguish between corporal punishment and the less severe imprisonment. Certainly a monetary fine would be a still lesser punishment.

52. To describe and evaluate all the discussions of this problem would be beyond the scope of this article. The interested reader may obtain an historical survey in the following books: Rabbi Berkowitz, *supra* n. 48; Professor Z. Falk, *supra* n. 34. A most interesting article on the subject of conditional marriage by Rabbi A.I. Kook can be found in his book *Ezrat Cohen* (Jerusalem: Mosad Harav Kook, 1969), 160–172.

53. The Biblical law has indeed made one exception. The father may give in marriage his young daughter—up to the age of 12½—to anyone he pleases, but this was prohibited by the Rabbis. See *Kidd.* 41a. The Council of the Chief Rabbinate in Israel has prohibited the marriage of a girl under the age of 16. See B. Schereschewsky, *Dine mishpahah* (Jerusalem: Reuven Mass, 1958), 2 ed., 432. Israeli law prohibits the marriage of a girl under 17: Marriage Law 1950, 4 *Laws of the State of Israel* 158. See also Elon, *Israel Law Review* 4 (1969), 113.

54. For all kinds of stipulations see *Shulhan Arukh, Even Ha'ezer* 54. The stipulations there mentioned are made by the man, since this was the usual case in those times, but the rules would equally apply to stipulations made by the woman.

55. *Ket.* 73a.

56. *Ibid.*

57. *Shulhan Arukh, Even Ha'ezer* 38:35.

58. See *Rosh* on *Ket.* 73. *Maimonides, Hilkhot Ishut* 7–23; *Rema, Ibid.*

59. See *Maimonides, Hilkot Ishut* 7–23, who maintains that this presumption applies only in a few cases and only to a religious person.

60. *Takanah* passed by the Council of the Chief Rabbinate of Israel, 1950. See Schereschewsky (*supra* n. 53), 431.

61. See *Mishneh Lemelekh, Gerushin* 10:18.

62. *B.K.* 110, 111. See *Tosephot Ketuboth* 47b. Also make a "hair-splitting" distinction between the *Yavam* and the husband.

63. The writer hopes that he shall not be criticized for oversimplifying the intricate problems, without explaining the various opinions of the early and later *Poskim*. This article was intended only to set out the problems and to make some suggestions for the consideration of the authorities, who are fully aware of the difficulties involved.

Bibliography

(abbreviated titles in parentheses)

All England Reports (A.E.R.)

Annotated Law Reports (A.L.R.) published during the Mandatory Period.

Ba'er Heiteiv (commentary on *Even Ha'ezer*)

Bet Shemuel (commentary on *Even Ha'ezer*)

Bible: Genesis, Leviticus

Brambley, P.M., Family Law (English) 4th ed. (London, Butterworth, 1971)

Caro, J., *Shulhan Arukh: Even Ha'ezer, Yore Dea, Hoshen Hamishpat*

Chigier, M., Rabbinical Courts in Israel, "Laws in Ancient and Modern Israel" (New York, Ktav, 1972); 2 Israel Law Review (1967) 147–171.

Divrei Knesset (D.K.). Record of *Knesset* proceedings.

Drayton, R.H., The Laws of Palestine (London, Waterlow and Sons, 1934)

Dukhan, Laws of Palestine 1918–1925 (Tel Aviv, Rotenberg, 1933)

Edward, C., The World's Earliest Laws (Thinkers Library, 1934)

Falk, Z.W., Religious Law and the Modern Family in Israel, 6 School of Oriental and African Studies (London, George Allen and Unwin, 1968).

Goitein, S.D., *Hamishpat Hamuslimi B'medinat Yisrael* (Jerusalem, *Gvilim* 1957)

Hapraklit, published by the Israel Bar Association

Hatzaot Hok proposed laws

Institute of Justinian. Translated by J.B. Moyle, 5th ed. (Oxford, Clarendon Press, 1945)

Israel Law Review (I.L.R.) published by Hebrew University, Jerusalem
Kovetz Takanot, official gazette for secondary legislation
Laws of the State of Israel (L.S.I.)

Lee, R.W., Elements of Roman Law (London, Sweet and Maxwell, 1949); Roman Dutch Law (Oxford, 1948)

Layish, A., Women and Islamic Law in a non-Muslim State (Jerusalem, Keter, 1975).

Mehlita, Mishpatim
Maimonides, *Yad Hahazaka*

Ostrowsky, *Irgun Hayishuv Hayehudi* B'eretz Yisrael (Jerusalem, 1941)

Palestine Law Reports (P.L.R.) published during the Mandatory period.

Piskei Din (P.D.), Law Reports of the Supreme Court (published by the Ministry of Justice, Jerusalem)

Piskei Din shel Batei Hadin Harabani'im Beyisrael (P.D.R.)
Piskei Din shel Batei Mishpat Mehozi'im (P.M.)
Pithei Teshuvah (commentary on *Shulchan Aruch*)

Psakim Elyonim (P.E.), Law Reports of the Supreme Court published by the Israel Bar Association.

Qur'an (The Glorious). Translated by M. Pickthal (Hyderabad-Deccan, Government Central Press, 1938).

Salmond, Jurisprudence, 10th ed. (London, Sweet and Maxwell, 1947)

Schacht, J., An Introduction to Islamic Law (Oxford, Clarendon Press, 1964)

Scheftelowitz, E.E., Family Law (Hebrew) (Tel Aviv, Gvilim, 1965)

Schereschewsky, B.Z., *Dinei Mishpaha* (Jerusalem, Rubin Mass, 1967)

Sefer Hahukim (S.H.), Laws of Israel (Hebrew)
Shai Lamoreh (commentary on *Even Ha'ezer*)
Shakh (*Siftei Cohen*), commentary on *Shulhan Arukh*)

Sheinbaum, E., Personal Law, *Sidrei Shilton Umishpat* (Tel Aviv, Yahdav, 1971).

Silberg, M., *Hama'amad Ha'ishi Beyisrael* (Jerusalem, Hebrew University, 1961)

Sutton and Shannon on Contract, 4th ed. (London, Butterworth and Co., 1949)

Talmud Babbli (T.B.): *Arakhin, Baba Kamma, Baba Batra, Kedushin, Ketuboth, Shevuoth, Yevamoth, Nedarim.*

Tosephta, Ketuboth.
Tur Even Ha'ezer
Uziel, B., *Mishpetei Uziel, Yore Dea*

Vitta, E., The Conflict of Laws in Matters of Personal Status in Palestine (Tel Aviv, 1947)

Warhaftig, Z., *Dat Umedina B'hakika* (Jerusalem, Government Publishers, 1973)

Weinberg, J.J. *Tnai Benasuin u'veget* (Jerusalem, Mosad Harav Kook, 5727)

N.B.
The long list of the Court cases was omitted, as it is unlikely that the English reader will be interested to read them in the Hebrew. Those who will be interested can find them in the notes . . . or in the Hebrew book by the same author.

IV

Literary Sources

9
Taibele and Her Demon

Isaac Bashevis Singer

I

In the town of Lashnik, not far from Lublin, there lived a man and his wife. His name was Chaim Nossen, hers Taibele. They had no children. Not that the marriage was barren; Taibele had borne her husband a son and two daughters, but all three had died in infancy—one of whooping cough, one of scarlet fever, and one of diphtheria. After that Taibele's womb closed up, and nothing availed: neither prayers, nor spells, nor potions. Grief drove Chaim Nossen to withdraw from the world. He kept apart from his wife, stopped eating meat and no longer slept at home, but on a bench in the prayer house. Taibele owned a dry-goods store, inherited from her parents, and she sat there all day, with a yardstick on her right, a pair of shears on her left, and the women's prayer book in Yiddish in front of her. Chaim Nossen, tall, lean, with black eyes and a wedge of a beard, had always been a morose, silent man even at the best of times. Taibele was small and fair, with blue eyes and a round face. Although punished by the Almighty, she still smiled

Translated by Mirra Ginsburg.

easily, the dimples playing on her cheeks. She had no one else to cook for now, but she lit the stove or the tripod every day and cooked some porridge or soup for herself. She also went on with her knitting—now a pair of stockings, now a vest; or else she would embroider something on canvas. It wasn't in her nature to rail at fate or cling to sorrow.

One day Chaim Nossen put his prayer shawl and phylacteries, a change of underwear, and a loaf of bread into a sack and left the house. Neighbors asked where he was going; he answered: "Wherever my eyes lead me."

When people told Taibele that her husband had left her, it was too late to catch up with him. He was already across the river. It was discovered that he had hired a cart to take him to Lublin. Taibele sent a messenger to seek him out, but neither her husband nor the messenger was ever seen again. At thirty-three, Taibele found herself a deserted wife.

After a period of searching, she realized that she had nothing more to hope for. God had taken both her children and her husband. She would never be able to marry again; from now on she would have to live alone. All she had left was her house, her store, and her belongings. The townspeople pitied her, for she was a quiet woman, kindhearted and honest in her business dealings. Everyone asked: how did she deserve such misfortunes? But God's ways are hidden from man.

Taibele had several friends among the town matrons whom she had known since childhood. In the daytime housewives are busy with their pots and pans, but in the evening Taibele's friends often dropped in for a chat. In the summer, they would sit on a bench outside the house, gossiping and telling each other stories.

One moonless summer evening when the town was as dark as Egypt, Taibele sat with her friends on the bench, telling them a tale she had read in a book bought from a peddler. It was about a young Jewish woman, and a demon who had ravished her and lived with her as man and wife. Taibele recounted the story in all its details. The women huddled closer together, joined hands, spat to ward off evil, and laughed the kind of laughter that comes from fear.

One of them asked: "Why didn't she exorcise him with an amulet?"

"Not every demon is frightened of amulets," answered Taibele.

"Why didn't she make a journey to a holy rabbi?"

"The demon warned her that he would choke her if she revealed the secret."

"Woe is me, may the Lord protect us, may no one know of such things!" a woman cried out.

"I'll be afraid to go home now," said another.

"I'll walk with you," a third one promised.

While they were talking, Alchonon, the teacher's helper who hoped one day to become a wedding jester, happened to be passing by. Alchonon, five years a widower, had the reputation of being a wag and a prankster, a man with a screw loose. His steps were silent because the soles of his shoes were worn through and he walked on his bare feet. When he heard Taibele telling the story, he halted to listen. The darkness was so thick, and the women so engrossed in the weird tale, that they did not see him. This Alchonon was a dissipated fellow, full of cunning goatish tricks. On the instant, he formed a mischievous plan.

After the women had gone, Alchonon stole into Taibele's yard. He hid behind a tree and watched through the window. When he saw Taibele go to bed and put out the candle, he slipped into the house. Taibele had not bolted the door; thieves were unheard of in that town. In the hallway, he took off his shabby caftan, his fringed garment, his trousers, and stood as naked as his mother bore him. Then he tiptoed to Taibele's bed. She was almost asleep, when suddenly she saw a figure looming in the dark. She was too terrified to utter a sound.

"Who is it?" she whispered, trembling.

Alchonon replied in a hollow voice: "Don't scream, Taibele. If you cry out, I will destroy you. I am the demon Hurmizah, ruler over darkness, rain, hail, thunder, and wild beasts. I am the evil spirit who espoused the young woman you spoke about tonight. And because you told the story with such relish, I heard your words from the abyss and was filled with lust for your body. Do not try to resist, for I drag away those who refuse to do my will beyond the Mountains of Darkness—to Mount Sair, into a wilderness where man's foot is unknown, where no beast dares to tread, where the earth is of iron and the sky of copper. And I roll them in thorns and in fire, among adders and scorpions, until every bone of their body is ground to dust, and they are lost for eternity in the nether depths. But if you comply with my wish, not a hair of your head will be harmed, and I will send you success in every undertaking . . ."

Hearing these words, Taibele lay motionless as in a swoon. Her heart fluttered and seemed to stop. She thought her end had come. After a while, she gathered courage and murmured: "What do you want of me? I am a married woman!"

"Your husband is dead. I followed in his funeral procession myself." The voice of the teacher's helper boomed out. "It is true that I cannot go to the rabbi to testify and free you to remarry, for the rabbis don't believe our kind. Besides, I don't dare step across the threshold of the rabbi's chamber—I fear the Holy Scrolls. But I am not lying. Your husband died in an epidemic, and the worms have already gnawed away his nose. And even were he alive, you would not be forbidden to lie with me, for the laws of the *Shulchan Aruch* do not apply to us."

Hurmizah the teacher's helper went on with his persuasions, some sweet, some threatening. He invoked the names of angels and devils, of demonic beasts and of vampires. He swore that Asmodeus, King of the Demons, was his step-uncle. He said that Lilith, Queen of the Evil Spirits, danced for him on one foot and did every manner of thing to please him. Shibtah, the she-devil who stole babies from women in childbed, baked poppyseed cakes for him in Hell's ovens and leavened them with the fat of wizards and black dogs. He argued so long, adducing such witty parables and proverbs, that Taibele was finally obliged to smile, in her extremity. Hurmizah vowed that he had loved Taibele for a long time. He described to her the dresses and shawls she had worn that year and the year before; he told her the secret thoughts that came to her as she kneaded dough, prepared her Sabbath meal, washed herself in the bath, and saw to her needs at the outhouse. He also reminded her of the morning when she had wakened with a black and blue mark on her breast. She had thought it was the pinch of a ghoul. But it was really the mark left by a kiss of Hurmizah's lips, he said.

After a while, the demon got into Taibele's bed and had his will of her. He told her that from then on he would visit her twice a week, on Wednesdays and on Sabbath evenings, for those were the nights when the unholy ones were abroad in the world. He warned her, though, not to divulge to anyone what had befallen her, or even hint at it, on pain of dire punishment: he would pluck out the hair from her skull, pierce her eyes, and bite out her navel. He would cast her into a desolate wilderness where bread was dung and water was blood, and where the wailing of Zalmaveth was heard all day and all night. He commanded Taibele to swear by the bones of her mother that she would keep the secret to her last day. Taibele saw that there was no escape for her. She put her hand on his thigh and swore an oath, and did all that the monster bade her.

Before Hurmizah left, he kissed her long and lustfully, and since he was a demon and not a man, Taibele returned his kisses and moistened his beard with her tears. Evil spirit though he was, he had treated her kindly . . .

When Hurmizah was gone, Taibele sobbed into her pillow until sunrise.

Hurmizah came every Wednesday night and every Sabbath night. Taibele was afraid that she might find herself with child and give birth to some monster with tail and horns—an imp or a mooncalf. But Hurmizah promised to protect her against shame. Taibele asked whether she need go to the ritual bath to cleanse herself after her impure days, but Hurmizah said that the laws concerning menstruation did not extend to those who consorted with the unclean host.

* * *

As the saying goes, may God preserve us from all that we can get accustomed to. And so it was with Taibele. In the beginning she had feared that
her nocturnal visitant might do her harm, give her boils or elflocks, make
her bark like a dog or drink urine, and bring disgrace upon her. But
Hurmizah did not whip her or pinch her or spit on her. On the contrary, he
caressed her, whispered endearments, made puns and rhymes for her.
Sometimes he pulled such pranks and babbled such devil's nonsense, that
she was forced to laugh. He tugged at the lobe of her ear and gave her love
bites on the shoulder, and in the morning she found the marks of his teeth on
her skin. He persuaded her to let her hair grow under her cap and he wove it
into braids. He taught her charms and spells, told her about his night-
brethren, the demons with whom he flew over ruins and fields of toadstools,
over the salt marshes of Sodom, and the frozen wastes of the Sea of Ice. He
did not deny that he had other wives, but they were all she-devils; Taibele
was the only human wife he possessed. When Taibele asked him the names
of his wives, he enumerated them: Namah, Machlath, Aff, Chuldah,
Zluchah, Nafkah, and Cheimah. Seven altogether.

He told her that Namah was black as pitch and full of rage. When she
quarreled with him, she spat venom and blew fire and smoke through
her nostrils.

Machlath had the face of a leech, and those whom she touched with her
tongue were forever branded.

Aff loved to adorn herself with silver, emeralds, and diamonds. Her
braids were of spun gold. On her ankles she wore bells and bracelets; when
she danced, all the deserts rang out with their chiming.

Chuldah had the shape of a cat. She meowed instead of speaking. Her
eyes were green as gooseberries. When she copulated, she always chewed
bear's liver.

Zluchah was the enemy of brides. She robbed bridegrooms of potency. If
a bride stepped outside alone at night during the Seven Nuptial Benedic-
tions, Zluchah danced up to her and the bride lost the power of speech or was
taken by a seizure.

Nafkah was lecherous, always betraying him with other demons. She retained his affections only by her vile and insolent talk, which delighted his heart.

Cheimah should have, according to her name, been as vicious as Namah
should have been mild, but the reverse was true: Cheimah was a she-devil
without gall. She was forever doing charitable deeds, kneading dough for
housewives when they were ill, or bringing bread to the homes of the poor.

Thus Hurmizah described his wives, and told Taibele how he disported
himself with them, playing tag over roofs and engaging in all sorts of

pranks. Ordinarily, a woman is jealous when a man consorts with other women, but how can a human be jealous of a female devil? Quite the contrary. Hurmizah's tales amused Taibele, and she was always plying him with questions. Sometimes he revealed to her mysteries no mortal may know—about God, his angels and seraphs, his heavenly mansions, and the seven heavens. He also told her how sinners, male and female, were tortured in barrels of pitch and caldrons of fiery coals, on beds studded with nails and in pits of snow, and how the Black Angels beat the bodies of the sinners with rods of fire.

The greatest punishment in Hell was tickling, Hurmizah said. There was a certain imp in Hell by the name of Lekish. When Lekish tickled an adulteress on her soles or under the arms, her tormented laughter echoed all the way to the island of Madagascar.

In this way, Hurmizah entertained Taibele all through the night, and soon it came about that she began to miss him when he was away. The summer nights seemed too short, for Hurmizah would leave soon after cockcrow. Even winter nights were not long enough. The truth was that she now loved Hurmizah, and though she knew a woman must not lust after a demon, she longed for him day and night.

II

Although Alchonon had been a widower for many years, matchmakers still tried to marry him off. The girls they proposed were from mean homes, widows and divorcees, for a teacher's helper was a poor provider, and Alchonon had besides the reputation of being a shiftless ne'er-do-well. Alchonon dismissed the offers on various pretexts: one woman was too ugly, the other had a foul tongue, the third was a slattern. The matchmakers wondered: how could a teacher's helper who earned nine groschen a week presume to be such a picker and chooser? And how long could a man live alone? But no one can be dragged by force to the wedding canopy.

Alchonon knocked around town—long, lean, tattered, with a red disheveled beard, in a crumpled shirt, with his pointed Adam's apple jumping up and down. He waited for the wedding jester Reb Zekele to die, so that he could take over his job. But Reb Zekele was in no hurry to die; he still enlivened weddings with an inexhaustible flow of quips and rhymes, as in his younger days. Alchonon tried to set up on his own as a teacher for beginners, but no householder would entrust his child to him. Mornings and evenings, he took the boys to and from the cheder. During the day he sat in Reb Itchele the teacher's courtyard, idly whittling wooden pointers, or cutting out paper decorations which were used only once a year, at Pentecost, or modeling figurines from clay. Not far from Taibele's store there was a well, and Alchonon came there many times a day, to draw a pail of water or to take a drink, spilling the water over his red beard. At these times, he would throw a quick glance at Taibele. Taibele pitied him: why was the man knocking about all by himself? And Alchonon would say to himself each time: "Woe, Taibele, if you knew the truth!"

Alchonon lived in a garret, in the house of an old widow who was deaf and half-blind. The crone often chided him for not going to the synagogue to pray like other Jews. For as soon as Alchonon had taken the children home, he said a hasty evening prayer and went to bed. Sometimes the old woman thought she heard the teacher's helper get up in the middle of the night and go off somewhere. She asked him where he wandered at night, but Alchonon told her that she had been dreaming. The women who sat on benches in the evenings, knitting socks and gossiping, spread the rumor that after midnight Alchonon turned into a werewolf. Some women said he was consorting with a succubus. Otherwise, why should a man remain so many years without a wife? The rich men would not trust their children to him any longer. He now escorted only the children of the poor, and seldom ate a spoonful of hot food, but had to content himself with dry crusts.

Alchonon became thinner and thinner, but his feet remained as nimble as ever. With his lanky legs, he seemed to stride down the street as though on stilts. He must have suffered constant thirst, for he was always coming down to the well. Sometimes he would merely help a dealer or peasant to water his horse. One day, when Taibele noticed from the distance how his caftan was torn and ragged, she called him into her shop. He threw a frightened glance and turned white.

"I see your caftan is torn," said Taibele. "If you wish, I will advance you a few yards of cloth. You can pay it off later, five pennies a week."

"No."

"Why not?" Taibele asked in astonishment. "I won't haul you before the rabbi if you fall behind. You'll pay when you can."

"No."

And he quickly walked out of the store, fearing she might recognize his voice.

In summertime it was easy to visit Taibele in the middle of the night. Alchonon made his way through back lanes, clutching his caftan around his naked body. In winter, the dressing and undressing in Taibele's cold hallway became increasingly painful. But worst of all were the nights after a fresh snowfall. Alchonon was worried that Taibele or one of the neighbors might notice his tracks. He caught cold and began to cough. One night he got into

Taibele's bed with his teeth chattering; he could not warm up for a long time. Afraid that she might discover his hoax, he invented explanations and excuses. But Taibele neither probed nor wished to probe too closely. She had long discovered that a devil had all the habits and frailties of a man. Hurmizah perspired, sneezed, hiccuped, yawned. Sometimes his breath smelled of onion, sometimes of garlic. His body felt like the body of her husband, bony and hairy, with an Adam's apple and a navel. At times, Hurmizah was in a jocular mood, at other times a sigh broke from him. His feet were not goose feet, but human, with nails and frost blisters.

Once Taibele asked him the meaning of these things, and Hurmizah explained: "When one of us consorts with a human female, he assumes the shape of a man. Otherwise, she would die of fright."

Yes, Taibele got used to him and loved him. She was no longer terrified of him or his impish antics. His tales were inexhaustible, but Taibele often found contradictions in them. Like all liars, he had a short memory. He had told her at first that devils were immortal. But one night he asked: "What will you do if I die?"

"But devils don't die!"

"They are taken to the lowest abyss . . ."

That winter there was an epidemic in town. Foul winds came from the river, the woods, and the swamps. Not only children, but adults as well were brought down with the ague. It rained and it hailed. Floods broke the dam on the river. The storms blew off an arm of the windmill. On Wednesday night, when Hurmizah came into Taibele's bed, she noticed that his body was burning hot, but his feet were icy. He shivered and moaned. He tried to entertain her with talk of she-devils, of how they seduced young men, how they cavorted with other devils, splashed about in the ritual bath, tied elflocks in old men's beards, but he was weak and unable to possess her.

She had never seen him in such a wretched state. Her heart misgave her. She asked: "Shall I get you some raspberries with milk?"

Hurmizah replied: "Such remedies are not for our kind."

"What do you do when you get sick?"

"We itch and we scratch . . ."

He spoke little after that. When he kissed Taibele, his breath was sour. He always remained with her until cockcrow, but this time he left early. Taibele lay silent, listening to his movements in the hallway. He had sworn to her that he flew out of the window even when it was closed and sealed, but she heard the door creak. Taibele knew that it was sinful to pray for devils, that one must curse them and blot them from memory; yet she prayed to God for Hurmizah.

She cried out in anguish: "There are so many devils, let there be one more . . ."

* * *

On the following Sabbath, Taibele waited in vain for Hurmizah until dawn; he never came. She called him inwardly and muttered the spells he had taught her, but the hallway was silent. Taibele lay benumbed. Hurmizah had once boasted that he had danced for Tubal-cain and Enoch, that he had sat on the roof of Noah's Ark, licked the salt from the nose of Lot's wife, and plucked Ahasuerus by the beard. He had prophesied that she would be reincarnated after a hundred years as a princess, and that he, Hurmizah, would capture her, with the help of his slaves Chittim and Tachtim, and carry her off to the palace of Bashemath, the wife of Esau. But now he was probably lying somewhere ill, a helpless demon, a lonely orphan—without father or mother, without a faithful wife to care for him. Taibele recalled how his breath came rasping like a saw when he had been with her last; when he blew his nose, there was a whistling in his ear. From Sunday to Wednesday, Taibele went about as one in a dream. On Wednesday she could hardly wait until the clock struck midnight, but the night went, and Hurmizah did not appear. Taibele turned her face to the wall.

The day began, dark as evening. Fine snow dust was falling from the murky sky. The smoke could not rise from the chimneys; it spread over the roofs like ragged sheets. The rooks cawed harshly. Dogs barked. After the miserable night, Taibele had no strength to go to her store. Nevertheless, she dressed and went outside. She saw four pallbearers carrying a stretcher. From under the snow-swept coverlet protruded the blue feet of a corpse. Only the sexton followed the dead man.

Taibele asked who it was, and the sexton answered: "Alchonon, the teacher's helper."

A strange idea came to Taibele—to escort Alchonon, the feckless man who had lived alone and died alone, on his last journey. Who would come to the store today? And what did she care for business? Taibele had lost everything. At least, she would be doing a good deed. She followed the dead on the long road to the cemetery. There she waited while the gravedigger swept away the snow and dug a grave in the frozen earth. They wrapped Alchonon the teacher's helper in a prayer shawl and a cowl, placed shards on his eyes, and stuck between his fingers a myrtle twig that he would use to dig his way to the Holy Land when the Messiah came. Then the grave was closed and the gravedigger recited the Kaddish. A cry broke from Taibele. This Alchonon had lived a lonely life, just as she did. Like her, he left no heir. Yes, Alchonon the teacher's helper had danced his last dance. From Hurmizah's tales, Taibele knew that the deceased did not go straight to Heaven. Every sin creates a devil, and these devils are a man's children after his death. They come to demand their share. They call the dead man Father and roll him through forest and wilderness until the measure of his punishment is filled and he is ready for purification in Hell.

From then on, Taibele remained alone, doubly deserted—by an ascetic and by a devil. She aged quickly. Nothing was left to her of the past except a secret that could never be told and would be believed by no one. There are secrets that the heart cannot reveal to the lips. They are carried to the grave. The willows murmur of them, the rooks caw about them, the gravestones converse about them silently, in the language of stone. The dead will awaken one day, but their secrets will abide with the Almighty and His judgment until the end of all generations.

10

Agunot

Shmuel Yosef Agnon

And they never drew near. Month comes and month goes. In numbers the scholars assembled, to attend the law from Ezekiel's lips, and the academy was filled with holy lore. Gracious learning was on his tongue, and whatever his mode of expounding—simple or subtle or mystic—bright angels gathered around him, shedding the light of the law on his brow. But even as he teaches, anguish gnaws at his heart, as though—God forbid!—he lacks gratitude for having been deemed worthy to go up to the Holy Land.

And Dinah—Dinah sits, despondent. At times she goes out for a while, and stands by the spot where Ben Uri had wrought, and stares at his implements, which are gathering dust. She clasps her hands, and murmurs some few of the songs Ben Uri had sung, sings until her eyes are dimmed by tears. Her soul weeps in secret for her pride. Once, as Rabbi Ezekiel was passing by, he heard a pleasing melody rising within that chamber. When he paused to listen, they told him that it was no mortal voice he heard singing, but rather the evil spirits that had been created out of Ben Uri's breath as he sat and sang at his work. Rabbi Ezekiel hastened away. Thenceforth, when forced to walk in that part of the house, he averted his head, in order to avoid lending his ears to the chants of such as these.

Toward evening, Rabbi Ezekiel goes to walk in the hills. The mighty ones of Israel walk out at that hour, and their retainers go before them, striking the earth with their staffs, and all the people hasten to rise in awe and deference before them, and the sun casts purple canopies over each of the righteous as it goes down to greet its Creator. The elect, who are deemed worthy of this, are granted the privilege of finding their place in the Holy Land in their lifetime, and not only this, but those deemed worthy of dwelling there in their lifetime are privileged to enjoy the Holy Spirit for ever and ever. But Rabbi Ezekiel? His feet are planted in the gates of Jerusalem, and stand on her soil, but his eyes and his heart are pledged to houses of study and worship abroad, and even now, as he walks in the hills of Jerusalem, he fancies himself among the scholars of his own town, strolling in the fields to take the evening air.

It is told that once they found there Freidele sitting with her friends, singing:

> They have borne him far away
> To wed a dowered maiden.
> His father did not care to know
> Our hearts were heavy laden.

One day an emissary of the rabbis returned to Jerusalem from the diaspora, and brought a letter for Rabbi Ezekiel. His father was pleased to inform him that he had negotiated the home journey in safety, and now, as ever before, was bearing up under the burdens of justice and learning in their town. In passing, he thought his son might care to know that Freidele had found her mate and had moved—together with her mother—to another city, so that the sexton's wife was therefore looking after his needs. Rabbi Ezekiel read the letter and began to weep. Here was Freidele, decently wedded, and here was he, fancying her still. And his own wife? When they pass each other she stares off in one direction, he in another.

Month comes, month goes, and the academy grows ever more desolate. The scholars, one by one, steal away. They cut a staff from some tree in the garden, take it in hand, and set off on their separate ways. It is obvious for all to see—Heaven help us!—that Rabbi Ezekiel's soul is tainted. Sire Ahiezer perceived that his works had not prospered, that the couple was ill-matched, that the marriage, in fact, was no marriage at all.

The couple stand silent before the rabbi, their eyes downcast. Rabbi Ezekiel is about to divorce his wife. And just as he did not look at her at the hour of their marriage, so he does not look at her in the hour of their parting. And just as Dinah did not hear his voice as he said to her, "Lo, thou art sanctified unto me," so she does not hear it as he says, "Lo, I cast thee forth." Our sages of blessed memory said that when a man puts his first wife away from him, the very altars weep, but here the altars had dropped tears even as he took her to wife. It was not long that Sire Ahiezer left Jerusalem with his daughter. He had failed in his settlement there; his wishes had not prospered. He went forth in shame, his spirit heavy within him. His house was deserted, the House of Study stood desolate. And the quorum that had gathered in the synagogue to honor Sire Ahiezer so long as he was there, now did not assemble there for even the first round of afternoon prayers on the day of his departure.

11

Till Death Do Us Part

Rochelle Majer Krich

The night air was surprisingly cool for July. Deena Vogler hugged her arms as she hurried from her car and searched for the Alcott Street address. There it was. At the front door, she reached for the bell, then hesitated.

Tonight's appointment was probably pointless. Another tease, looking for help from a well-meaning rabbi who would listen to her in a paneled room filled with authoritative volumes of the Bible, the Talmud, and their related commentaries. She'd spent several sessions in another paneled room with another well-meaning rabbi, and the wealth of knowledge contained in the richly bound tomes that filled the air with their leathery perfume hadn't provided her with any answers.

But Alan Krantz, her summer employer and her best friend's husband, had pushed her. "This rabbi's different," he'd insisted. "He's aggressive, and I hear he has new ideas for women in your predicament. What do you have to lose?"

She rang the bell. Don't expect anything, she told herself, then smiled wryly, because of course she did, or why would she be here?

Moments later, Deena was standing inside a small room. It wasn't paneled, she noticed, but the books were there, overfilling the shelves that lined the walls.

"I'm glad you came, Mrs. Vogler," Reuben Markowitz said. There was warmth in his voice and his brown eyes. "Please, have a seat." He gestured to a folding chair in front of a wood-toned Formica desk, then noticed the Cabbage Patch doll that was occupying it. "My best listener," he told Deena as he moved the doll to his already cluttered desk and took his seat. "Never criticizes my sermons. Unfortunately, I have to share her with Tamar. She's our three-year-old." He smiled. "Let me get a pen and paper and we'll get started."

She watched dubiously as he searched under staggered, pagodalike layers of books and papers that seemed precariously close to toppling onto the carpeted floor. She pictured Rabbi Brodin's rosewood desk, always immaculate, cleared of everything except a leather-bound calendar, a brass stand that held a gold Mont Blanc fountain pen, and a pad of cream-colored, linen-weave paper that bore a calligraphied inscription in raised charcoal-gray ink: "From the desk of Rabbi Morton Brodin." *He never even gave me one of his personalized notes,* Deena realized suddenly. *But then, with all his efficiency and organization, he had nothing to tell me.*

Rabbi Markowitz was much younger than Rabbi Brodin, probably in his early thirties. There was no gray in the trim beard or the curly brown hair capped by a black suede yarmulke. He was dressed more casually, too, dark slacks and a knit polo shirt instead of a three-piece suit. Rabbi Brodin, she was sure, would not approve.

"Found it!" Rabbi Markowitz held up a pad of yellow lined paper and a ballpoint pen. "You mentioned on the phone that you're having difficulties with your husband. For counseling, it's always better—"

"My ex-husband," Deena interrupted quickly. "Well, that's the problem, really. I got my civil divorce months ago, although we still haven't made a property settlement. But Jake won't give me a religious divorce."

A *get*. Without it, she could never remarry. Rabbi Brodin had sat, swiveling gently in his beige upholstered armchair, reminding her in his carefully modulated voice that she couldn't initiate the *get*, that Jake had to sign it and hand it to her voluntarily in the presence of witnesses, that no rabbi could usurp that authority.

And the curious thing was that she'd listened with disbelief and mounting horror, as though this was all new to her, as though she'd never heard stories about women whose husbands refused to give them a *get*. The stories had troubled her, but in a detached sense, much the same way that she was troubled hearing that some person unknown to her had been stricken with a disease. "How awful," she always said. "What a bastard!" And she meant it. But now she was the woman in the story, and it was all shockingly new.

"So I'm Jake's property, his chattel, subject to his whim?" she'd demanded of Rabbi Brodin, already knowing the answer. "Well, I wouldn't put it exactly like that," he'd murmured. He had avoided her eyes, had doodled on the linen-weave paper.

But what other way was there to put it?

Rabbi's Markowitz's lips tightened. "Is it a question of the property division? Is he using the *get* as leverage?"

"My attorney, Brenda DiSalvo, thinks so. She says that explains Jake's demands." Eighty percent of the value of their three-bedroom house in Beverlywood, an upscale residential L.A. neighborhood adjoining Beverly Hills. True, as a real estate broker, Jake had had the inside track on the house, but without the downpayment from her parents, Jake and Deena would never have been able to buy it. He wanted the dining room set, the stereo system, the TV, the VCR. And the cobalt dishes. "But every time I've compromised – against my attorney's advice – Jake has increased his demands. And frankly, I'm angry about having to give up what's rightfully mine. It's not the things," she added quickly. "Things are replaceable. But I hate giving in to blackmail."

"You shouldn't have to," Markowitz said firmly. "No one should. Has your husband told you what he wants?"

"Jake has this insane idea that we should get married again. He claims he still loves me, but it isn't that, it's – " She stopped, searched for the words. How could she explain it to someone else when it wasn't always clear to her? "Jake doesn't like to lose, Rabbi Markowitz. He's a real estate broker, very aggressive, very successful. He never lets a deal slip through his hands if he can help it. I think he sees the divorce like that. I'm a challenge again."

"Again?" He looked puzzled.

She brushed her hair away from her forehead, as if to clear her thoughts. "I thought he loved me, at least at first. Now I'm not so sure." She sounded wistful. "I think, you know, that he saw me as intriguing, different from the other women he knew. Jake is ten years older than I am, did I mention that? He's much more experienced."

And extremely handsome, she added silently, with thick black hair, penetrating gray eyes, and a slow, sensuous smile that had invited intimacy the first time they met. Deena had never lacked dates – she knew men found her more than pretty; they always told her so, complimented her figure, her long, thick, coppery hair, her green eyes. But they hadn't prepared her for Jake. The mutual physical attraction had been immediate, intense. And he'd been funny and exciting and sophisticated and spontaneous, lavish with gifts and flowers. And incredibly charming when he wanted to be – which had been always during their courtship and engagement. She'd been caught up in the illusion of romance, had mistaken flash for substance.

"But we had a lot in common – similar backgrounds, interests. We're both only children of Holocaust survivors; we both come from Orthodox homes." Was she explaining to Rabbi Markowitz, she wondered, or defending herself?

"So where did you and Jake meet?"

"At his realty firm. Two years ago, before I started law school, my dad got me a summer job there. My dad's friendly with the senior partner, Ben Kasden." It was an arrangement that Max Novick had bitterly regretted from the moment Deena told him she was going out with Jake. *"Just one time," she had told her father. "What's the harm?"*

"How long were you married?"

"A little under a year." She watched him write the information on the yellow pad.

"Do you have any children?" His pen was poised, waiting.

"No, I—no." She avoided his eyes, felt herself blushing even though she knew he couldn't read her mind. She'd felt guilty using birth control; as a devout Orthodox Jew, she knew it was prohibited. And she'd wanted to get pregnant, to have Jake's child. But Jake had insisted, and she'd given in. Even then, he'd been irrationally worried about her becoming pregnant, frequently demanding assurances before they made love that she was using her diaphragm.

At the time, she'd been hurt, disappointed, puzzled by his reluctance. Now, she was thankful. A child would have made everything so much more difficult.

"Mrs. Vogler, why did you want the divorce?"

Irreconcilable differences, Brenda DiSalvo had told the judge. Usually, that was a vague, catch-all phrase; in this case, it was absolutely true. "I'm very committed to being Orthodox. It isn't just something I grew up with. It's what I am. Jake didn't want to be religious anymore."

"That's rough," Markowitz agreed. He tapped his pen against his palm. "This was a sudden change?"

"Not exactly. Jake gave up religion in his teens. When he met me, he became observant again, but after we were married, he became lax—about daily prayers, about keeping kosher, about *Shabbas*. Everything. He mixed meat and dairy dishes, brought home food he knew wasn't kosher. He stopped going to *shul* on *Shabbas* and did things he knew would upset me. He turned on lights, watched TV, drove his car." All of which are forbidden on the Sabbath.

"Did you talk to him about it?"

She nodded. "We argued constantly."

"What did he say?"

"I'm tired of all these goddamn rules, sick of this antiquated crap! This is the twentieth century, or maybe you haven't noticed. And I'm fed up with having you look over my shoulder, spying on me. Saint Deena."

"Jake, you knew from the start how important this is to me. We had an agreement. You promised—"

"Yeah, well, it's time to change the agreement, sweetheart. You don't like it, sue me."

"Basically, that he wanted to live in the modern world," Deena told Rabbi Markowitz. "He said that I could live the way I wanted, but that I had no right to force my life-style on him." She hesitated. "Sometimes I had the feeling he did it all to annoy me, to get even."

"What do you mean?" He frowned.

She felt her cheeks getting hot. It was difficult discussing this with a stranger. "He . . . uh . . . was very unhappy with our . . . sex life. He resented the restrictions." According to the laws of *taharat hamishpacha*, family purity, a husband and wife have to separate each month from the onset of her period. After her period, she counts seven clean days, then immerses herself in a *mikvah*, a ritual bath.

Deena still remembered in detail the first time she'd gone to the *mikvah*, the night before the wedding. Pearl had accompanied her, and Deena had been nervous yet excited.

The attendant had led Deena to a private room outfitted with a full-sized tub and separate tiled shower, a commode, and a sink and vanity area attached to a mirrored wall. Neatly folded thick, white towels and disposable slippers sat on the counter next to a large tray holding shampoo, nail polish remover, baby oil, and acrylic containers filled with cotton balls and Q-Tips. One drawer revealed scissors, emery boards, and pumice stone; another, combs, brushes, and a blow dryer.

The *mikvah* itself was in a separate tiled area. Deena walked down the steps to the center of the heated pool. She immersed herself completely for a few seconds and bobbed up. The attendant nodded her approval. Deena recited the blessing in Hebrew, and it seemed to her that her voice echoed in mystic resonance. She immersed herself again, recited another, longer blessing; she stumbled a little on the words, but the attendant smiled her encouragement. Then Deena submerged herself a final time. When she climbed out of the pool, the attendant stood, her face modestly averted, extending a robe to Deena.

Deena had felt special. Pure, somehow. Convinced that this would start their marriage off right.

Rabbi Markowitz said, "But he knew about these rules before you were married?"

"Of course! And I told him it was something I'd never compromise on." Was that why she'd given in on the birth control? Probably. "The first few months, Jake was fine. Then he became more and more difficult." He'd been alternately demanding, cajoling, insulting, petulant, a spoiled child who couldn't have his way. Twice, she'd had to physically fight him off and spend the night sleeping on the den couch.

"Being Orthodox involves continuous commitment and faith," Rabbi Markowitz remarked. "And enormous self-control. Even then, it isn't always easy. We follow rules that govern our daily actions, tell us how to dress, what to eat, when to have sex. Some people can't handle that."

"But Jake didn't even try, Rabbi Markowitz! And I should have known it wouldn't work. That's what really bothers me. Everybody warned me — my parents, my friends." She paused. "I was worried too. I told Jake it wouldn't work if he was doing it just for me, but he said he was committed, and I believed him." She studied her hands. "I know what you're thinking, that I believed him because I wanted to. I see that now."

"Listen, I don't know anyone who hasn't done that at least once. Including me. You think your husband fooled you? Maybe you're right. But he probably fooled himself too, or he wouldn't have married you. You made the terms clear, right?"

She nodded.

"And you know, there's something awfully compelling and romantic about saving someone's soul. I should know." Markowitz grinned.

She flashed a half-smile. "Maybe." The thought had crossed her mind. "But I still feel pretty stupid."

"You have to put that behind you," he said firmly. "So okay. Things weren't working out and you separated?"

"No." She shook her head. "No, I went to Rabbi Brodin for help. He's the one who instructed Jake when he was becoming Orthodox again. He married us."

"And?"

"He told me to be patient. He said Jake was probably going through a phase; everything would work out. I wanted to believe him. I wanted more than anything for the marriage to work. And then . . . and then . . ." She felt a familiar tightening in her chest. "I found out Jake was having an affair."

"I'm sorry," Markowitz said gently. "That must have been very painful."

"I was devastated," she said softly. Even now, the hurt and humiliation were still there, and the sense of inadequacy, too. Because of course she'd asked herself countless times what had driven him to Annie.

She shifted in her seat. "But it was the best thing that happened, learning the truth. It made me see that marrying Jake was a terrible mistake. And I thought, you know, that the divorce wouldn't be a problem, because he obviously wasn't happy either, right? But he won't give me the *get*."

"What about your in-laws? What's their position on this?"

"The Vogelanters are fine people, but—"

"Vogelanter?" Rabbi Markowitz interrupted.

"Jake shortened his last name." He had lopped off the last syllables with the same nonchalance that he'd abandoned his tradition. "To answer your question, they haven't helped. I think Joe, Jake's father, feels bad about all this. And Ida, well, she dotes on Jake." My Jackie, Ida always called him.

"Have you tried talking to anyone else?"

"Rabbi Brodin." Again. "At first he said I should wait until we had the property settlement. I followed his advice, and it was a terrible mistake. I don't have the *get* or a settlement. Now he says I should be patient, that he's sure Jake will see reason." She smiled grimly. "But I know Jake, Rabbi." She saw again Jake's grin, remembered their last encounter.

"According to Jewish law, you're still my wife, you know. Nothing the judge said changed that. You can't even date another man, let alone marry someone." A note of triumph had crept into his voice.

"Why are you doing this, Jake? What can you gain by refusing to give me a get *besides making me miserable?"*

"I told you. I want you to take me back. That's all I've ever wanted! Not the house, not the money."

"That's not going to happen! You're living in a fantasy."

"Maybe. But I'm in no rush." He paused. "Are you?"

"What?"

"What's the matter, Deena? Is there a boyfriend I don't know about? Some cute law student who carries your books?"

"Don't be ridiculous!"

He got up and made his way to the front door.

She followed him. "What about the property settlement?"

"Make me an offer, Lady Dee." He smiled jauntily and left.

Deena leaned forward. "Rabbi Markowitz, I can't tell you how helpless I feel, how . . . trapped. From the time I wake up until the time I go to sleep, all I can think about is the *get*. Sometimes—" She stopped. "Sometimes, I'm so angry that I just want to walk away from it all. I tell myself that I'll marry without it, that God will forgive me."

"But you can't." It wasn't a question; it was a fact.

"No. I wish I could, but I can't." She would be denying her very essence. She took a breath. "So can you help me?"

Reuben Markowitz capped the pen and placed it on the yellow pad. To Deena, it seemed like an eternity before he spoke.

"I'm not going to pull any punches. You're in a tough situation," he said quietly. "I hope you didn't come here expecting an immediate solution."

"No, of course not," she lied. Had it been a wasted evening after all? For a while, she'd thought, maybe. . . . She blinked back tears.

"But it isn't hopeless." He got up, walked around the desk, and half-sat on the edge. "It probably won't be simple, judging from what you've told me about your husband. And I can't tell you how long it'll take. But I'm going to do everything I can to help you."

"Thank you." Her voice quavered.

"Don't thank me yet." He smiled. "Right now you're what the Talmud calls an *agunah*—literally, someone who is 'tied' or 'bound.' There are certain procedures, a specific schedule of events, that we have to follow to undo those ties."

"But I will have my *get*?"

He met her eyes. "I can't guarantee that. I've helped a number of women in your situation, but I don't have a perfect success record. Far from it. I've helped a few men, too."

"Men?" Deena frowned.

"The husband has to initiate the *get*, but the wife has to accept it. I know of women who have refused to accept the *get*, but that's not as common. But back to your case. One, I'm going to present it to the local *beth din*, the Jewish court of arbitration. The *beth din* will issue a summons ordering your husband to appear."

She shook her head. "Jake won't do it. Why should he?"

"I don't expect him to. Even religious men often ignore the summons. But we have to follow the process. The *beth din* will issue two more summonses. If Jake ignores the third one, the *beth din* will issue a contempt citation, a *seruv*, stating that he's refused to appear. The document will be publicized."

"But how will that help me?"

"It paves the way for community action. The rabbis can talk about the husband from the pulpit, restrict ritual honors, bar him from services. Jewish tradesmen can refuse to deal with him. The community can ostracize him. The works."

"Jake doesn't go to *shul*, Rabbi Markowitz. He isn't—"

He smiled. "I know. Buying kosher food isn't exactly a priority for him, is it? It's too bad he's not involved in the Jewish community. But there are other ways of persuasion. We can harass your husband with phone calls and pickets at his place of work, at his home. Everywhere."

"Why didn't Rabbi Brodin tell me any of this?" She felt a rush of anger against Brodin and the time he'd let her waste.

"He probably hopes the problem will resolve itself. It isn't easy dealing with an angry, sometimes vindictive husband, family members, friends—some of whom may be influential. It can get ugly. To be fair, though, most rabbis feel frustrated by the situation and sorry for the wife. And because they honestly don't see another solution, they encourage her to give the husband whatever he wants in exchange for the *get*." Rabbi Markowitz shook his head. "To me, that's encouraging blackmail. And I think it's only going to perpetuate the problem. That's why we're trying to do something about it."

We? "You make it sound as though there's an organization that handles this."

"There is, in New York. They really get the community involved, and they've been successful in many cases. We're trying to follow their example here in Los Angeles. Ideally, of course, national Jewish organizations would come out with edicts banning these husbands from any involvement in Jewish affairs. That would take the pressure off the individual rabbi. So far, though, that hasn't happened."

"And you're personally going to walk in a picket line in front of Jake's office?" Deena looked at him.

"If that's what it takes. I know a lot of people who'll join me. Men *and* women. This isn't just your problem, you know. This issue is an embarrassment to Judaism, a perversion of the law. The *get* was intended to protect the wife, to make sure that if her husband divorced her, he would honor the provisions of the *ketubah*, the marriage document."

"Right now I don't feel very protected." She hesitated. "To be honest, I'm having a difficult time dealing with this on a philosophical level. I mean, I've always loved Judaism because it's so concerned with human rights, with justice, with kindness. How can the same Torah that commands special protection and compassion for widows and orphans and strangers, that even forbids us to take birds out of their nest while their mother is present, that—" She stopped and shook her head. "This just doesn't make sense to me."

"It's not the law that's at fault," Markowitz said gently. "It's unscrupulous men like your husband who circumvent the intention of the law and use the *get* for revenge or blackmail. Sometimes both. We have to put a stop to this. But we have to do it within the framework of the law."

"But you don't know Jake. He's very stubborn, Rabbi Markowitz. What if he stands up to all this pressure?"

"There are other ways," he said quietly. "Under certain circumstances a *beth din* could administer physical punishment—lashes—to someone like Jake. Today, in Israel, he'd be imprisoned until he gave you the *get*."

"But—"

"But this isn't Israel. You're right. And a *beth din* doesn't have authority here, and the Torah commands us to follow the laws of the country where we live." He paused. "Nevertheless . . ."

"Oh." The word was half-whisper, half-exclamation. She pictured Jake forced to his knees, his arms yanked behind him, his once handsome face battered, his lips caked and bleeding. The idea sickened and excited her. "But isn't it dangerous?" she managed.

"I doubt that it will come to that. But yes, it's dangerous. Harassment is dangerous, too. I've had threatening calls from husbands, from other rabbis. I've had lots of calls from the police." He shrugged.

"Have you ever . . . ?"

"Been in jail? No, but I've come close, and I figure it'll probably happen one day. My wife isn't thrilled about it, but she understands that this is something I have to do." His eyes were dark and pensive.

"But let's not get ahead of ourselves," he said briskly. "If your husband is sensible, he'll realize that it's to his advantage to give you your *get*. We can make life pretty miserable for him without resorting to extremes. Let me get started with the *beth din*. Unfortunately, they're not usually quick to take action. And I'm going to put you in touch with a support group of *agunot*. You'll find it helpful talking to women who understand exactly what you're going through."

"I don't know." The thought of revealing her intimate life to strangers made her uncomfortable.

"I insist; you'll thank me. The leader is Faye Rudman. Here's her phone number." He returned to his seat, scribbled a number on the bottom of the note-covered pad, tore the fragment unevenly, and handed it to Deena.

She glanced at the paper and put it into her purse. "How long has Mrs. Rudman been waiting for her *get*?"

He hesitated. "Her case is unusual. Her husband is in a mental institution. If he's not legally competent, he can't legally give her a *get*. She's been an *agunah* for eleven years." His voice was heavy with sadness.

Eleven years! "So what can you do for her?"

"Very little, I'm afraid. She'll have to wait until he's sane enough to be judged competent, even for a short while. A day, an hour. Or until he dies." Markowitz shook his head.

"That's horrible!" she whispered.

"It is. But Faye is amazing. You'll see when you meet her. And please, do yourself a favor. Don't compare yourself to her. Jake is not insane, and you won't have to wait until he's dead to remarry."

"Who knows, right?" The thought chilled her. But for the first time in many months, she felt a glimmer of hope.

It was ten-thirty by the time Deena pulled into her driveway on Guthrie. The pale gray stucco house, wrapped in shadows except for the triangle of light at the front entrance, seemed lonely and uninviting, and much too large for a solitary occupant. Our dream home, she thought.

She turned off the ignition and sat in the sudden stillness, preoccupied with what Rabbi Markowitz had told her. When she left her car a few minutes later, she didn't notice the red Porsche down the street or the figure who sat in it, watching her as she made her way up the brick path to the front door.

V

Confrontations

12

Agunot:
Is the System Working?

EDITOR'S NOTE: The word agunah *sends a shudder through most Orthodox Jews. When hearing that a woman is unable to remarry because her estranged husband will not grant her a Jewish divorce, we are appalled by the willingness of some men to oppress their wives via the instrument of Jewish law.*

The following two articles address themselves to the agunah *issue. In the first article, three directors of Agunah, Inc., a women's advocacy organization, depict systemic problems which they believe exist. (The* Agunah, Inc. article does not represent the view of *The Jewish Homemaker.) In the second article, a leading arbiter of Jewish law responds to issues raised by Agunah, Inc., and discusses the role of Jewish courts in divorce matters.*

AGUNAH, INC.: "NO"

Susan Aranoff, Rivka Haut, and Susan Alter

Arranging a wedding is easy. We've all attended one and we know what to expect. Arranging a divorce is a far different matter. Divorce, representing failed dreams and frustrated hopes, often brings out the worst in people. It can create a tense, combative situation, leading to power struggles, financial wars, and custody battles.

The Imbalance of Power

According to *halacha* (Jewish law), the power to grant a *get*, a bill of divorce, lies with the husband, who must do so freely and without coercion. The phenomenon of husbands using the *get* as a bargaining chip with which to win unfair and undeserved concessions from wives has made the *get* process one of the most disgraceful and painful aspects of contemporary Jewish life.

By Jewish law, a marriage is not ended until a *get* has been given by the husband and received by the wife. A civil divorce, while necessary for other reasons, is irrelevant from the religious perspective.

Remarriage without a *get* damages the wife more than the husband. She is considered an adulteress: any children born of her second union are *mamzerim* — illegitimate — unable to marry anyone except converts or other *mamzerim*. Should a husband refuse to grant a *get,* the wife remains an *agunah*, a chained woman, tied to a "dead" marriage, unable to remarry for the rest of her life.

In medieval times, attempts were made to redress the imbalance in divorce law. The rabbis enacted a *takanah* (legislative decree) which declared that a woman cannot be divorced against her will; she has to accept the *get* willingly.

However, if she refuses, there are remedies available to the husband. He can try to obtain a *heter me'ah rabbanim* (lit., permission of a hundred rabbis), which will suspend for him the *cherem d'Rabbeinu Gershom* — the medieval injunction against polygamy — thus allowing him to take another, additional wife. He is required to deposit a *get* for his wife with a *beit din,* rabbinic court, so that it is available to her when she chooses to accept it. He is then permitted to remarry.

There is another way available to a husband whose wife refuses to accept a *get*. He may obtain a *get al vedei zikuv*. If a *beit din* is convinced that it is to the wife's benefit to be divorced from her husband (for example, if she is committing adultery), the husband may deposit a *get* with the *beit din,* and he is considered divorced from her and able to remarry. His wife is informed that her *get* can be obtained at the *beit din.*

While these processes take some time and money, they at least indicate viable solutions for the husbands of recalcitrant wives. Many men, in fact, have availed themselves of these remedies.

For women no such correctives are available. Women may not, under any circumstance, have more than one husband at a time. If a woman cannot obtain a *get,* she remains an *agunah* forever.

This imbalance can leave wives at the mercy of their husbands. Unlike the situation in civil divorce, where both parties start the process as equals, in the religious arena the wife enters the divorce proceedings at a decided disadvantage. She needs to obtain a *get* more than the husband needs to give it. This leaves women vulnerable to financial extortion, to aggravated custody and visitation battles, to psychological tension, and to anxiety.

Sadly, women often emerge from such battles more damaged than they do from civil court divorce proceedings. Today it is almost always the case that civil court settlements reflect greater understanding and compassion for the welfare of women and children than the settlements proposed by rabbinic courts.

Agunot: The Magnitude of the Problem

In the times of the Talmud, the classic *agunah* was one whose husband's whereabouts were unknown. He may have disappeared on a trip, or was missing in battle. In the absence of witnesses to testify to his death, his wife became an *agunah*. The case of the classic *agunah* did not involve sinful behavior.

Today's *agunot* are, for the most part, women who know where their husbands are. These men are willfully withholding a *get,* intentionally keeping their wives in a state of limbo.

The numbers of such cases are rising dramatically. There are thousands of *agunot* in the world today: *The Jerusalem Report* of March 5, 1991, calculates that there are presently 10,000 *agunot* in Israel. Although we do not have reliable statistics for other countries, there are certainly thousands of *agunot* in the U.S. alone. All parties versed in this issue agree that the number of *agunot* rises every year, as does the number of divorces among Jews. We have now reached a crisis situation.

Agunah, Inc.

Agunah, Inc., an organization formed and directed by women, tries to aid wives who are having trouble obtaining a *get*. Over the past four years we have assiduously studied the contemporary problems encountered in Jewish divorce. As advocates for wives, we have guided them through the *get* process and educated them as to what to expect when they go before a *beit din* and how to secure the rights guaranteed them by *halacha*.

We have interviewed and surveyed various *batei din* in the New York Metropolitan area and discovered significant differences among them. We have also found that the *beit din* system as a whole is in a state of terrible disrepair.

The Process

Upon initiating a *get* proceeding, a couple chooses a *beit din* to adjudicate their case. There are a number of possibilities. Many chassidic groups have their own rabbinic court (e.g., Lubavitch and Satmar). In addition, some courts are connected to larger bodies (e.g., Rabbinical Council of America [RCA], Rabbinical Alliance of America).

Then there are some private *batei din*. There is also a type of *beit din* called a *zabla*. This term comes from the acronym for the Hebrew phrase *"zeh borer lo echad,"* in which each of the litigants selects one *dayan* (judge), and those two *dayanim* choose a third. This type of *beit din* is an *ad hoc* one, formed for one particular case.

Sometimes a couple goes to a *beit din* only for the *get*, agreeing to resolve all other issues in another manner (such as by mediation, civil litigation, legal settlements, etc.). These cases are relatively simple to expedite. The fees range from $250 to $500 (not much, considering the high cost of lawyers for civil actions). And there are fee schedules for those who cannot pay even these modest amounts.

The proceeding is relatively fast, about two hours, and is handled by the *mesader haget* (the rabbi), two witnesses, and a *sofer* (scribe). For this kind of procedure any rabbinic court will do, and women need not concern themselves with which one to use. But for anything more than a simple *get* proceeding, a woman must do serious research before going to a particular *beit din*.

If either spouse desires to litigate marital assets or custody of children before a *beit din*, the other must agree to go. This does not mean that a wife must accept the *beit din* of her husband's choice. If his *beit din* is not acceptable, she may summon him to another. However, once either party insists upon litigating in a *beit din*, a *din Torah* (arbitration according to Jewish law) is necessitated.

Women are usually underprepared to present their case in *beit din*. Men are more accustomed than women to dealing with rabbis. Many men involved in these cases have gone to yeshiva. Additionally, there are a handful of *dayanim* who are known to force women to agree to a settlement which favors the husband. It is critical that men and women alike investigate before agreeing to use a particular *beit din*.

If children are involved, there is further cause to be cautious. When deciding such critical issues as child custody and visitation rights, *batei din*, in contrast to civil courts, do not consult psychologists and social workers. They use their own judgment and criteria.

Here too, women particularly must become knowledgeable about the track records of the various *batei din*. When both parents want custody, it is important to carefully explore the positions of *batei din* on this issue. For example, one very fine *beit din*, Rabbi Leib Landesman's, in Monsey, N.Y., has told Agunah, Inc. that, when both parents are deemed "equally good parents," it will, following its interpretation of *halacha*, award daughters, and sons under the age of six, to the mother, with boys above six going to the father.

Not every *beit din* follows this rule. Some, such as the RCA *beit din*, usually give mothers custody, with fathers receiving generous visitation privileges (On the average, fathers get more generous visitation privileges from rabbinic courts than they do in civil court.)

There is an additional factor of which women are often unaware. When the parties go to a *beit din*, they sign a *shtar berurin*, a document which binds them to the *beit din*'s decision. When this happens, the *beit din* assumes the role of a legal arbitrator, and its decision is legally as well as halachically binding on the parties.

It cannot be stressed enough how important it is for women to research the *beit din* system, or ask for help, before signing the *shtar berurin*.

Can women lose custody? Yes. Agunah, Inc. was involved in a case where the RCA *beit din* awarded custody to the mother on the condition that she dispose of her TV. Were she to again obtain a TV, the *beit din* would reopen custody hearings. This *psak* (decision) was changed upon being challenged, but it would have stood had the mother not gone outside the *beit din*, to rabbis who complained on her behalf.

Agunah, Inc. was also involved in a New York case where the mother stood to lose custody of her son because she had remarried and was moving to a state where the only yeshiva (run by Torah U'Mesorah) had co-ed classes until grade six. The *beit din* decided to remove the young boy (then six years old) from his mother's care and put him not with his father—who all agreed was not a fit parent—but with a *foster mother*, in order to keep him in New York! Only upon going to civil court to challenge the ruling did the mother retain custody.

Another frightening aspect of choosing a *beit din* is the fact that not all *dayanim* are honest and ethical. In one case, a *dayan* told a woman that for an extra two thousand dollars he would make a greater effort to procure her *get* by Rosh Hashanah.

This in itself was completely unethical, but the story gets worse. When Rosh Hashanah came and went without a *get*, the woman told the *dayan* that the deal was off. Nevertheless, when the *get* was finally given, the *dayan* demanded the extra two thousand dollars, and was incensed when the woman refused to pay. It is obvious that this venality undermines the halachic process.

Many individuals who work in this field are aware of the corruption that exists. We know of a recent attempt by a rabbi to protest this type of corruption by refusing to participate in a *din Torah* with a *dayan* he knew to be unethical.

And yet, courageous though it is, this attempt is not sufficient to deal with the magnitude of the problem. Women who are victims of this corruption are often afraid to make their plight known, because they fear that the rabbinic court will retaliate by ruling against them.

Sometimes, and lately more frequently, women (and men) have been challenging decisions of *batei din* in civil court. They often win. However, doing this takes quite a bit of money, for it involves complicated litigation. The further cost in despair and anguish when the welfare of one's children is threatened by hardhearted rulings of *batei din* is incalculable.

The *Ketubah*

All of us who have attended a wedding or been married ourselves know that a great deal of attention is given to the *ketubah*. The *ketubah* is essentially a contract given by husband to wife, promising her a sum of money upon his death or upon divorce.

The Talmud informs us that the *ketubah* was created to protect the wife, making it financially difficult for her husband to divorce her at will. Moreover, the *ketubah* money was to serve as a financial cushion for the woman, tiding her over until she was able to support herself or to remarry.

This halachic device is almost universally ignored today. Very few divorced women ever receive their *ketubah* money. So unused is the *ketubah* that we have discovered that few rabbis and *batei din* even know the monetary value of the standard Ashkenazic *ketubah*.

It is true that a wife forfeits her right to the *ketubah* in some instances. For example, if she is a *moredet* (rebellious), refusing to live with her husband or to have marital relations with him, then she forfeits her *ketubah*. If she has engaged in forbidden behavior (e.g., adultery), or if she desires the divorce and he does not want it, then she usually forfeits her *ketubah*. If she receives support or alimony, that generally supplants the *ketubah*.

However, there are many cases where none of these factors apply and yet women do not receive what is rightfully theirs. An example is the case of a woman we shall call Shoshanah. Shoshanah was to receive neither alimony nor child support (there were no children). At the *get* proceeding she was asked by the *beit din* to renounce the value of the *ketubah*—to "be *mochel* the *ketubah*." Shoshanah readily agreed, because she was so anxious to obtain her *get* that she did not wish to complicate matters. Consequently she was deprived of her halachically deserved *ketubah* money; in effect, Shoshanah paid for her *get*.

At Shoshanah's *get* proceedings, an Agunah, Inc. representative asked the presiding rabbi how much the *ketubah* (that Shoshanah was renouncing) was worth. She was told: "I don't know." After asking who in the *beit din* did know, she was told that nobody there knew. Thus, Shoshanah was asked to renounce an asset of undetermined monetary value, which is questionable from a halachic standpoint.

In an effort to determine what a *ketubah* is worth, the directors of Agunah, Inc. asked Rabbi Gedalia Schwartz, the *rosh beit din* of the RCA, for this information. He gave us a formula devised by Rabbi Moshe Feinstein, *zt'l,* which the RCA uses to make the calculation. According to Rabbi Feinstein, the *ketubah* is worth 100 pounds of silver. Therefore, a *ketubah* today would be worth about $6,000.

We asked Rabbi Kenneth Auman, of the *beit din* of the Vaad Harabonim of Flatbush, Brooklyn, how much a *ketubah* is worth. He replied that it is worth a minimum of $10,000 and a maximum of $20,000. We were told by one *dayan* on a Brooklyn *beit din* that, although women hardly ever receive their *ketubah,* he recently adjudicated a case of a woman who did. How much, we asked, was the amount paid? He replied that it was $4,000, in accordance with Rabbi Feinstein's calculation.

Usually the *ketubah* is not mentioned in the proceedings until the woman is asked to renounce its value. There may indeed be cases where it is to the woman's benefit to give up the *ketubah*. But it is improper for *batei din* to assume from the outset that such will be the case. The disturbing fact is that this is precisely what happens.

At every *chupah* (wedding ceremony) the *ketubah* is carefully read aloud. Is it or is it not of value? If it is, let us know its value, and let women who deserve it collect it. If it has lost its value today, for whatever reason, we should know that too.

Getting the Community Involved

It is impossible in one article to discuss all the problems found in this complicated area. There are many things that can and should be done by the Jewish community to remedy some of the problems.

One of Agunah, Inc.'s proposals is to have the Jewish community monitor *batei din*. These operate in a closed system, wherein there is no appeal and for whom there is no official oversight agency. We would like to see the community appoint a committee, composed of rabbis as well as lay people, including women, to act as an impartial panel where complaints can be brought. We feel this would go far toward instilling more confidence in the *beit din* system.

There have been various attempts at civil remedies. The New York State *Get* Law is such an attempt. In reality, it helps few.

Pre-nuptial agreements dealing with the *get* issue are another attempt at a remedy. The engaged couple signs a statement agreeing that, if they eventually separate, they will submit their case to a particular rabbinic court and abide by its decision. The hope is that such an agreement would be enforceable in civil court should either of the parties refuse to keep his/her word.

The pre-nuptial agreement has not as of yet been widely adopted. We suggest that anyone getting married should find out about such an agreement and sign one.

Agunot Need Our Help

Agunot are all around us. They are our neighbors. All of us are vulnerable to this problem—our daughters, sisters, granddaughters. These women suffer because of their commitment to Torah and *halacha*. They are paying too high a price. They need and deserve the help of the Torah world.

The Torah exhorts us to help the oppressed, particularly widows and orphans. Today's *agunot* are oppressed beyond words. We must begin to hear their silent weeping. We cannot ignore them any longer.

What Can Be Done?

Agunah, Inc. was established in 1987 to seek societal and halachic solutions for *get* problems. To this end, the organization undertook a survey of the *beit din* system.

Many problems became evident from this review. As a result, Agunah, Inc. promulgated a number of proposals in order to respond to what it considered unsuccessful and often unfair practices on the part of some rabbinic courts.

The proposals are as follows:

1. Urge pulpit rabbis and community leaders to respect and support *seruvim* (contempt citations) of *batei din* by ostracizing recalcitrant spouses from

synagogues. [This was adopted two years ago by Lincoln Square Synagogue in New York City, one of America's most prestigious congregations, and more recently by Agudath Israel for all its member synagogues. — *Ed.*]

2. Standardize the *beit* din procedure so that all *batei din* function in basically the same way.
3. Computerize *gittin*.
4. Have another woman present at the *beit din* session when sexual matters are discussed. Otherwise, an uncomfortable situation is made even more difficult.
5. End extortion. Blackmail is rife in the system. Women too often have had to pay for *gittin*. This must be stopped. Recalcitrant husbands should not profit from abusing *halacha*, and rabbis should not encourage this practice.

A BEIT DIN RESPONDS: "YES"

Leib Landesman

EDITOR'S NOTE: Rabbi Leib Landesman is the rosh beit din *of the Kollel Horabonim Beit Din, in Monsey, NY. His* beit din *has presided over cases involving some of the most complicated halachic issues, especially in the field of matrimonial law. Rabbi Landesman has been involved with thousands of divorce cases, and has personally administered approximately 500* gittin. *In an interview with the* Jewish Homemaker's *managing editor, Avraham M. Goldstein, Rabbi Landesman responded to a variety of points raised by the directors of Agunah, Inc. in their article.*

Agunah, Inc.'s primary contention is that a "crisis" exists today regarding the matter of Jewish divorce. Rabbi Landesman disputed this claim. He challenged the statistic printed by the *Jerusalem Report* that there are 10,000 *agunot* in Israel, and the extrapolation from that figure by Agunah, Inc. to the effect that there are thousands in the U.S. as well. [The *Jerusalem Report* figure comes from a film by the Israel Women's Network— *Ed.*]

Rabbi Landesman questioned the premise that there are more *agunot* today than, say, twenty years ago. He attributed this perception to "individuals and organizations that have made all this into an issue, so there's more exposure. It doesn't necessarily mean there are more cases now."

A critical area at issue, he noted, is how to define an *agunah*. "It's a colloquial phrase," Rabbi Landesman said, "that's used today for someone who wants a *get* but doesn't have a *get*. But it's used in very broad terms. It's used to describe someone who has followed the proper procedures and after a certain amount of time still doesn't have a *get*. But it's used as well for someone who hasn't done things right. It also is used for someone who wants a *get* on demand and it's not forthcoming instantly. She decided last week that she wants a *get,* and she doesn't have it within a day or a week."

Pressed regarding the figure given by the *Jerusalem Report,* Rabbi Landesman pointed out that there is a great difference between the Israeli system and ours. In Israel, *batei din* have jurisdiction over matrimonial matters. If the problem between the couple is limited to financial support, the *batei din* are on an equal footing with the secular court system. If a *get* is involved, then the *beit din* has sole jurisdiction over all matters, however ancillary, which are related to the *get,* including but not limited to custody, child support, and property.

He continued that, just as with the secular courts in the U.S., the *beit din* system in Israel suffers from overload, which has created a backlog. A contested divorce may take from two to five years. Rabbi Landesman added that lawyers and *to'anim* (client representatives before a *beit din*) often have no desire to expedite their cases, since the more time is spent, the greater is their fee.

Rabbi Landesman stated that, if there is any truth to the 10,000 figure, it refers to all cases currently within the *beit din* system, regardless of their status, and that it is improper to categorize a woman whose case is going through the process as an *"agunah."*

He added: "In almost every case I've known about, when there are major issues at stake, where they're really fighting, it takes a few years until it's resolved. But once everything is resolved, the issue of the *get* is resolved too. The *get* is one of twenty issues that have to be resolved."

Rabbi Landesman said that he would be very surprised if one could compile a list of 50 women in the U.S. at any given time who have followed the proper procedures and not received a *get*.

According to the rabbi, a critical error is the failure to follow these procedures at the outset. It often takes a long time until the wife takes her estranged partner to *beit din*. While she may consider herself an *agunah* even before instituting a *get* proceeding, he believes this is an inaccurate appraisal.

As an example, he says that he once remarked to an *agun* (a man whose wife refused to accept a *get*), "Whose fault is it that your problems of eight years have first been brought to the *beit din*'s attention twenty minutes ago?"

Rabbi Landesman emphasized that he holds in great esteem organizations which exist for the purpose of helping *agunot*. "Even if they help one person who is truly in need, it is worth all their efforts," he noted. Moreover, "The fact that these organizations exist does at times speed things up. For example, instead of taking a year or two until the recalcitrant spouse realizes it's over, it may speed things up by a few months." He said that the number of *agunah* cases may have decreased in recent years because of the efforts of groups such as Agunah, Inc.

Rabbi Landesman took strong exception to the allegation that *batei din* are unfair to women. He emphasized that, at least in his own *beit din,* both parties are treated equally. He rejected the idea that the woman is made to feel uncomfortable or cannot compete on an equal footing in the halachic arena, and stated that a female *to'en* would be welcomed at the Kollel Horabonim Beit Din. (There are, to his knowledge, no female *to'anim* in the U.S. His *beit din* generally disdains *to'anim,* believing they do little to advance the case of the party they are representing, and that they will often resort to impressive-sounding but halachically vacuous arguments in order to justify their fee.)

Rabbi Landesman also took strong issue with Agunah, Inc.'s insinuations that the secular courts are fairer than *batei din*. He said: "The article gives a very rosy picture of the court system and a very shoddy picture of the *beit din* system. This is very misleading. People think the court system is the epitome of righteousness, but being privy to many confidential matters, I can clearly state that I know more than one judge who belongs in jail. And I know of cases which have been 'fixed' between the judge and one of the lawyers."

He did acknowledge that in many *batei din*—although not in the Kollel Horabonim Beit Din—there is a lack of decorum, which may lead to the perception that *batei din* are not as meticulous as the secular courts. Yet this is "a problem of color, not of substance," he declared, saying that *batei din* are much more scrupulous than secular judges, and that "judges and lawyers are much more corrupt than any *beit din* or *dayan* can be subjectively perceived to be, even in the worst possible case." The rabbi agreed with Agunah, Inc. that different *batei din* have different halachic standards. He stressed that it is up to the litigants to do their homework before selecting a particular *beit din*.

Rabbi Landesman pointed out that American *batei din* do not have the power to force compliance with their decisions. Therefore, what Agunah,

Inc. sees as *beit din* problems are almost all implementation problems. For example, he insisted that the fact that it is the husband who has to give the *get* does not put the wife at a disadvantage as far as the *psak* is concerned. He declared that a *beit din* decides its cases based solely on halachic criteria. It is in cases of noncompliance (which, he says, when taking all differences, not just the *get,* into account, happens about equally between husbands and wives) where implementation of the *psak* becomes difficult. He said that almost all recalcitrants eventually comply, and that in many cases the husband's tactic is merely to wait the wife out, hoping she will compromise on some of the areas where the *psak* was favorable to her.

While this is certainly an example of the *get* being used as a weapon, Rabbi Landesman explained that, if a woman is patient and is unwilling to be defeated by the husband's tactic, the entire *psak* will eventually be implemented in almost every case.

Rabbi Chaim Malinowitz, who sits on the Kollel Horabonim Beit Din, opined that, if all methods short of physical coercion were properly applied, any husband in his right mind would give a *get*. These methods include ostracism from the community and using all legal devices available to make the husband support his estranged wife financially, as he must do according to *halacha*. According to Rabbi Malinowitz, the financial strain alone is usually enough to bring about compliance.

Commenting on Agunah, Inc.'s assertion that a man has the option of a *heter me'ah rabbanim*, Rabbi Landesman said that such a *heter* is rarely issued. Therefore, the husband is just as stuck by the lack of a *get* as the wife. The exception to this is, he said, where the parties are not strict about religious observance. Since the woman's sin would be much greater than the man's, the lack of a *get* may not prevent the husband from finding an outlet for his desires. This, however, is a commentary not on Jewish law, but on the lack of observance in some circles.

Rabbi Landesman noted that he knew of one case where the husband had to pay over a million dollars to convince his wife to accept a *get*. No *heter me'ah rabbanim* was granted him.

Agunah, Inc. charges that the *ketubah* has become essentially a worthless document and that it is almost never paid. Rabbi Landesman responded that, in his *beit din,* if the *ketubah* is claimed and is due, it is paid. At times, he noted, the *ketubah* is considered when the general financial matters are arranged. But there is no standard policy in his *beit din* of asking the wife to forego the *ketubah*.

Regarding the value of the *ketubah,* Rabbi Landesman explained that there are several formulas through which the worth of the standard Ashkenazic *ketubah* is calculated, and that the formula used depends on the facts involved in each particular *din Torah*. He said that the highest *ketubah* amount his *beit din* has awarded is $7,938.

He disputed Agunah's view that the *ketubah* is a critical component of the proceedings, noting that it is a simple financial document. He stated that a couple can fix the amount of their *ketubah* by writing in whatever figure they choose.

Rabbi Landesman acknowledged that when immediate implementation is a problem his *beit din* may counsel the aggrieved party, and may suggest that it is in her (or his) interest to forego certain items to which she is halachically entitled in order to expedite the total dissolution of the marriage. (The same is done in the secular legal world to avoid extended litigation.) However, he stressed, if she says she wants what halachically is coming to her, the *beit din* will stand by its *psak*.

Rabbi Landesman accepted the premise that *zablas* occasionally leave something to be desired. Noting that the *dayan* picked by each party is, by *halacha,* expected to do his best for his litigant, Rabbi Landesman said that some such *dayanim* will skirt the boundary which separates a *zabla dayan* from a *to'en*. Still, he declared that even the worst *zabla beit din* is more honest than a secular court. Asked about a *zabla dayan* from Williamsburg, Brooklyn, who is known to represent husbands and to refuse to convene the court until the woman's *dayan* accedes to his choice of the third, supposedly neutral, judge, Rabbi Landesman stated that the woman's *dayan* must play a waiting game if such is the case.

When a *psak* is not followed, the *beit din* issues a *seruv* (contempt citation). Rabbi Landesman was emphatic in stating that it is much more difficult to enforce a *seruv* in the Modern Orthodox community than it is in more right-wing communities. While refusing to generalize, he decried the fact that many Modern Orthodox men "are too busy playing baseball" while their wives "are too busy playing tennis" to take an interest in their friends' marriage difficulties.

He cited a case in New Jersey, where a recalcitrant husband worked in a firm along with 70 other Orthodox Jews, most of them Modern Orthodox. His *beit din* was unable to convince them or their rabbi to implement the particulars of the *seruv* which had been issued.

Rabbi Landesman lauded Agunah, Inc.'s call for a system that will computerize *gittin,* and supports having a fund to help destitute women. [The Vaad HaRabbonim of Far Rockaway has recently established such a fund.—*Ed*.] However, he disagreed with Agunah's opinion that the New York State *Get* Bill has not helped many women obtain a Jewish divorce, declaring that he has personally presided over 150 cases where the bill led to the issuance of a *get*.

Rabbi Landesman said that a matter often glossed over is the difficulty some husbands find in exercising the visitation rights which have been accorded them. He said: "I would be inclined to think that there are as many problems with fathers' visitation rights as there are with *gittin* for women." He cited cases where ex-husbands have rarely or never seen their offspring after having given a *get,* including a case where a man spent $32,000 in court in an unsuccessful attempt to have his rights enforced. Asked what can be done, he replied, "I don't know; I am baffled. Most people don't have the thousands of dollars it costs to go to court, or they don't have the mental endurance needed."

Are Orthodox divorces rising in number? And what can be done to avoid divorce?

Rabbi Landesman disputed recently published statistics that say divorce in the Orthodox community is rising. He said that, at least in proportional terms, the incidence of divorce has declined over the last two decades.

In his opinion, the primary reason for this trend is that "people now realize divorced life is not all that rosy, especially for the woman. The second time around, it's basically a man's market. Women have friends who are divorced. They speak with them and see that it's difficult—financially and in other respects." According to the rabbi, people today "don't rush for a *get* like they used to," a phenomenon he applauds. He said: "If there is an unbearable situation involving health, religion, or physical abuse, where objectively one just cannot remain in the marriage, divorce is an alternative. But if there's a personality clash, including disliking one's character or just not liking the person, these are subjective tastes, and they are things one can learn to change."

Rabbi Landesman said that women who come to him seeking a divorce are encouraged to first speak with divorcees and remarrieds so that they will have a better understanding of divorced life. He asserted that women have to decide whether it may be better to remain in a non-ideal marriage, and that, if there are children, the *nachas* derived from them often makes the marriage worth saving.

Rabbi Landesman had other suggestions for reducing divorce among Orthodox Jews. He said that, in over half of divorce cases involving Modern Orthodox couples with which he has been involved, the parents of the woman were opposed to the match in the first place. He told one such wife: "When you go to buy a fur coat, you first ask the opinion of someone else. But with something as important as marriage, you have the attitude that you don't need to inquire."

The rabbi emphasized that potential mates frequently do not understand the commitment involved in a marriage. Were they to recognize that marriage "is not a game," they would be more careful when selecting a partner. He said that this deficiency can be found in all kinds of Orthodox *shidduchim*.

Furthermore, he noted that the Steipler Rav, Rabbi Yaakov Kanievsky, *zt'l*, voiced concern for the fact that yeshiva students often have not learned how to interact with others. Rabbi Landesman said that early problems in a marriage often occur because the husband needs time to learn how to act towards his wife — a difficulty that can be ironed out with time, patience, and hard work.

A further step toward reducing divorce, he said, would be if people realized that the *beit din* system can be used to resolve problems short of divorce. The husband especially has certain obligations to his wife, and she can take him to *beit din* if he is not meeting those obligations. Were a small issue nipped in the bud, it might not become a larger one, leading to a divorce, over which, the Talmud says, the altar sheds tears.

The Ground Rules

When is a *get* called for? Is one entitled to a *get* upon demand? These and related questions were put to Rabbi Chaim Malinowitz, who sits on the Kollel Horabonim *beit din* with Rabbi Landesman. The following is a summary of his response.

According to the *Shulchan Aruch* (Code of Jewish Law), even when a *get* is desirable, there are varying ways in which the *beit din's* decision may be expressed. The kind of *psak* which will be issued depends upon the circumstances of each particular case.

At one extreme, the *beit din* will direct that there must be a *get,* and that the husband may be coerced, even physically, to divorce his wife. Grounds for this kind of *psak* may include physical abuse, financial non-support by the husband, and refusal to have marital relations.

At the other extreme, the *beit din* may advise the parties that a *get* is desirable, but will not declare that the husband is obligated to grant the *get* or that the wife is obligated to accept it.

There are varying degrees which lie between these extremes. A common one is a *psak* which obligates the husband to give a *get* and permits all forms of pressure, short of acts which would constitute coercion, for the purpose of implementing the *psak*. The types of pressure include total ostracism from the community and forcing the husband to financially support his estranged wife.

Grounds for this sort of *psak* are looser than for a decision which permits coercion. Examples are a lesser degree of financial non-support by the husband or a lesser degree of the wife being unable to live with him.

Generally, if the *beit din* considers a marriage "dead," as determined through the rules set out by the *Shulchan Aruch,* a *psak* will be issued obligating the husband to give his wife a *get* and obligating her to accept it.

Rabbi Malinowitz says he is convinced that in "99 out of 100 cases" proper implementation of steps such as ostracism and forcing the husband to support his wife would result in a *get.* He says that "anyone in his right mind" would give a *get* rather than paying thirty or forty thousand dollars a year to a woman with whom he is not living. Rabbi Malinowitz feels that the problem lies in the unwillingness of Jewish society to totally ostracize recalcitrant husbands, and the difficulty of implementing a *psak* of financial support in a society where church and state are separate.

Rabbi Malinowitz sums up: "Not always when a woman decides she doesn't want to live with this man or vice versa is the marriage dead. The Torah views marriage as an obligation between two parties, and it can't be revoked just because one party wants out; there have to be certain safeguards.

"The *Shulchan Aruch* decides what a dead marriage is. If a marriage is practically dead from an objective viewpoint and can be seen by the *beit din* as being objectively dead, the *halacha* calls for a *psak* of obligation, with or without various types of pressure short of actual coercion."

False Hope

Over the last few years, there have been calls for *batei din* to retroactively annul weddings where the husband adamantly refuses to give his wife a *get.* In Talmudic parlance this is termed *hafka'at kiddushir.*

Rabbi Menachem Elon, a respected Torah scholar and author of *Ha-Mishpat Halvri,* a landmark work on Jewish law, believes that, if there were one *beit din* with responsibility for all matrimonial matters worldwide, *hafka'at kiddushin* would be halachically feasible.

Even in the unlikely event that a central *beit din* could be constituted, Rabbi Elon's position is subject to question. Of more practical import is the assertion made by two writers that Rabbi Moshe Feinstein, *zt'l,* the leading *posek* of our time, annulled weddings. Emanuel Rackman, in his *Jewish Week* column, has made this false claim on numerous occasions. The same is true of Sholom Klass, who has so written in the *Jewish Press* (although Rabbi Klass recently conceded that he was wrong).

It is true that Rabbi Feinstein freed countless women from their *agunah* status. He did not, however, resort to annulment. Rather, he permitted them to remarry when he was able to determine that one of two factors was operative. If there was a material defect in the original wedding ceremony, especially if there were no Orthodox witnesses, Rabbi Feinstein would rule that the couple had never been married. (He did insist that an attempt first be made to secure a *get*.) Alternatively, if the husband had, at the time of the wedding, hidden facts from his wife which would have led her to reject him as a mate, Rabbi Feinstein was willing to rule that the marriage was grounded in error—*kiddushei ta'us*.

The differences between Rabbi Feinstein's actions and *hafka'at kiddushin* are crystal clear. In cases of *kiddushei ta'us*, there is a material problem at the time of the marriage. In most *agunah* cases today, the problem occurs at the end of the marriage; the marriage itself was performed in a halachically acceptable way.

Kiddushei ta'us involves a finding by a proficient Torah scholar that the wedding ceremony was lacking; a *beit din* is not involved. Annulment must be done by the act of a *beit din*. Thus, Rabbi Feinstein acted in his role of scholar, not *dayan*.

In fact, in 1986, Rabbi Nisson Alpert, who was Rabbi Feinstein's top student, wrote a letter to the *Jewish Week* from his own deathbed, declaring in stark terms that Emanuel Rackman was misstating Rabbi Feinstein's position.

One can only hope that Emanuel Rackman will come to appreciate that he is giving *agunot* false hope, and that, admirable as his aims may be, he cannot actualize them by distorting the views of our greatest contemporary halachic decisor.

— Avraham M. Goldstein

LETTER TO THE EDITOR: FALSE ACCUSATION BY AGUNAH, INC.

As an activist for nearly a decade in helping women secure *gittin*, I applaud *The Jewish Homemaker's* interview with Rabbi Leib Landesman

(Oct. 1992), which puts into perspective the reality of the *agunah* problem in America. Unfortunately, Agunah, Inc., founded with the most worthy intention of helping people obtain gittin, has sought to advance its cause through its entirely counterproductive approach of engaging in a vendetta against *batei din* and ad hominem attacks on individual rabbis. Intentionally or otherwise, they have turned a legitimate communal problem into a general attack on the leaders, institutions, and principles of Orthodox Judaism. Their article in the same issue is a perfect example.

They attempt to demonstrate dishonesty and unethical behavior by *dayanim,* noting a case where a dayan allegedly tried to extort $2,000 from a woman to procure a *get* for her by a certain date. I know that what they are claiming is totally untrue because of my personal involvement in the case.

The facts are that the woman seeking the *get* felt great appreciation for the efforts of a rabbi who had given much time in attempting to negotiate a monetary settlement so that both sides would be satisfied. She felt that it was not fair that the lawyers in the case should be paid for their efforts and their time while the rabbi was expected to do everything gratis. She therefore offered him $2,000, which was to be paid out of the money that she would receive in the settlement of the case. It is also important to note that this rabbi was not involved as a dayan in the case; the article implies otherwise.

It is sad that Agunah, Inc., in its zeal to discredit rabbis and *batei din*, has resorted to false stories to prove its point. If anything, my experience has been that rabbanim are often the unsung heroes, giving much time and effort to resolve very sticky and complex issues in a dedicated and caring fashion.

Efforts to resolve the *agunah* problem must include mediation, attempts at reconciliation, counseling, community action in ostracizing recalcitrant spouses, and many other approaches. What it does not need is a one-sided smear campaign of exaggeration, distortion, and falsehood.

Labish Becker
Brooklyn, NY

EDITOR'S NOTE: The Jewish Homemaker *has confirmed that Labish Becker's version of the story is correct.*

13
Tragedy Compounded: The *Aguna* Problem and New York's Controversial New "*Get* Law"

Chaim Dovid Zwiebel

Introduction

Approximately one year ago, in the summer of 1992, New York State enacted a new "*get* law"—legislation designed with the most commendable of intentions to help alleviate the tragic plight of the modern-day "*aguna*."

However, the new law has generated a great deal of rabbinic opposition. Prominent halachic authorities, including the most universally respected *poskim* of our day, have ruled that the approach embodied in the new legislation raises serious halachic problems affecting the most sensitive and stringent aspects of Jewish family life, and have insisted that the law not be permitted to stand as enacted.

In the nearly 10 years I have been privileged to work for Agudath Israel of America, no issue that I can recall has occupied as much of the time and attention of the *Moetzes Gedolei HaTorah* (Council of Torah Sages) of America as has the 1992 "*get* law" matter. Under their constant guidance, Agudath Israel has sought to help reach a constructive resolution of the problem—a resolution that will enjoy the broad consensus support of all recognized halachic authorities, while making a positive contribution toward addressing the wrenching problem of the *aguna*.

In so doing, the *Moetzes Gedolei HaTorah* has directed Agudath Israel to steadfastly avoid engaging in potentially destructive public debates. On the contrary: The one public statement issued by Agudath Israel concerning the 1992 legislation (reprinted in the Shevat 5753/February 1993 issue of *The Jewish Observer*) expressly called upon all segments of the community "to cease and desist from issuing inflammatory statements that can only further exacerbate tensions over this issue, and make it more difficult to resolve the problem constructively."

Unfortunately, however, the controversy surrounding last year's "*get* law" continues to generate a great deal of public confusion, distortion and misinformation; and the law itself remains on the books, unamended and undisturbed. The time has clearly come, in the view of the *Moetzes Gedolei HaTorah*, to present to the public the full background of the law and the reasons our leading Torah authorities feel as strongly about it as they do. This article represents my effort to address this need.

Readers hoping to find personal fingerpointing and name-calling will be disappointed; I have done my best to avoid any of that in the pages that follow. Nor is there any extensive halachic analysis of the various issues raised by the 1992 legislation. *The Jewish Observer* is not the proper format, and I am not the proper exponent, to engage in such analysis. The few basic halachic points set forth in the article are only those necessary for a rudimentary understanding of the complex issues involved.

I am grateful to the many *rabbonim* with whom I have had the privilege of discussing the subject of the 1992 "*get* law," and more generally the terrible problem of the modern-day "*aguna*." Their input and insight have made a major contribution to this article, and I only hope that I have been a faithful student of their lessons.

I

The wrenching problem of the modern-day "*aguna*" is one of the most pressing issues on Orthodox Jewry's contemporary communal agenda. For many reasons:

First, and most obviously, when a recalcitrant husband acts out of spite or greed and improperly withholds a *get* from his wife, he exacts an enormous toll in human suffering. All too many Jewish women are experiencing unbearable anguish and agony while trapped in a state of marital limbo from which they see no escape. Innocent children are caught up in the emotional vortex of their mothers' devastation. Loving parents and family members are shattered by their daughters' and sisters' tragic plight. The personal tragedies are incalculable, and would be more than reason enough for the community at large to take urgent notice of the problem.

But the human factor is not the only serious concern; at stake also is *k'vod Shamayim*. When the plight of the *aguna* stirs the creative imagination of television programmers and pulp novelists; when individual cases become the subject of feature articles in such mass media publications as *New York* magazine and *The Village Voice*; when prominent *rabbonim* and *batei* din, and even *Hashem*'s holy Torah itself, are publicly portrayed as insensitive and inhumane—the *chillul Hashem* is terrible.

There is also the matter of *kedushas Yisroel*—the sanctity of the Jewish people, preserved throughout the *golus* millennia through strict adherence to Torah laws governing marriage and divorce, but jeopardized considerably by the growing number of failed Jewish marriages in which the husband refuses to give his wife a *get*. A non-observant Jewish woman who otherwise would prefer to receive a *get*, to ensure her ability to remarry a more observant Jewish man, will often satisfy herself with a civil divorce at the slightest sign of *get*-recalcitrance by her husband. Reportedly, even some Orthodox women trapped in marital limbo are so desperate for a way out of their excruciating circumstances that they eventually succumb to temptation and rebel against halacha by remarrying (or entering into less formal but equally illicit liaisons) without the benefit of a *get*, and then drifting entirely away from Torah observance.

To be sure, there is ample basis to cast a skeptical eye on the claims that have been advanced by certain "*aguna* activists" about the alleged magnitude of the problem within the Orthodox Jewish community. There is also good reason to beware the larger agenda of some of these activists, whose rhetoric often cultivates disrespect for established halachic procedures and rabbinic leaders, and who use the *aguna* issue to promote some of the most insidious anti-Torah values of contemporary secular feminism.[1]

We would also do well to recall the adage that there are two sides to every story—perhaps even the *aguna* story. No doubt there are situations where a husband may be fully justified in not wanting to give his wife a *get*, or where a wife is not entirely without blame herself for her husband's recalcitrance.

And when the champions of modern marital egalitarianism lecture us about the "archaic inequities" of Jewish divorce law, perhaps we should suggest that they glance in the mirror and survey the devastation of the broken homes and broken lives that litter the contemporary American family landscape. *Ashreinu mah tov chelkeinu*—fortunate are we, how wonderful is our lot, how proud the Torah community can be of the strong sense of family structure that characterizes the *bayis ne'eman b'Yisroel*.

Be all that as it may—the objectionable excesses and hidden agendas of some activists, the complexities of individual cases, the overall strength of Torah family life—we dare not lose sight of the seriousness of the *aguna* problem, and of the urgent moral imperative it places on us. Trite though it may sound, it is true: even one *aguna* is one *aguna* too many, one more than we can afford to tolerate. When the stakes include heartrending human suffering, massive *chillul Hashem* and the undermining of basic foundations of *kedushas Yisroel*, burying our communal head in the sand is simply not an acceptable policy.

II

Little wonder, therefore, that some of the most outstanding *rabbonim* and *askonim* of our time have devoted so much thought and energy toward helping resolve the painful plight of the modern-day *aguna*. But solutions to thorny problems never come easily.

The halachic nub of the *aguna* problem is the fundamental principle that a *get* must be given as a matter of the husband's own free will; otherwise it is a *"get me'useh"* (a forced *get*) and not valid.[2] In the large majority of cases— including cases in which a *beis din* rules that the husband should give a *get*, or even is *obligated* to give a *get*—neither the *beis din* nor anyone else has the halachic authority to *force* a husband to do so. Only in certain extraordinary circumstances, discussed in *Shulchan Aruch Even Ho'ezer 154*, may a *beis din* authorize the use of physical force or some other form of duress to compel a *get* by "persuading" the husband that he really wants to divorce his wife after all (*"kofin oso ad she'yomar rotzeh ani"*). (See Rambam, Hilchos Geirushin 2:20.) And even in those extraordinary *kofin* cases, the only permissible role for independent non-Jewish force is if the force is directed at compelling the husband to comply with the *beis din*'s directive; an independent secular court order directing the husband to give a *get*, for example, is halachically unacceptable, no matter what the circumstances.

That is not to say that pressure tactics may never be employed to convince an unjustly recalcitrant husband to give his wife a *get*. *Halacha* recognizes that many forms of pressure are not so overbearing as to deprive the husband of his free will in deciding whether to divorce his wife, and thus raise no concerns of *get me'useh*. (See *Rama, Even Ho'ezer 154:21.*) Obviously, it is critical that whatever pressure is imposed not rise to the halachic level of compulsion, lest the *get* be deemed invalid as *me'useh*. The line between permissible pressure and impermissible compulsion is one that only *rabbonim muvhakim*, experts in *tiv gittin v'kiddushin*, are capable of drawing, as the halachic factors are complex and the halachic stakes enormous — so enormous that if a woman "remarries" after having received a *get me'useh*, her relationship with her new "husband" will be deemed adulterous (*aishes ish*), and their children will bear the stigma and disability of illegitimacy (*mamzeirus*).

The first prerequisite in devising a communal strategy for pressuring unjustly recalcitrant husbands, therefore, must be authoritative halachic guidance to ensure that the pressure does not cross over the compulsion line and result in *get me'useh*.

In this connection, it is also critical that the validity of *gittin* given as a result of the pressure be recognized by a broad base of halachic consensus. Were *gittin* to be given under circumstances that certain *rabbonim* might find them acceptable but others would not, some women may discover that their marital status is considered halachically questionable and that their ability to remarry is severely impaired. When a proposed solution to the *aguna* problem fails to gain broad consensus support among recognized authoritative *poskim*, it may well lead to a tragic split in *Klal Yisroel* — and is thus no solution at all.

The validity of the *get* is not the only halachic issue to be considered. Even if a form of pressure does not rise to the level of impermissible compulsion, *halacha* may independently prohibit its use. To take an extreme example, assume that an act involving *chillul Shabbos* is undertaken to pressure a recalcitrant husband to give his wife a *get*. Or, to take a more common example, assume that the pressure comes about as a result of the wife's unauthorized resort to secular court (*arkaos shel nochrim*) when *halacha* would require her to adjudicate the dispute before *beis din*. (See *Choshen Mishpat* 26:1.) In these cases, the *get* given by the husband may be halachically valid, but the means employed to impose the pressure are anti-halachic. Thus, a second prerequisite in devising a responsible communal approach to the *aguna* problem is to ensure that the proposed means of imposing pressure on recalcitrant husbands does not itself create independent halachic concerns.

There is yet another point that should be considered a prerequisite. Although the *Shulchan Aruch* delineates circumstances where halacha would encourage a husband to divorce his wife, the general preference of *halacha* is that marriages be preserved. For example, in a case where a woman simply states that she is no longer happy in her marriage and wants out on vague grounds of "incompatibility," the *beis din* may well fully support a husband's refusal to terminate the marriage by *get*. "No-fault divorce" and "divorce on demand," though popular in secular society, are concepts entirely alien to the values of Torah.[3] This, too, complicates the search for a viable means of dealing with the *aguna* problem. Any "solution" that enables a woman to pressure her husband into giving her a *get* where *halacha* would seek affirmatively to preserve the marriage may undermine the entire Torah approach to marriage and divorce, and has no place on our communal agenda.

III

Among the several approaches that have been devised to address the *aguna* problem is secular legislation—laws that seek to utilize the secular courts in civil divorce proceedings as a means of pressuring a recalcitrant husband to give his wife a *get*. New York State has enacted two such laws.

The first "*get* law" was enacted in 1983. It is predicated on the proposition that no person who wants a civil divorce should be able to obtain one if he or she simultaneously refuses to participate in a *get* proceeding. Thus, says the law (section 253 of the New York Domestic Relations Law), no final judgment of civil divorce shall be entered until the party seeking such divorce first files an affidavit stating that, "to the best of his or her knowledge, he or she has . . . taken all steps solely within his or her power to remove all barriers to the other party's remarriage." The law specifically defines "barrier to remarriage" to include a barrier imposed by halachah: "any religious or conscientious restraint or inhibition . . . that is imposed on a party to a marriage . . . by reason of the other party's commission or withholding of any voluntary act."

The 1983 law had its genesis around a conference table in the former 5 Beekman Street national headquarters of Agudath Israel of America, where a group of *rabbonim* and lawyers convened in 1981 at the organization's behest to try to develop a strategy that would enlist the secular legal system as an ally in dealing with the *aguna* problem. It was understood, of course, that such an alliance must be carefully crafted so as not to create any potential for halachic problems. Accordingly, when a concrete proposal was developed, it was submitted for the consideration of a broad array of leading *poskim* and *gedolei Yisroel* from various circles in the Torah community. These prominent rabbinic figures offered their halachic endorsement of the basic concept embodied in the proposal, and unanimously encouraged Agudath Israel to pursue such legislation.[4] After two years of hard work, including certain technical revisions in the proposal designed to overcome various legal objections that had been raised, the first "*get* bill" became the law of New York State.

Evaluating the 1983 legislation by the three broad criteria outlined above confirms its soundness as an appropriate communal response to the *aguna* problem. With respect to the issue of *get* validity, the many *poskim* consulted by Agudath Israel all agreed that the approach of this first "*get* law" created no potential for *get me'useh*. This is so because the only form of pressure the law exerts on a recalcitrant husband to give a *get* is that a certain benefit he seeks to obtain from the court—i.e., the civil divorce—can be withheld if he refuses to participate in the *get* process. Since the court has no power under the law to take away something from the husband that rightfully belongs to him, his free will remains halachically intact. And, because the pressure it creates will be felt only by a husband who affirmatively seeks a civil divorce, the 1983 law cannot be said to encourage the improper use of *arkaos shel nochrim* or any other antihalachic methodology. Nor can it be said that the law promotes the giving of a *get* in a situation where *beis din* would support a husband's efforts to preserve the marriage; the husband's approach to the secular court for a civil divorce shows he has no interest in maintaining *shalom bayis*.

The 1983 law has spared or freed a number of women from the chains of *igun*. Although figures are hard to come by, one New York area *dayan* who handles many *gittin* was recently quoted as stating that he has personally presided over some 150 cases where the law contributed to the giving of a *get*.[5] However, as helpful as the 1983 law has apparently proven to be, there are many *agunos* for whom it provides absolutely no assistance. The law imposes its affidavit obligation only on the party seeking the civil divorce. Thus, the law is an effective tool only where the recalcitrant spouse is the one who seeks a civil divorce. Frequently, though, the *aguna* is the one who commences the civil divorce proceeding, and the recalcitrant spouse contests the case. The law is powerless to deal with that particular scenario of *igun*.

For this reason, and others that are beyond the scope of this article, New York's 1983 "*get* law" is not "*the* solution" to the *aguna* problem. It can be helpful in certain cases, but by no means all cases. And so, concerned activists searched for additional ways by which the secular legal system might assist in alleviating the tragic plight of *agunos*.

IV

In all New York State civil divorce cases, if husband and wife fail to reach agreement on the various financial aspects of the divorce, the court will impose its own economic terms. Section 236 of New York's Domestic Relations Law establishes thirteen separate factors that courts are obligated to consider in making "equitable distribution" of "marital property" (i.e., "all

property acquired by either or both spouses during the marriage . . . regardless of the form in which title is held"). The first twelve of these factors relate
to purely economic considerations. The thirteenth is "any other factor
which the court shall expressly find to be just and proper."

In March 1992, a New York State Supreme Court judge interpreted the
equitable distribution statute in a manner that has direct bearing on the
problem of *aguna*. (In New York, the "Supreme Court" is the court of *lowest*
general jurisdiction.) The case, *S. v. S.*, involved a civil divorce proceeding
commenced by the wife and contested by the husband—thereby rendering
the 1983 *get* law irrelevant—which culminated in a judgment of divorce. At
that point, the husband pressed for equitable distribution of the marital
assets, the bulk of which were held in the wife's name. The wife argued that
the husband should be denied equitable distribution because of his refusal to
give her a *get*.

The court declined to deny equitable distribution entirely, but stated that
its statutory authority under factor 13 to consider "any other factor which the
court shall expressly find to be just and proper" would enable it to consider
evidence in the equitable distribution hearing about the husband's alleged
refusal to give his wife a *get*, and to award the wife a greater share of the
marital assets than it otherwise would. Said the court:

> Obviously, the misuse of a power differential between the parties be it a
> monetary differential or otherwise (i.e. the withholding of a Get or withhold-
> ing one's appearance before a Beth Din) can be taken into account by a court in
> equity. Thus, such misuse of a power differential may be a factor in determin-
> ing equitable distribution.[6]

The court's interpretation of its authority under the equitable distribution
statute was apparently the first time any court had announced its willingness
to take into account the *get* factor in making its allocation of marital assets.
But the concept was not entirely new. It had been proposed as legislation
as early as *1984*, one year after the original "*get* law" had been enacted,
when a bill was introduced in the New York State Assembly (without
Agudath Israel's knowledge or input) that would have required a court,
"where appropriate, [to] consider the effect of a barrier to remarriage" on
the factors governing equitable distribution of marital assets (as well as the
factors governing "maintenance," i.e., support payments from one spouse
to another).

However, the bill engendered considerable halachic controversy from the
start. One distinguished *moreh hora'a*, Rabbi Yitzchok Liebes שליט"א,
wrote a lengthy *teshuva* nine years ago setting forth his view that such a law
might be acceptable—specifically, that a *get* given to avoid the potential loss

of assets in equitable distribution, at least in cases where a *beis din* has ruled that a husband is obligated to give a *get*, is not considered *me'useh*. (*She'eilos U'teshuvos Bais Avi, Even Ho'ezer 169*.) At the same time, however, in reviewing the *she'eila*, he wrote that he had been informed "*she'donu b'she'eila zo gedolei z'maneinu v'lo hiskimu l'hatir bo'zeh*," that leading halachic authorities of the time had considered the proposal but had refused to support it. Rabbi Liebes further indicated that "*mi'kivan she'zeh inyan Klal Yisroeli*," since this is a matter that affects the entire Jewish community, he himself was also not prepared to issue a *p'sak* in support of the proposed legislation without the additional backing of two "*rabbonim muvhokim b'hora'a d'peki'i sh'meihu*," outstanding halachic decisors whose reputation is well established. Without such backing, wrote Rabbi Liebes, "*harei d'vorai rak b'toras hatza'a*," my words are only to be taken as a suggestion.

No other "*rabbonim muvhakim*" were prepared to lend their halachic support to the measure. And so the bill remained dormant, gathering dust in the state legislature for eight long years, without ever being brought up for vote. Because the proposal was no longer under active "front burner" consideration, and because it had already been opposed by the "*gedolei z'maneinu*" referred to in Rabbi Liebes' *teshuva*, Agudath Israel did not find it necessary to take steps during these years to make further halachic inquiries about the matter.

After the decision in *S. v. S.*, however, the bill was dusted off and revitalized, now promoted by its proponents as a "codification" of the court's ruling. The bill passed through the state legislature; and, on July 17, 1992, was signed into law.

This article is not the place to get into a detailed discussion of the full chronology of all the events surrounding the passage of the 1992 "*get* law"; there is little to be gained by dwelling on this painful history.[7] One bottom-line point is worth emphasizing, however, because it has important ramifications for future legislative undertakings:

It has been a longstanding policy of Agudath Israel, established years ago when the *Moetzes Gedolei HaTorah* was under the chairmanship of Rabbi Moshe Feinstein זצ"ל and reaffirmed many times over the years (including by the current members of the *Moetzes Gedolei HaTorah*, שליט"א), that any secular law impacting upon *halacha* — which, like all secular laws, is binding upon all *segments of the Torah community* — must have a broad base of consensus support from authoritative *poskim* respected by all segments of the Torah community. That is why, as discussed above, the concept underlying the original 1983 "*get* law" was first shown to a wide array of *poskim* from various circles, and only after each of these diverse *rabbonim* gave his halachic approval was the law advanced through the legislative process.

Sadly, no such procedure was followed with respect to the 1992 "*get* law." In fact, the law was advanced through the legislature and presented to the Governor for signature without any authoritative written halachic backing; in the face of clearly articulated opposition by at least one of the halachic authorities consulted by the bill's proponents; and despite full knowledge that Agudath Israel had undertaken to seek definitive halachic guidance on the proposal in the expectation and belief that final action on the legislation would be put on hold until such guidance would be forthcoming. Thus were sown the seeds of disaster.[8]

V

It has by now become abundantly clear that the idea of utilizing the secular equitable distribution process as a means of pressuring a recalcitrant husband into giving his wife a *get* does not enjoy broad halachic support. Quite the contrary: The two leading *poskim* of our time, Rabbi Shlomo Zalman Auerbach שליט"א and Rabbi Yosef Sholom Elyashiv שליט"א, along with numerous other *rabbonim* from broad circles (including *rabbonim* who are heavily involved in *siddur gittin* in the United States), have expressed substantial halachic concerns with the concept embodied in the 1992 law.

The rulings of Rabbi Auerbach and Rabbi Elyashiv came in response to a *she'eila* presented last summer by Agudath Israel. After weeks of strenuous efforts to ascertain the precise meaning and potential ramifications of the new law, these two universally respected *gedolei haposkim* each issued a *teshuva* indicating their opposition to the law.[9] The *teshuvos* emphasize that economic duress—in the form of a threat to the husband that assets which rightfully belong to him will be taken away if he does not give his wife a *get*—can rise to the level of improper coercion, which would nullify the husband's free will and invalidate the *get* as *me'useh*. Thus, they ruled, by formalizing the authority of the court in equitable distribution to consider the effect of a husband's failure to give his wife a *get*, the 1992 law institutionalized the potential for coercive *issuy*. In Rabbi Auerbach's words, the law is not a *takona* (a positive step) but a *sakona* (a danger).

Rabbi Auerbach and Rabbi Elyashiv had occasion to reconsider their views several months ago. They were asked to do so in light of a suggested new interpretation of the 1992 law—an interpretation radically different from the one the law's co-draftsman had put forward when the *she'eila* was first presented. While a full discussion and evaluation of this suggested new interpretation is beyond the scope of this article, its essence is that the law's definition of the term "barrier to remarriage"—a barrier that exists because of a spouse's withholding of a "voluntary act" — automatically safeguards against any possibility of coercive *issuy*, because a husband acting under coercion is incapable of a "voluntary act." Under this reading, the law would preclude a court in equitable distribution from taking into consideration a husband's failure to give a *get* if such failure is based on a *beis din*'s concern that the husband is under improper coercion — even coercion created by the law itself.[10]

Shortly after *Shavuos* this year, the two *ziknei haposkim* issued *teshuvos* reiterating their *p'sak* that the 1992 law was not acceptable and must be changed. Rabbi Elyashiv's *teshuva* challenges the logic of the proposed new interpretation of the statute, and questions how a law whose very purpose is to utilize the pressure of the equitable distribution mechanism to help an *aguna* receive her *get* could be read to contain a built-in provision that prohibits utilization of that mechanism because the pressure amounts to halachic *issuy*. If that is how the law will be interpreted, queries Rabbi Elyashiv, "*mah ho'ilu be'takonosom*," what was accomplished by its passage? His conclusion, and that of Rabbi Auerbach, is that the law may well lead to *get me'useh*, and must not be allowed to stand as is.[11]

It is further apparent, as Rabbi Elyashiv and other *rabbonim* have observed, that the 1992 legislation also fails to meet the other prerequisites outlined above for appropriate communal responses to the *aguna* problem. Entirely apart from the issue of the *get*'s halachic validity, the means of pressure created by the new law raises potential halachic problems of its own — most obviously, the incentive it creates for a woman to resort to *arkaos shel nochrim*. This most serious halachic prohibition is implicated if, as a result of a woman's desire to utilize the law as a means of pressuring her husband into giving her a *get*, she improperly and without a *beis din*'s authorization submits the economic issues of asset division and spousal support to a secular court rather than a rabbinic tribunal. Moreover, these *rabbonim* have noted, the law could be used to pressure husbands into giving *gittin* even in situations where there is absolutely no halachic basis even to encourage divorce, let alone compel divorce.[12]

VI

The 1992 "*get* law" has found some post-enactment rabbinic support. Most notably, the Rabbinical Council of America, at its June 1993 convention, passed a resolution endorsing the legislation, and urging that other states follow the New York model. But there is less here than meets the eye.

From releases and press reports on the subject, it appears that the RCA's endorsement of the 1992 legislation does not mean that the rabbinical

organization embraces the equitable distribution mechanism as a halachically appropriate means of pressuring a recalcitrant husband into giving
a *get*. Even the RCA, it appears, would agree with the basic premise of the
law's halachic opponents that a *get* given to avoid potential economic losses
under the 1992 law may be invalid as a *get me'useh*. The RCA nonetheless
supports the law, and is not concerned that such legislation will lead to
problems of *me'useh*, because it is confident that individual *batei din* will be
able to make a case-by-case determination as to whether the husband would
in any event have wanted to give a *get* voluntarily. If such determination
leads in any given case to the conclusion that the husband's willingness to
give a *get* is attributable to his concern about the potential economic
consequences of the new law, the *beis din* will simply refuse to be *mesader*
the *get*.

With all due respect, however, once it is conceded that fear of economic
loss in equitable distribution can negate a husband's free will and preclude a
beis din from being *mesader* a *get*, it is difficult to understand why anyone
would embrace the 1992 "*get* law" as a favorable development—let alone
endorse it as a model for other states to follow. It is true that the legislation
may prompt a recalcitrant husband to respond more quickly than he otherwise would to a summons of a *beis din*. But once he arrives in *beis din*, and
tells the *rabbonim* why he has come—to remove a barrier to his wife's
remarriage, so that he will retain his assets in equitable distribution—the
beis din will be unable to go forward with the *get*. Stated simply, by
enshrining in statute a factor which *halacha* regards as *issuy*, invalidating
coercion, *the law itself creates an impediment* to the giving of a *get*, and is
thus of no real assistance to the suffering *aguna*.

Indeed, if the law is interpreted as its proponents have recently suggested—that a judge has no authority under the statute to reduce the husband's share of the assets if his failure to give a *get* is caused by a *beis din*'s
determination that he is subject to coercive *issuy*—then not only is the law
unlikely to *help agunos*; it may affirmatively *harm* them. Under this interpretation, the law provides a wily recalcitrant husband with yet an additional
weapon in his arsenal to ensure that his wife will not receive her *get*. All he
needs to do so is tell the *beis din* that he wants to give his wife a *get* in order to
avoid losing assets in equitable distribution—secure in the knowledge that
the *beis din* will refuse to be *mesader* the *get* because of the *issuy* factor, and
that the court will not reduce his assets because of the *beis din*'s conclusion.

Moreover, is there really basis for such confidence that all *batei din* will
uniformly recognize the *issuy* factor created by the legislation and never be
mesader a *get* that is motivated by the husband's fear of economic loss? At a
minimum, the 1992 law imposes an exceedingly difficult task on even the

most competent *batei din*; in many cases that come before them, perhaps in *all* cases that come before them, they must now probe in great depth the state of mind of a husband who tells them he wishes to give his wife a *get*, so that they can determine whether he is truly motivated by his own free will or rather by his desire to avoid a loss of assets. Little wonder that many *rabbonim* have expressed concern that the law might lead to *gittin* whose status is under a halachic cloud.

In short, the 1992 law is problematic no matter how it will be interpreted or implemented. *At best* — if *batei din* will uniformly refuse to be *mesader gittin* which husbands seek to give in order to avoid a potential loss of assets in secular court — the law is a cruel hoax: of little or no benefit to *agunos*, and possibly of substantial benefit to recalcitrant husbands. And, *at worst* — if some *batei din* will be *mesader* such *gittin* — the legislation raises the horrifying specter of the proliferation of *gittin* of questionable validity, of *she'eilos* involving issues of *aishes ish* and *mamzeirus*, of an Orthodox Jewish community divided amongst itself on basic questions of *yichus*.

VII

When Rabbi Auerbach and Rabbi Elyashiv issued their *teshuvos* late last summer, the *Moetzes Gedolei HaTorah* of America called upon the law's chief legislative sponsor to take steps to try to amend the statute in conformance with the *p'sak*.[13] They renewed their request several times over the course of the year, most recently early this summer when the two *ziknei haposkim* reiterated their original ruling that the law is unacceptable in its current form.

Unfortunately, the legislative sponsor has declined to comply with this request, claiming (among other things) that any effort to change the law would engender "overwhelming opposition" and would be futile. This may or may not be an accurate assessment. Realistically, though, given the sponsor's high rank in the state legislature, it seems clear that his bottom-line is right; any effort to change the law without his affirmative support would surely be doomed to futility.

Of course, things can change. It is possible that the courts will eventually determine the law to be unconstitutional. Or the courts may issue a definitive interpretation that demonstrates conclusively the law's potential for *issuy*, in which case whatever support the legislation currently enjoys would presumably evaporate. And it is conceivable that sober reflection will persuade the law's supporters — some of whom, including the chief legislative sponsor, have long records of outstanding service to *Klal Yisroel* — that the law is problematic no matter how it is interpreted and should be changed. I, for one, am hopeful.

In the meantime, we must redouble our efforts to find other ways of dealing with the tragic *aguna* problem, communal approaches that enjoy the halachic support of all circles. It is noteworthy, in this regard, that the RCA adopted two other *aguna*-related resolutions at its recent convention: one calling for the imposition of synagogual sanctions against recalcitrant spouses who refuse to respond to the summons of a *beis din*[14]; the other endorsing the use of a written contractual agreement entered into between bride and groom prior to marriage, binding them to submit to the jurisdiction of a *beis din* in the event they ever *chas v'Sholom* cease to dwell together as husband and wife, and obligating the husband upon such cessation to pay his wife a certain fixed sum of daily support for the duration of the Jewish marriage.[15] It remains to be seen whether these approaches, and others that have been prepared by other individuals and groups, will gain widespread rabbinic support and communal implementation. At a minimum, though, they deserve to be given careful study by all who recognize the gravity of the problem and the urgency of its compelling demand for attention and amelioration.

To permit the frustrations of the 1992 legislative experience to cause us to throw up our hands in despair, and simply assign the *aguna* problem to the "Tsk, Tsk, What a Shame" file, would be one of the saddest legacies of the entire sorry episode.

Notes

1. See Rabbi Yissocher Frand, *"Where There's a Rabbinic Will, There's a Halachic Way": Fact or Fiction?*, *The Jewish Observer*, Cheshvan 5751/October 1990.

2. It is true, since the *"takonas Rabbeinu Gershom,"* that a *get* also must be received by the wife voluntarily. However, if a wife unjustifiably refuses to accept a *get*, the husband may go through the process of obtaining a *"hetter me'ah rabbonim"*, which would permit him to remarry. (See *Bach, Tur Even Ho'ezer* 1.) Admittedly difficult though that process may be, no comparable procedure is available to women whose husbands unjustifiably withhold a *get*.

3. It appears, though, that with the growing evidence of the terrible long-term social costs of divorce – to children, to the husband and wife, to society at large – the pendulum may be swinging back even in secular circles to make civil divorce less easily available. See Wallerstein & Blakeslee, *Second Chances: Men, Women, and Children a Decade After Divorce* (Ticknor & Fields, 1989); Whitehead, *Dan Quayle Was Right, The Atlantic Monthly*, April 1993.

4. The files in Agudath Israel's archives include written statements of support from Rabbi Moshe Feinstein זצ"ל and Rabbi Yaakov Kamenecki זצ"ל (each of whom

wrote that the 1981 proposal created no concerns of *get me'useh*, and offered strong words of encouragement that such legislation be enacted); and, *yibadlu l'chaim.* Rabbi Shimon Schwab שליט״א, Rabbi Moshe Stern שליט״א, Rabbi Yecheskel Roth שליט״א, and Rabbi Dovid Cohen שליט״א.

5. See the interview with Rabbi Leib Landesman, head of the Bais Din of the Kollel Horabbonim in Monsey, in *The Jewish Homemaker, Tishrei-Cheshvan* 5753/ October 1992.

6. The decision in *S.* v. *S.* is reported at 583 N.Y.Supp.2d 716.

7. Suffice it to note, for the record, that various rumors and allegations about Agudath Israel's purported failure to communicate its concerns about the legislation prior to enactment, or about Agudath Israel's purported ulterior organizational motives in opposing the legislation, are false. With the benefit of 20-20 hindsight, as the person within Agudath Israel who has primary responsibility for legislative affairs, I do regret that I did not take certain additional, more forceful steps prior to the enactment of the law to try to ensure that it would not move forward without broad-based authoritative halachic backing. However, based on my conversations during the spring and summer of 1992 with the bill's main proponents, I believed— justifiably, I think (though, as it turned out, naively)—that they too were in full accord with our view that no legislation in this area should be enacted without broad halachic support. In retrospect, I was obviously mistaken.

8. A critic recently took Agudath Israel to written task for seeking to impose "halachic correctness" on the entire Jewish community through its insistence that the 1992 law should be changed to meet the objections of its halachic opponents. Considering the respective statures of the halachic opponents of the legislation and its supporters, there are dangerous elements of halachic anarchy in this criticism. In any event, the ironic truth is precisely the contrary of this critic's complaint. The proponents of the law are the ones who are doing the imposing, by insisting that whatever modicum of rabbinic support the equitable distribution approach may enjoy justifies the promulgation and enforcement of statewide legislation that affects all Jews from all circles. Respect for legitimate halachic diversity is not advanced through the promotion of a universally binding *takonas hatzibbur*, in the form of a secular law, that does not enjoy universal halachic support.

9. After Agudath Israel presented the *she'eila* to the *gedolei haposkim*, Rabbi Elyashiv assigned two American-born *rabbonim* now residing in Yerushalayim (who frequently serve as "aides" to this *gaon*) to determine all the facts surrounding the new law, to ensure that all aspects of the *she'eila* would be properly understood and considered. Over the next month-and-a-half or so, numerous telephone conversations and fax correspondence went back and forth between *Eretz Yisroel* and America, as these two learned "*shamoshim*" posed a variety of questions to several American attorneys—including one of the codraftsmen of the legislation—to clarify all aspects of the law and of the *she'eila*. It was only after this extensive process that Rabbi Auerbach and Rabbi Elyashiv issued their *teshuvos* calling for changes in the law.

Thus, the suggestion that has appeared in the press that these two non-English speaking *gedolei haposkim* issued their *teshuvos* about the 1992 law without first taking steps to assure themselves that they fully understood the *she'eila* is flatly contradicted by an impressive record of extensive communications and clarifications that preceded their *piskei halacha*. Indeed, it is frankly a gross insult to the great stature and uncompromising integrity of these two halachic giants to even entertain such a suggestion.

Agudath Israel's approach to Rabbi Auerbach and Rabbi Elyashiv was made pursuant to the policy of the *Moetzes Gedolei HaTorah* of America, who regard these two great *rabbonim* in Yerushalayim as the pre-eminent *poskim* of final resort in our day. Over the past several years, in fact, the *Moetzes Gedolei HaTorah* has referred a number of complex communal *she'eilos* to Rabbi Auerbach and Rabbi Elyashiv.

10. This may sound confusing. To help understand this new interpretation advanced by the law's defenders, let us consider a specific scenario:

Assume that an *aguna* commences a civil divorce proceeding. Her husband, aware of the 1992 legislation, goes to a *beis din* and states that he is now at long last prepared to give his wife a *get* in order to avoid loss of assets in court. The *beis din*, however, responds that it is unable to be *mesader* the *get* under the circumstances, because such a *get* would not be the product of the husband's own free will and would thus be invalid as a *get me'useh*. The *beis din* puts its position in writing.

The husband then appears before the court, explaining that he did attempt to give his wife a *get* but that the *beis din* refused to allow him to give it. He shows the court the *beis din*'s written statement that it was unable to be *mesader* the *get* because the potential loss of assets in court nullified the husband's free will and therefore would have invalidated the *get* as a product of coercion. Under the interpretation advanced by the law's defenders, the court under these circumstances may not take the *get* factor into consideration, and the husband will lose no assets.

Whether or not this is the way the courts are likely to interpret the law has been the subject of discussion and debate among legal experts. A number of distinguished experts in family law have expressed their view that a court faced with a wife whose future financial circumstances will be affected by her inability to remarry may well make adjustments in equitable distribution and maintenance irrespective of a *beis din*'s determination that any *get* given to avoid such adjustments would be a *get me'useh*. I, too, share that view.

11. Rabbi Elyashiv's *teshuva* also addresses a second argument advanced in the request for reconsideration of the original *p'sak*: that the new law would permit a court to award additional assets to the spouse facing a "barrier to remarriage" only in cases where her future financial circumstances would likely be affected by her inability to remarry; and that since a husband is in any event halachically required to support his wife, the court would simply be imposing upon him an obligation that *halacha* fully recognizes. Rabbi Elyashiv points out, however, that the court's statutory authority under the new law goes far beyond that which is recognized under *halacha*, and accordingly can rise to the level of *issuy*.

Shortly after receiving them from Yerushalayim, Agudath Israel circulated copies of both sets of Rabbi Auerbach's and Rabbi Elyashiv's *teshuvos* to *rabbonim* and *batei din* involved in *gittin*. Interested readers who wish to obtain copies may request them through the editorial offices of *The Jewish Observer*.

12. These points have been most forcefully articulated in a series of *teshuvos* and proclamations issued by the Bais Din of the Kollel Horabbonim in Monsey.

13. Total repeal of the 1992 legislation would not necessarily resolve the problem. As noted above, the New York State Supreme Court in *S. v. S.* interpreted the original equitable distribution statute — particularly the court's authority under factor 13 of the statute to divide marital assets on the basis of "any other factor which the court shall expressly find to be just and proper" — as authorizing consideration of the *get* factor in dividing the assets. Were the 1992 law simply repealed, the original statute would still be in place; and courts in future cases might follow the interpretation of *S. v. S.*, thereby still presenting problems of potential *issuy*. The ideal solution, therefore, would be to amend the statute so as to preclude any possibility of judicial compulsion through equitable distribution.

14. According to the news release published by the RCA at the conclusion of its convention, these sanctions would include "preclusion from holding membership or office in the synagogue, being called to the Torah or any other honor, and the announcement of the names of recalcitrant spouses on a regular monthly basis in synagogues in the local community at the conclusion of Sabbath services." Similar (though not identical) resolutions have been adopted by the Conference of Rabbonim of Agudath Israel Synagogues (as described in greater detail in my *Teves* 5753/ January 1993 *J.O.* article, *Batei Din vs. Secular Courts: Where Do We Seek Justice?*), by the Council of Young Israel Rabbis, and by several other rabbinic groups and individual shuls. See *Darchei Moshe*, *Tur Choshen Mishpat* 19; *Rama*, *Even Ho'ezer* 154:21.

15. A full discussion of pre-nuptial agreements generally, and of the specific form endorsed by the recent RCA resolution, is beyond the scope of this article. One general point is worth noting, however: Rabbi Moshe Feinstein's *teshuva* in *Iggros Moshe*, IV *Even Ho'ezer* 107, suggests that all proposed pre-nuptial agreements be evaluated by two distinct criteria: whether they may raise potential *halachic* problems; and, even if they pass that most basic test, whether they may raise potential *personal* problems between husband and wife.

14

The *Agunah* Problem and the So-Called New York State *Get* Law: A Legal and Halachic Analysis

Marvin E. Jacob

Preface

I have elaborated more than I had to in this matter . . . because I know that a few of the scholars of our generation are in the habit of removing any conceivable doubt before ruling . . . that is good and proper in all other kinds of rulings, but in the case of an *Agunah* that is not my approach, instead I follow the path of the early and later scholars who sought every possible alternative with every ounce of their strength to be lenient in the case of an *Agunah*.

— *T'shuvos Masaas Binyomin*, *Siman* 109, p. 222

Nowadays, if one frees a single *agunah* from the chains of her *Iygun,* it is as if he rebuilt one of the desolate places of Jerusalem on high.

— *T'shuvos Maharsham* in the name of the *T'shuvos HaBach Hachadoshos,* Part 1, *Siman* 84

I am indebted to my partner, Carlyn S. McCaffrey, Esq., for her insightful comments relative to the Domestic Relations Law. Mrs. McCaffrey has practiced and lectured extensively in the field of Family Law and is an Adjunct Professor of Law at New York University Law School.

It is a matter of greatest importance, and may God bring success to all those
who toil in these great matters involving remedies for the daughters of Israel.
                                            — *Igros Moshe, Even HaEzer,* Part 4, *Siman* 106

Introduction

The *Agunah*[1] problem has become widespread in the State of New York in
the last fifteen or twenty years. Legislative solutions, among others, have
been proposed to alleviate the problem. In particular, laws were enacted in
New York, in 1983 and 1992. However, the 1992 law has been criticized as
contrary to Halacha. This article is devoted to a detailed explanation of the
1992 law and its background with a view to demonstrating that the criticism
stems from a misunderstanding of the true meaning of the law.

In July 1992, the New York State legislature amended the Equitable
Distribution Law of 1980 by providing that upon dissolution of a marriage the
court shall, where appropriate, consider the "effect" of a "barrier to remarriage" in determining the disposition of marital property and the setting of
maintenance (spousal support).[2] Although the amendments proceeded for
months through the state legislature accompanied by extensive front-page
newspaper publicity, no opposition to the law was interposed in the state
legislature prior to passage. However, immediately after passage, Agudath
Israel of America (hereinafter referred to as "Agudah") unilaterally obtained
rulings from two distinguished Israeli Rabbis, which rulings called for the
amendment or repeal of the new law. Noting that a *Get* which is executed out
of fear of monetary penalty is Halachically invalid, the rulings are premised
upon the legal misperception advanced by Agudah's legal staff, that the new
law mandates that matrimonial courts impose monetary penalties upon any
husband who does not grant his wife a *Get*. On reconsideration of their
rulings, again at Agudah's request, one of the two Israeli Rabbis dropped his
call for repeal and no longer opposes the law, while the other continued to
urge that the new law be amended.

A description of the new law and its background is set forth in the
discussion which follows. Also set forth is a description of the Canadian *Get*
Statutes and the proposed Israeli *Get* Statute. It is hoped that an analysis of
all of these provisions will be of aid in understanding the issues in dispute
relative to the new law. In fact, it is the law, *not the Halacha*, that is in
controversy here. In other words, *it is the M'tzius* (the factual background)
which is in issue, not the applicable Halacha. In fact, there has never been
any question that a *Get* given under the compulsion of monetary penalty is
Halachically invalid. The dispute has always revolved around a misin-
terpretation which Agudah's legal staff has attributed to the new law.

Properly construed, however, the new law should be free of any taint of Halachic invalidity.

The Equitable Distribution Law of 1980

The 1992 Amendments, about which there has been considerable controversy, were enacted in the form of two brief additions to an otherwise comprehensive statute governing property and support rights in divorce which was enacted in 1980. Thus, the 1992 Amendments should not be interpreted in isolation as one would interpret a discrete piece of legislation. Rather, the 1992 Amendments should be interpreted consistent with the objectives of the comprehensive statute of which they are a part.[3] This comprehensive statute, commonly referred to as the Equitable Distribution Law,[4] overhauled the New York statutes dealing with alimony, property division, and child support. Prior to its enactment in 1980, property was generally divided among spouses in a divorce on the basis of legal title. Upon dissolution of a marriage, a spouse who held legal title to property was entitled to the entire property, while the nontitled spouse would receive nothing. In the view of the New York State legislature, the title concept often worked great hardship upon the wife whose husband accumulated property in his own name during the marriage, notwithstanding the contributions made toward the property or the marriage by the wife. Accordingly, the Equitable Distribution Law was enacted in New York State which, among other things

> conceptually views the marriage relationship as an "economic partnership" upon dissolution of which property accumulated during the marriage is distributed *based upon the needs and circumstances of the parties regardless of which spouse actually holds title*; and directs the court to consider 13 factors[5] in determining an equitable and fair distribution of marital property among the parties and 11 factors[6] in setting the amount and duration of maintenance.[7] As one commentator has put it: "[t]he Equitable Distribution Law requires that the court distribute property 'equitably,' upon consideration of specific statutory factors, other just factors, and upon the circumstances of the case and of the parties."[8]

As is evident, the Equitable Distribution Law of 1980 was not enacted to compel the giving or acceptance of a *Get*, but that statute granted broad equitable powers to matrimonial courts which were used by one judge as a basis for holding that he could inquire into the inequitable conduct of a husband who misused the *Get* for economic gain. More about this later in this article.

New York's First So-Called *"Get* Law"

In June 1983, three years after enactment of the Equitable Distribution Law, New York enacted Section 253 of the Domestic Relations Law, the first so-called *"Get* Law." *This statute had nothing to do with equitable distribution.* Unlike the 1992 Amendments, Section 253 was a discrete statute, and its primary purpose was to deny a civil divorce to a husband who denies his wife a *Get.* In other words, Section 253 was designed to compel Jewish spouses, especially men, "voluntarily" to accede to religious divorces or be precluded from obtaining a civil divorce decree, whether the husband seeks a civil divorce decree by initiating a divorce action therefor or counterclaims for such relief in a divorce action initiated by the wife.[9]

Section 253 introduced for the first time the concept of "barrier to remarriage," words which later became the centerpiece of the 1992 Amendments. However, Section 253 uses the term "barrier to remarriage," not as it would be used in ordinary, everyday conversation, but rather as a term of art or law *which requires special statutory definition.* To constitute a "barrier to remarriage," the statute requires a showing that the barrier (i) was imposed on one party to the marriage by reason of the other party's commission or withholding of a "voluntary act" and that (ii) the "barrier" is capable of being removed by such other party's voluntary act.[10]

For Halachic as well as constitutional reasons, in its definitional provisions, Section 253 expressly confines itself to "voluntary acts." The statute also makes clear that the steps required to be taken by the spouse refer to "all steps solely within" the "power" of a spouse.

In addition, "barrier to remarriage," as defined, apparently took into account that although a *Get* must actually come from the husband and a *Bais Din* cannot give a *Get,* a *Bais Din* can effectively deny a *Get* to a husband by refusing to officiate at a *Get* proceeding.

As indicated above and as more fully described hereinafter, it is this *special statutory definition* which was incorporated into, and became the heart of, the above-described 1992 Amendments to the 1980 Equitable Distribution Law. This definition governs any determination by a matrimonial court, under Section 253 or the 1992 Amendments, that a "barrier to remarriage," in fact, exists.

One fact should be kept in mind throughout this discussion: the 1983 Law, which is the centerpiece of the 1992 Amendments, was universally approved by Halachic authorities, including HaGaon Harav Moshe Feinstein, *zt"l,* the paramount Halachic authority of the past several decades. In other words, the 1992 Amendments, about which there has been so much controversy, created nothing new in a conceptual or Halachic sense regarding voluntariness in giving or accepting a *Get*, since the core of 1992 Amendments had already been part of the law since 1983.

Justice Rigler's Decision in the Schwartz Case

Schwartz v. *Schwartz* (the so-called Rigler decision)

Unfortunately, Section 253 was perceived by many as having accomplished little regarding a solution to the *Agunah* problem. For, that statute only covered situations where the husband felt the need to seek a civil divorce. For the most part, however, husbands did not seek civil divorces, which left most wives without any legitimate leverage with which to counteract a recalcitrant husband's refusal to give a *Get*. To ameliorate the problem, in 1984, Assemblyman Sheldon Silver introduced in the New York State Assembly a new bill (which ultimately was enacted into law in July 1992). Virtually no progress was made on enacting that bill into law for approximately eight years.[11] Fortuitously, in March 1992, Justice William Rigler of the New York State Supreme Court, issued a landmark decision in which he held that the withholding of a *Get* by a husband, for inequitable reasons, can be taken into account by a matrimonial court in determining the equitable distribution of marital assets upon dissolution of a marriage.[12]

In his decision, Justice Rigler found that the *Get* procedure gives "tremendous power to a husband in a divorce proceeding"; the husband can virtually "dictate the terms of any agreement." This "disparity of power" is used by "unscrupulous spouses" who use their denial of a *Get* "vindictively" or as "a form of economic coercion" and thereby impose on the wife "enormous anguish." Justice Rigler further found that matrimonial courts possess traditional equity powers, and that the Equitable Distribution Law implies that the purpose of that statute is "to do equity."[13]

Justice Rigler observed that the courts in dividing marital property under the Equitable Distribution Law must consider 13 factors and, "most importantly," factor Number 13, which requires that the court consider "any other factor the court shall expressly find to be just and proper." Thus, Justice Rigler concluded that factor Number 13 "permits the court to review *all the equities* in the case when dividing marital property" (emphasis added). Accordingly, Justice Rigler held that the misuse of the "power differential" arising from the withholding of a *Get* may be a factor in determining equitable distribution under factor Number 13.[14]

Justice Rigler's decision made clear that inherent in the Equitable Distribution Law of 1980 was the judicial power to review a " . . . spouse's actions in relation to a *Get* . . . " and that " . . . those actions may be considered by the court when it equitably distributes the marital property."

In sum, although the Equitable Distribution Law of 1980 was not enacted with the objective that matrimonial courts should consider inequitable conduct which accompanies the withholding of a *Get*, its provisions possessed precisely that potential.

Justice Rigler's decision was hailed as a breakthrough in the battle for the rights of *Agunos*. Indeed, it was a creative legal approach to a resolution of the *Agunah* problem. However, although it raised no Halachic issues in the *Schwartz* case (as the wife owned substantially all of the assets), according to some it raised potential Halachic issues regarding *Get Me'usah* generally. Among other things, it suggested that matrimonial courts had discretion to impose monetary penalties upon husbands who "misused" the leverage of a *Get*.[15]

New York's Second So-Called *"Get* Law"

At this juncture, after proceeding for more than 4 months through the New York State legislature (accompanied by continuous front-page newspaper publicity), the 1992 Amendments were enacted without any opposition from any person or organization in the Jewish community.[16] The texts of the Amendments are quite brief and provide, in pertinent part, that a court shall, where appropriate, consider the *effect* of a "barrier to remarriage," *as defined in the 1983 Law*, on the 13 factors enumerated in the Equitable Distribution Law of 1980 regarding equitable distribution of marital property and the 11 factors regarding maintenance.[17] The amendments accomplished several things. First, they made clear that only where a husband is Halachically competent to give a *Get*, and refuses to do so, should a "barrier to remarriage" arise as a matter of law. Second, the 1992 Amendments did not codify the holding in *Schwartz, supra*. Rather, the Amendments defined (and narrowed) the matrimonial court's equitable power regarding "barriers to remarriage" in specific statutory terms.[18] Finally, the amendments made clear that a court could not issue orders which, directly or indirectly, interfered with the determination of a *Bais Din* not to officiate at a *Get* proceeding. A more detailed discussion of these three points is set forth hereinafter.

"Barrier to Remarriage" Defined

As indicated above, the words "barrier to remarriage" are not to be construed as they might be used in everyday speech, which had been the misperception of many, including Agudah, when it hastily sought rulings from the distinguished Israeli Rabbis. It is, as described above, a term of art specially defined in Section 253(6) of the Domestic Relations Law (the 1983 Law). As defined, a "barrier to remarriage" arises by reason of the voluntary act or omission of the spouse and must be capable of removal by voluntary act of that spouse. In other words, Section 253(6) not only defines what constitutes a "barrier to remarriage" but also what does not. Additionally, "voluntary act" is used in the context of what is "solely within the power" of the spouse to perform. Thus, where a *Bais Din* refuses to arrange a *Get* for a husband because it is Halachically impermissible to do so, and thereby effectively denies him a *Get*, the husband is not capable of removing the *Bais Din's* decision by mere "voluntary" act.[19]

In effect, therefore, the 1992 Amendments repose in the *Bais Din*, not in the court, the ultimate decision of whether the wife's inability to remarry will be taken into account in determining the distribution of marital assets.[20] For, the denial of a *Get* by a *Bais Din* effectively removes the "barrier to remarriage" as a matter of civil or secular law, as the husband has now done all he can "voluntarily" do by appearing before the *Bais Din* and stating his willingness to give a *Get*. Removal of the barrier arising from the *Bais Din's* judgment to deny the *Get* is not "solely within the power" of the husband to accomplish.[21] Surely, it makes no sense whatsoever to punish a husband for failure to carry out a court order, which is impossible for him to perform,[22] especially where it is the very compulsion of the court order that creates the impossibility of performance. The 1992 Amendments should not, indeed cannot, be construed to create such an untenable and inequitable result.

Thus, there is no merit to the contention that despite the adverse ruling of a *Bais Din*, a New York court would still consider the husband as the cause of the "barrier to remarriage." Remarkably, the opponents of the 1992 Amendments have, in effect, suggested that the husband could lie to the *Bais Din* when he is asked to describe the factors that comprise his decision to settle and give the *Get*. Clearly, the failure to lie to a *Bais Din* cannot be construed as the failure to do a "voluntary" act. Nor is there any substance to Agudah's view that the focus of the statute on "voluntary" or words of like import as described above, was intended to protect Catholics, not Jews. First, no such legislative intent is expressed in the statute or elsewhere. Also, it makes no sense to argue that similar facts will yield different results depending on whether a husband is Catholic or Jewish. Legislation should not and cannot, constitutionally, work that way. *See Church of Lukumi Babalu Aye, Inc.* v. *City of Hialeah*, 113 S. Ct. 2217 (1993); *Larson* v. *Valente*, 102 S. Ct. at 1683–84. The 1992 Amendments treat Catholic and Jewish husbands alike. In both cases, the inability of the wife to remarry because of religious barriers does not result in the imposition of monetary sanctions upon the husband.

The Focus of the Law on "Effect"

The 1992 Amendments focus on "effect," not on the "barrier to remarriage" itself or the husband's conduct in relation to it. In other words, under the 1992 Amendments the court may consider only the *effect* of a "barrier" (if one exists as a matter of law) on the thirteen legislative factors. As has been observed, "[w]hile the barrier to remarriage issue is not a direct legislative factor on equitable distribution, it is to be considered as a factor which *may* influence the statutory factors." (Emphasis added.)[23]

A "barrier to remarriage" can affect factor Number 8,[24] but it is difficult to see how the barrier affects other factors in equitable distribution, including Number 13 (which was the factor utilized by Justice Rigler).

Indeed, women who have substantial independent resources or income may not gain from a finding of a "barrier to remarriage." That is one of the reasons for inclusion in the statute of the words "where appropriate." Since a "barrier to remarriage" does not affect all of the 13 factors, and, in any event, the court must take into account all of the equities, the court is directed only, "where appropriate," to consider the effect of such a barrier.

Moreover, from a constitutional standpoint, the 1992 Amendments are neutral in their application. They focus only on the needs and circumstances of the spouse who is affected by the inability to remarry and avoid touching upon questions of religious doctrine which arise inevitably when courts must impose consequences solely for refusal to give or accept a *Get*.

In sum, "barrier to remarriage" is an indirect factor, not a direct, 14th legislative factor. When considering the equitable distribution of marital assets the court may only assess the impact of a "barrier to remarriage" on "the probable future financial circumstances" of the wife.[25] If the wife's future needs so indicate, the court may make an additional allocation to her from the marital assets to compensate for her inability to obtain support from another husband because of her *Agunah* status. This is in contrast to the holding in *Schwartz, supra*, where the refusal to give a *Get* was considered a direct (13th) factor in equitable distribution.

By Its Terms, the New Law is a *"Mezonos"* (Support) Provision

The "effect" approach of the statute, and its focus on the probable future financial circumstance of a wife who cannot remarry, has significant Halachic implications. For, if the court makes an additional distribution to a wife because of her inability to access support from another husband, that additional allocation is, in reality, intended to provide the wife with *Mezonos* or support. And, if a husband gives a *Get* to relieve himself of a *Mezonos* or support obligation, the *Get* he gives is not considered a *Get Me'usah*. For example, HaGaon Rav Moshe Feinstein, *zt"l*, issues the following ruling with regard to court orders dealing with *Mezonos* or support:

> With regard to your second question, if a secular judge imposes the responsibility upon a husband, when he refuses to give his wife a *Get*, to make a payment of money to her for her *Mezonos* and all of her needs, is such a *Get* considered a *Get Me'usah*? Behold, until he divorces his wife, he is responsible for her *Mezonos* and all of her needs according to the *Din*, *and she is even permitted to petition the secular courts for an order to compel him to provide her with Mezonos and all of her needs*, and even though the secular courts will order more than would a *Bais Din*,[26] because those courts will compel him to support her even if she works and profits, when those courts order him to provide her with her *Mezonos* and with all of her needs *under any circumstances, it is obvious* ["Poshut" in the original] that if he divorces her in order to rid himself of his responsibility, that such a *Get* is not considered a *Get Me'usah, and that it is a Kosher Get L'chatchilah." Igros Moshe, Even HaEzer*, Vol. 4, *Siman* 106 (translated from the Hebrew, emphasis and bracketed material added).[27]

The views of Rav Feinstein, *zt"l*, are fully in accord with the *T'shuvos Bais Meir, Even HaEzer, Siman* 154; *T'shuvos Chasam Sofer, Even HaEzer*, Part 2, *T'shuva* 60; *T'shuvos Mahara Ashkenazy, Siman* 18; *T'shuvos Rav Pealim*, Vol. 4, *Siman* 9; *T'shuvos Bnei Binyamin, Siman* 34; and *T'shuvos Shael V'mayshiv*, Vol. 2, Part I, *Siman* 28; all of which are predicated on the *T'shuvos Hamabit* and the *Tashbatz*, as discussed therein.[28] According to these *Poskim* (and there are none to the contrary on the issue), coercing a husband to fulfill his support obligation is different from coercing a husband to give a *Get*. In the former, the husband gives the *Get* in exchange for relief from his obligation of support, much the same as he would be paid a sum of money to give a *Get*. In either case the wife relinquishes property or rights in exchange for a *Get* which raises no issue of *Get Me'usah*, according to these *Poskim*.[29]

Under *Get* legislation recently proposed in Israel (*see* discussion at page 171 *infra*), *Botei Din* would be empowered to increase support payments for the benefit of an *Agunah* which exceed any amount owed by reason of Halacha or agreement, for the purpose of compelling a husband to give a *Get*.[30] The proposed legislation is broadly supported by the *Poskim* and

Botei Din in Israel and appears to be premised on, among other things, the views of the above *Poskim*. In any event, the 1992 Amendments are "needs" oriented and, therefore, orders issued thereunder would focus solely on the wife's needs for support, as distinguished from amounts that exceed her needs which are designed to compel a *Get*. Clearly, therefore, the 1992 Amendments should present no Halachic problem.

Significantly, the *Mezonos* point was not addressed in the *T'shuvos* of Rav Auerbach or Rav Elyashiv, *Shlita*.[31] However, subsequent to the issuance of those Response, Rabbi Dovid Arye Morgenstern, one of the *"Meshumashim"* of Rav Elyashiv, *Shlita*, sent a brief note to Agudah, summarily dismissing the *Mezonos* point for two reasons. Rabbi Morgenstern's brief note states that it was written with the *"Haskamah"* of Rav Elyashiv, Shlita. It is evident, however, that Rabbi Morgenstern's two reasons are premised upon the same misperceptions of the law discussed above.

Rabbi Morgenstern argues that whereas, Rav Moshe, *zt"l*, ruled only in circumstances where the husband was obligated to furnish *Mezonos*, under the new law the judge can order an additional allocation to the wife, even where the wife is not entitled to *Mezonos*.[32] Clearly, however, if a judge were to issue such an order, the *Bais Din* could and would deny the *Get* to the husband because he would be acting under compulsion of *"issuy,"* and, as shown above, there would be no adverse consequences to the husband. In other words, if the wife was not Halachically entitled to *Mezonos* because of her status as a *"Moredes,"* the order would be a distribution order, not a *Mezonos* order.

In his second point Rabbi Morgenstern makes the unsubstantiated claim that a distribution order can never be characterized as a *Mezonos* order for Halachic purposes, even where the order is predicated upon the wife's inability to remarry and her future financial needs resulting therefrom. (In this regard, it should be remembered that the court must make an explicit finding to that effect.) Not only is Rabbi Morgenstern's position in this regard contrary to the plain meaning of the law but also to the ruling of HaGaon Rav Feinstein, *zt"l*, as well as the other Poskim cited above.[33]

Agudah's Misperceptions about the New Law

Agudah's request for a ruling from Rav Elyashiv described the new law as a mandate to the court to take into account the refusal of a husband to give a *Get*, and that such refusal would invariably result in the confiscation of the husband's money. In its letter to Rav Elyashiv, Agudah states as follows:

. . . a new law has been enacted in the State of New York (without the approval of Agudah) which provides that the judge who rules upon the division of the marital assets upon dissolution of the marriage (Equitable Distribution), *must* take into account, among other things, the fact that the husband refuses to give his wife a Get, *and that fact will result* in the taking of a part of the husband's money to give to the wife. . . . (Translated from the Hebrew; emphasis added; parenthetical statement in the original.)[34]

As is evident from the foregoing, there is nothing in Agudah's statement that made clear to Rav Elyashiv that the new law is part of the Equitable Distribution Law, is therefore equitable in nature and not coercive, punitive or an automatic provision; that the 1992 Amendments conferred no new powers on matrimonial courts, but in fact narrowed them; that the husband is obliged to do only "voluntary" acts; that the *Bais Din* ultimately determines whether a *Get* may properly be given in any particular case; and that, in any event, the refusal by the *Bais Din* to arrange a *Get* for a husband may not be visited upon the husband.[35]

Moreover, Agudah's description of the new law is plainly wrong. There is no statute in New York which directs or authorizes, a court to deprive a husband of marital property based solely on his refusal to give a *Get*.[36] On the contrary, the Equitable Distribution law *directs* courts to distribute marital property "equitably" based upon "the circumstances of the case and of the respective parties." Nowhere does the statute direct courts to coerce *Gittin* or confiscate a husband's assets. Even prior to the 1992 Amendments, the matrimonial courts did not believe they possessed the power to do so.[37] As Justice Rigler stated in *Schwartz, supra*:

It is without question that when courts must touch upon questions of religious concerns, they may not consider religious doctrine. However, the courts may use "neutral principles of law" to resolve disputes touching on religious concerns.

The court will not grant plaintiff's [the wife's] application to stay the trial on the economic aspects of this case [Equitable Distribution] until defendant [husband] gives plaintiff a Get. *That request is far beyond the power of this court*. (Emphasis and bracketed material added; citations omitted.) 583 N.Y.S.2d at 718-719.

Agudah's misperceptions may have arisen from its prior encounter with the Canadian *Get* Laws. The Canadian statutes were enacted initially in 1986 (the Ontario Family Law Act, 1986 Amendments)[38] and on June 12, 1990 the Ontario law was incorporated into the federal Canada Divorce Act.[39] Under the two Canadian statutes, the failure by a husband to give a

Get within 15 days of a wife's demand (10 days under the Ontario Family Law), can result in the striking of *all* of the husband's claims and defenses in a divorce proceeding, including claims and defenses relative to custody, child and spousal support and the like. Unlike the new law, the Canadian law seems, by its terms, to be coercive and punitive. Failure to comply timely with the wife's demands can result in the forfeiture of all claims and defenses by the husband, which could also mean the forfeiture of money and/or property.[40]

The new law, on the other hand, is part of the Equitable Distribution Law and its purpose is not punitive, but, rather, to accomplish equity and fairness in dividing the marital estate upon dissolution of a marriage. As Justice Rigler observed, "[t]he very name of the statute implies the purpose of the statute, to do equity." *Schwartz, supra* 583 N.Y.S.2d at 718. There is no automatic forfeiture under any circumstances of claims, defenses, money or property. However, if a "barrier to remarriage" exists as a matter of law (as defined), the court is authorized to consider its "effect" on the "probable future financial circumstances" of the wife. Whether and to what extent there is an "effect" will turn upon the facts and circumstances of each case and the court must weigh the "effect," if any, together with all of the other equities in each particular case. No two cases should necessarily yield precisely the same result and, most importantly, there is nothing automatic, punitive or predictable with certainty about the result. As discussed hereinafter, from the standpoint of the *Halacha*, the existence of such a statute or a wife's threat to sue under it, should not invalidate any *Gittin* in this State. On the other hand, it does create a more level playing field insofar as the *Get* issue is concerned.[41]

In addition, the critics seem to have confused Section 253, the first so-called *Get* Law of 1983, with the 1992 Amendments, the second so-called *Get* Law. As explained above, the 1983 *Get* law is, undisputedly, coercive and punitive and may be viewed as targeting Jewish women and men as special objects of statutory protection.[42] Further, the 1983 *Get* Law was not enacted as part of the existing Equitable Distribution Law of 1980. However, the 1992 Amendments were different both in language and purpose. They were incorporated into, and made a part of, the Equitable Distribution Law of 1980 and merely authorize a matrimonial court, sitting as a court of equity, to consider, where appropriate, the economic effect, if any, of a "barrier to remarriage." There is nothing in the language of the 1992 Amendments which expressly, or otherwise, directs or even authorizes matrimonial courts to compel a husband to give a *Get* or to impose *penalties* for the failure to do so, and the law's critics have *never* pointed to any such language. Moreover, the 1992 Amendments create no new or special rights for Jewish women or men. The amendments merely assure that, within the existing comprehensive Equitable Distribution scheme, their "needs and circumstances" are not excluded or ignored. The Amendments merely made explicit what was already implicit since 1980.[43]

Legislation recently introduced in the Israeli Knesset,[44] which seeks to aid *Agunos*, also accentuates the difference between the remedial nature of the 1992 Amendments and laws which generally are designed to be coercive and punitive. The proposed Israeli legislation imposes sanctions upon any husband who refuses to comply with the ruling of a *Bais Din* that he give a *Get*. For example, such a husband can be denied a passport, the right to leave the country, a visa, a bank or checking account, a driver's license, a credit card, or employment in the civil service, army, police, local authority or any other public body. Also proscribed is work in any profession requiring a government license such as law or medicine. Significantly, this legislation has reportedly received widespread Rabbinic and communal support in Israel including the approval of the Degel HaTorah party, which is headed by the world reknowned, HaGaon Rav Eliezer M. Schach, *Shlita*. As stated above, the 1992 Amendments merely seek to provide an additional allocation for the support of women who are unable to remarry and find support through a new marriage. The proposed Israeli legislation, on the other hand, focuses on penalizing the husband in an effort to coerce him to give a *Get*. In the words of Rabbi Avraham Ravitz, Knesset representative of the Degel HaTorah Party, these sanctions are impossible for a recalcitrant husband to withstand. If the Israeli legislation is not Halachically objectionable despite its severe economic sanctions, why should the 1992 Amendments require amendment or repeal?

Conclusions Regarding the Distribution Aspects

In sum and substance, instead of the open-ended discretion that was available to matrimonial courts prior to the 1992 Amendments (relative to inequitable conduct) and the Halachic problems arising therefrom, the discretion of those courts is now circumscribed by a statute that incorporates within its equitable framework the definitional provisions of the Halachically approved 1983 Law as its centerpiece and provides the following:

(a) defines "barrier to remarriage," makes it a multi-tiered, defined term of art and sets forth specific limitations in statutory terms;

(b) unlike the 1983 law that pre-dated it, the 1992 Amendments are not punitive or coercive and their provisions do not operate in any automatic fashion;

(c) instead, the 1992 Amendments are remedial and religiously neutral, and focus only on the "economic effect" on the spouse arising from the inability to remarry;

(d) where a court finds that a "barrier to remarriage" exists, it may provide an additional support allocation; and

(e) in any event, whether the inability to remarry should be taken into account as an indirect factor in determining equitable distribution (or maintenance) effectively lies with the *Bais Din*, not the court.

The Reconsideration Request

In a request for reconsideration, made in April 1993 and transmitted by Agudah to the two distinguished Israeli Rabbis, the following was pointed out by Nathan Lewin, Esq., the author of the language of the 1983 Law:

"Barrier to remarriage" was defined *by my language* in the earlier law as including "any religious or conscientious restraint or inhibition . . . by reason of the . . . commission or withholding of any voluntary act." The third sentence of subsection (6) of Section 253 also declares: "It shall not be deemed a 'barrier to remarriage' within the meaning of this section if the restraint or inhibition cannot be removed by the party's voluntary act."

The word "voluntary" in each of these two sentences might appear superfluous, but it was deliberately inserted in the earlier law to insure that involuntary acts would not qualify. In other words, a husband maintains a "barrier to remarriage" only if he refuses to give a get that, if given, would be a "voluntary act." If the giving of the get is coerced – if it is, for this reason, not a "voluntary act" – withholding it is not, by definition, a "barrier to remarriage."

For this reason, it seems to me that the word "voluntary" in the two sentences defining "barrier to remarriage" automatically precludes the possibility of a get me'usah. If a *Bais Din* advises a court that the *Bais Din* will not officiate at a *get* because the husband is being coerced to give the get, the court may not, in my view, conclude that the husband's failure to give the *get*, is a "barrier to remarriage." Any other interpretation of Section 253 would, in effect, read out of the statute the word "voluntary." By including the word "voluntary" in the definition of "barrier to remarriage," Section 253(6) prevents a court from imposing any consequence – even the withholding of a civil divorce – if the husband's or wife's participation in a "*get*" results from coercion or "*issuy*."

For this reason, I believe a court advised by a *Bais Din* that a husband cannot give a get because, in the view of the *Bais Din*, he is acting under the compulsion of *"issuy"* — including *"issuy"* created by the new law — may not use the law to affect its decision on the distribution of marital property or on maintenance. A husband would, in my opinion, have valid grounds to set aside on appeal a court order giving him a smaller share of the marital property because he failed to provide a get after a *Bais Din* concluded that his reason for providing such a get was fear of a court order reducing his share of the marital property so that it was a *get me'usah*. (Emphasis added.)

Mr. Lewin also described his above-quoted views as not having been " . . . presented *at all* when the question was previously asked . . . " by Agudah of Rav Auerbach and Rav Elyashiv (emphasis added). Of course, by omitting the fact that "barrier to remarriage" was a carefully crafted term of art, the critics trivialized the transcendent point: the 1992 Amendments by their express terms automatically preclude the possibility of a *"Get Me'usah."*

However, in Rav Elyashiv's second *P'sak* of May 1993 (in response to Mr. Lewin) Mr. Lewin's views were rejected as erroneous. Based upon the information furnished by Agudah, Rav Elyashiv held that the overarching purpose of the new law was to coerce recalcitrant husbands to give *Gittin*. Thus, he concluded that a court would reduce a husband's share of the marital estate despite the *Bais Din's* refusal to arrange the *Get* because of *"issuy."* In addition, Rav Elyashiv held that a woman's threat to sue for a greater share of the marital estate could be carried out with absolute certainty. Since the very purpose of the new law was to coerce *Gittin*, the principle that the outcome of all litigation is, to one extent or another, uncertain, did not apply here.[45]

However, in his ruling of May 1993, Rav Auerbach did not appear to disagree with Mr. Lewin. Noting the "possible" invalidity of a *Get* given under the press of monetary sanctions, he stated that it "was necessary to see to it that the law is completely clear so that there is no fear whatsoever that a husband could be coerced to give a *Get*." Rav Auerbach's two and one-half line ruling is significant in two respects. First, it was a departure from his earlier call for repeal.[46] Second, by its very terms, it does not call either for amendments or changes to the current version of the law. It only requires that it be clear that the law does not result in *Gittin* which are coerced.

In my view, and speaking in my capacity as a lawyer, these two distin-guished *Poskim* seem to have been misinformed by Agudah as to the true meaning of the new law. That statement is not to be understood in any pejorative sense. On the contrary, I admire the dedicated work of the lawyers on Agudah's legal staff. In this instance, however, their analysis of these statutes is completely flawed.

The Controversy Relates to the Law, Not the Halacha

It should be evident from the foregoing, that there is no Halachic dispute concerning the 1992 Amendments. It is, in fact, well settled that a *Get* that is coerced, whether by physical means or economic penalty, is Halachically invalid. The controversy focuses *entirely* on the meaning of the law. For that reason, Agudah has been repeatedly urged to cease its attacks and allow the issue to be determined by the courts, whose job it is to interpret new statutes. Agudah has rejected that approach, although it had suggested initially that a test case be identified and pursued. Instead, it seeks to impose its view of the law (not the *Halacha*) on all other segments of the Jewish community. Clearly, Agudah's legal staff possesses no special expertise in matters of this kind, and their views on the law should not be given precedence, especially when they collide with those of the draftsmen and sponsors of the statute and senior, experienced counsel.[47]

The Passage of Time Has Demonstrated that the Reaction to Enactment of the New Law Was Unjustified and Unnecessary

The various *Botei Din* that officiate at *Get* proceedings in New York State have made clear that the vast majority of *Gittin* they arrange are not contested;[48] in other words, *Gittin* are generally not given during the pendency of litigation proceedings. Thus, the "dangerous scenarios" which have been advanced by the new law's critics as justification for their opposition are, in reality, a fiction. If, as the critics allege, the new law mandates that courts compel recalcitrant husbands to give *Gittin*, where are all of the cases of coerced *Gittin* since enactment of the new law in July 1992? In fact, in the 2 years since the new law has been in effect there has been no report of any case in which a judge has ordered a husband to give a *Get*. Neither has anyone pointed to a case in which a judge has confiscated a husband's assets for his refusal to give a *Get* or even threatened to do so. Moreover, there has not been a single case under this law in which a *Bais Din* has actually officiated at a *Get* proceeding under such circumstances. In sum, although a general alarm has been sounded by Agudah and others concerning a *Mamzeirus* epidemic, to date, no evidence to support that position has been adduced. Not only have events subsequent to enactment of the new law not borne out such forecasts, but also it should now be clear that coercion by a court to give a *Get* is rare (and, as shown above, improper), even if it may happen from time to time. However, for such rare occurrences, at most, guidelines for *Botei Din* would have sufficed. There was no need to call for amendment or repeal and there certainly is no demonstrable need or justification to continue the *Get* controversy.

Maintenance

So much for equitable distribution, or for the distribution aspects of the 1992 Amendments. Section 236B of the Domestic Relations Law also deals specifically with "maintenance" or support. In that regard, the statute sets forth eleven factors the court shall consider in setting the amount and duration of maintenance. In setting maintenance, the court is also directed to have "regard for the standard of living of the parties established during the marriage, whether the party in whose favor maintenance is granted lacks sufficient property and income to provide for his or her reasonable needs and whether the other party has sufficient property or income to provide for the reasonable needs of the other. . . . "

As in the case of distribution, the court shall, where appropriate, consider the *effect* of a *barrier to remarriage* as defined in Section 253(6) on the eleven factors. Of the eleven factors, only the fourth would appear to be affected by a barrier to remarriage. That factor requires the court to consider "the ability of the party seeking maintenance to become self-supporting. . . . "

In any event, it seems clear that a court may issue a maintenance order for a longer period or order permanent maintenance, if the court concludes that a barrier to remarriage exists, as defined in Section 253(6). If a husband decided to give a *Get* because of such an order, it is also seems clear that, according to the ruling of HaGaon Harav Moshe Feinstein, *zt"l*, and others, set forth above, such a *Get* would be free of any taint of *Get Me'usah* and *Kosher L'chatchilah*. Not surprisingly, therefore, the focus of the critics has been on the distribution provisions of the 1992 Amendments.[49]

Conclusion

Properly construed the 1992 Amendments seem free of Halachic invalidity for several reasons, including: they are *Mezonos* provisions; they automatically preclude the possibility of *Get Me'usah*; and they are not coercive or punitive. With regard to the last point, it bears emphasis that the new law is remedial and focuses on the religiously neutral principle of alleviating economic hardship, not on some coercive concept of punishing every husband who has refused to give a *Get*, whether or not he can find a competent *Bais Din* or Rabbi that will arrange one for him.

Apart from all of the above considerations regarding the meaning of the 1992 Amendments, the *Botei Din* in New York State have continued to arrange *Gittin* as before. The position of the *Botei Din* on this legislation is simple: regardless of the meaning of the law they are as competent as heretofore to determine the "voluntariness" of husbands on a case-by-case basis. The *Botei Din* recognize that each case turns upon its own particular facts and that, moreover, substantially all of the *Gittin* they arrange do not involve litigation as the *Schwartz* case or otherwise. Given the remoteness of the courtroom and the competence of the *Botei Din* to determine the "voluntariness" of husbands in any event, the *Botei Din* have generally not viewed themselves as dislocated by the questions that have been raised about the 1992 Amendments by those who clamor for amendment or repeal.[50]

Notes

1. In religious practice, a man must voluntarily give a *Get* and a woman must voluntarily receive it. Where a man refuses to give a *Get*, a woman becomes trapped in a "dead" marriage such that she is unable to remarry or even date other men. Accordingly, she is referred to in *Halacha* as an *Agunah*, which literally translated means "a chained woman." A man whose wife refuses to accept a *Get* is not referred to as "chained" since, in general, the consequences are not as severe and permanent for the man as they are for the woman.

2. The Amendments are hereinafter referred to interchangeably as the 1992 Amendments, the new law, or the New York *Get* Law.

The July 1992 Amendments (Section 236B(5) (h) and 236B(6) (d)) amended Section 236B of the Domestic Relations Law and became effective on August 16, 1992. The Amendments were initially introduced in identical form in the New York State Assembly in 1984. The bill passed the Assembly on March 23, 1992. The Senate bill was introduced on April 28, 1992 and passed on July 1, 1992. Governor Mario M. Cuomo signed the bill into law on July 12, 1992.

3. It is an elementary rule of statutory construction that all sections of a statute such as the one in question should be interpreted together. In fact, it is presumed that all matter in a statute must harmonize with all other sections and with the purpose of the legislation. Sutherland, *Statutory Construction*, Vol. 2A, ¶ 47.06. More about this later in this article.

4. Section 236B of the Domestic Relations Law.

5. The 13 factors include the duration of the marriage, the age and health of both parties, the income and property of each party at the time of the marriage and its dissolution, the probable future financial circumstances of each party, and any other factor which the court expressly finds to be just and proper.

6. The 11 factors include the income and property of each party, the duration of the marriage, the age and health of the parties, the ability of the party seeking maintenance to become self-supporting, contributions by the party seeking mainte-

nance to the career or career potential of the other party, and any other factor which the court expressly finds to be just and proper.

7. The Equitable Distribution Law was enacted for the benefit of the State and its citizens. Whether and to what extent the rule of *Dina D'Malchusa Dina* (Jews are bound by the laws of the state or nation in which they reside) is applicable to such a statute deserves consideration, but such a discussion is beyond the purview of this article. In this connection, *see e.g.*, Igros *Moshe, Even HaEzer*, Part 2, *Siman* 137.

8. Supplementary Practice Commentaries, McKinney's Consolidated Laws of New York Annotated, 1994 Cumulative Annual Pocket Part, Book 14, p. 111.

9. *See* Governor's Memorandum of Approval, McKinney's *1983* Session Laws of New York, pp. 2818-2819.

Section 253 received broad support from Halachic authorities, including HaGaon Rav Moshe Feinstein, *zt"l. See, e.g.*, *Igros Moshe, Even Ha'Ezer*, Part 4, *Siman* 106.

10. In the 11 years since enactment of Section 253 the courts have not interpreted the words "barrier to remarriage" or "voluntary."

11. However, between 1984 and 1992, comments were solicited from the *Botei Din* that arrange *Gittin* in New York, and numerous Rabbis and Rabbinical organizations, including Agudah. No criticism of the bill was offered.

12. *Schwartz* v. *Schwartz*, 583 N.Y.S.2d 716 (Sup. 1992).

13. Courts of equity are generally defined as courts that administer justice according to fairness as contrasted with rigidly formulated rules of law. Black's, *Law Dictionary*, 6th ed., 1990, p. 540.

14. Of course, such conduct may be a factor in determining equitable distribution under factor Number 8 as well, *see* fn. 24, *infra*, but in *Schwartz* the wife substantially owned the assets, making factor 8 largely, if not entirely, inapplicable.

15. Neither Agudah nor the other critics took a position against the decision.

16. In fact, in separate letters, three major Jewish organizations urged the Governor to sign the bill. They were the Orthodox Union, National Council of Young Israel, and the National Jewish Commission on Law and Public Affairs (COLPA).

17. The 1992 Amendments state as follows: "In any decision made pursuant to this subdivision the court shall, where appropriate, consider the effect of a barrier to remarriage, as defined in subdivision six of section two hundred fifty-three of this article, on the factors enumerated in paragraph d of this subdivision." Precisely the same amendment was enacted regarding maintenance. In addition, as was the case prior to the 1992 Amendments, a distributive award can be made in the form of a lump sum payment or in the form of payments over a period of time in fixed periodic amounts. Section 236b5(e).

18. *But, cf.* Justice Rigler's Memorandum of September 30, 1994, (dicta at) 6-7. In any event, when a statute creates a new right and specifies the remedy for the enforcement of such right the remedy is generally exclusive. *See, e.g.*, *Odom* v. *East Avenue Corporation*, 178 Misc. 363, 34 N.Y.S.2d 312, affirmed 264 App. Div. 985, 37 N.Y.S.2d 491 (1942).

19. It is also clear that a court could not interfere with the proceedings of a *Bais Din* by ordering the *Bais Din* to arrange a *Get* for a recalcitrant husband. In other words, a court might, directly or indirectly, compel a husband to appear before a *Bais Din*, but the court could not, constitutionally, order the *Bais Din* to perform any particular religious act involving its ecclesiastical functions. *Avitzur* v. *Avitzur*, 58 N.Y.S.2d 572, *cert. denied* 103 S.Ct. 76 (1983); *see also*, *Pal* v. *Pal*, 45 A.D.2d 738 (1974).

20. Some critics of the 1992 Amendments claim that it poses a danger nonetheless because an incompetent *Bais Din* or Rabbi might arrange a *Get* despite the existence of judicial coercion. (These critics also make the obvious point that it is not necessary for a *Bais Din* to arrange a *Get*, and that an individual Rabbi can do so.) There is no merit to such an argument for several reasons. First, it argues for doing nothing although Jews are exhorted to aid *Agunos*. *See* Preface, *supra*. It also goes beyond the views expressed by Rav Auerbach and Rav Elyashiv, who, at most, have sought amendment not repeal. Moreover, it is inconsistent with the view of Rav Moshe Feinstein, *zt"l*, who was intimately familiar with New York *Botei Din* and Rabbis. For example, fear of incompetence did not deter Rav Feinstein from endorsing the 1983 law or a similar law for South Africa. *Igros Moshe*, *Even HaEzer*, Part 4, *Siman* 106.

To the extent incompetence exists (be the incompetent a *Bais Din* or a Rabbi), the new law did not create or cause it, and the focus should be where it properly belongs—on curbing incompetence, not on opposing Halachically valid laws which aid thousands of *Agunos*. In any event, judicial coercion is a rare phenomenon, especially in this state. It took 12 years for the *Schwartz* case to develop, and in the 2 years since enactment of the new law, there has been no reported case of judicial coercion, or a *Bais Din* or Rabbi that has yielded to it.

21. The argument that the wife may bring a contrary *P'sak* from another *Bais Din* is of no moment. The court is in no position to determine the religious issues arising from the inconsistent rulings of *Botei Din*. (Section 253[9] of the Domestic Relations Law by its terms applies to Section 253[6].) In any event, it would be constitutionally impermissible for the court to become entangled in determinations of doctrinal disputes between *Botei Din*. *Jones* v. *Wolf*, 443 U.S. 595 (1979).

22. For example, if a court were to order a husband to give a *Get* within 30 days or suffer adverse consequences in equitable distribution, the husband would be incapable of carrying out the order because in giving the *Get* he would be acting under the compulsion of *"issuy."*

23. Supplementary Practice Commentaries, McKinney's Consolidated Laws of New York Annotated, 1994 Cumulative Annual Pocket Part, Book 14, p. 56.

24. I.e., the probable future financial circumstances of each party.

25. It seems clear, however, that where the *Get* has already been given but under circumstances that suggest economic duress, the matrimonial court is not precluded from inquiring into those circumstances and making appropriate adjustments in equitably distributing the marital property. It does not appear that the 1992 Amendments, which deal only with "barriers to remarriage" modified, in this regard, the

Equitable Distribution Law or the court's traditional equity powers. *Cf. Perl* v. *Perl*, 512 N.Y.S.2d 372 (A.D. 1st Dept. 1987); *Goldring* v. *Goldring*, 581 N.Y.S.2d 4 (A.D. 1st Dept. 1992).

26. It bears noting, however, that under the maintenance standards of Section 236B of the Domestic Relations Law, it is not likely that maintenance would be awarded to a wife who has independent resources or means of support. The standard enunciated in the statute focuses on "whether the party in whose favor maintenance is granted lacks sufficient property and income to provide for . . . her reasonable needs. . . . " In an earlier, more comprehensive *T'shuva* on this subject, Rav Feinstein, *zt"l*, demonstrated his awareness that court awards generally are not higher than *Bais Din* awards. On the contrary, Rav Feinstein, *zt"l*, is of the view in that *T'shuva* that courts generally award less maintenance than *Botei Din. Igros Moshe, Even HaEzer*, Part 2, *Siman* 137 (see discussion at fn. 26, *infra*, regarding Rabbi J. D. Bleich's misperceptions in this regard). Apparently, therefore, Rav Feinstein, *zt"l*, is referring in this *T'shuva* to isolated instances in which court awards exceed what a *Bais Din* would award. In the earlier *T'shuva*, Rav Feinstein, *zt"l*, also deals extensively with the principle that a *Get* which is exchanged for a *Mezonos* obligation, is *Kosher L'Chatchila*. The later, brief *T'shuva* quoted from above is premised upon the exposition of Halachic principles which is set forth in the earlier *T'shuva*.

27. In a memorandum on the new law, Rav Reuven Feinstein, *Shlita*, son of HaGaon Rav Moshe Feinstein, *zt"l*, has expressed his concurrence with the interpretation of the statute as a *Mezonos* provision and the applicability of his father's *T'shuva* thereto. Indeed, Agudah and its expert, Prof. Linda Silverman, of the New York University Law School, concur that the statute, by its very language, is a support provision.

The recent article (in the Hebrew language Torah journal, *Ohr Hamizrach, Nisan-Tamuz*, 5754) by Rabbi J. D. Bleich takes a contrary view. However, Rabbi Bleich's article does not contain an analysis of the law or any evaluation of the relative merits of the different interpretations. Rabbi Bleich simply adopts Agudah's interpretation *in toto*, and ignores the uncertainty which inevitably arises from the prospect that Agudah's interpretation of the law is incorrect and that the *T'shuvos Maharik* should therefore apply. *See* fn. 45, *infra*. Inexplicably, Rabbi Bleich relegates the critical *Mezonos* point to a footnote, wherein he misperceives the attitude of the courts regarding the size of maintenance awards. Finally, Rabbi Bleich fails to discuss the proposed Israeli *Get* Law, *infra*, the earlier comprehensive *T'shuva* of Rav Feinstein, *zt"l*, or the other *T'shuvos* cited above, all of which hold that a *Get* which is exchanged for a *Mezonos* obligation is not a *Get Me'usah*.

28. The rulings of the Bais Meir and Chasam Sofer were made in the context of an apostate (Mumor L'hachis) who refused to give a *Get*. Since there is a dispute whether an apostate can be coerced to give a *Get* (see Ramo, *Even HaEzer, Siman* 154, Paragraph 1), the remedy was devised by these *Poskim* to obtain decrees or orders from secular courts or authorities compelling the apostate to fulfill his support obligations to his wife. And, if the apostate gave the *Get* to rid himself of the

support obligation, there was no question of *Get Me'usah*. The rulings of the Mahara Ashkenazy and Rav Pealim were issued in the context of recalcitrant husbands (not apostates) who refused to give a *Get*, but ultimately agreed in order to rid themselves of support obligations. (In particular, the Mahara Ashkenazy, Bnei Binyamin and Shoel U'Mayshiv approve a lump-sum support payment as distinguished from periodic payments, contrary to the view expressed by Rav Elyashiv in his second *T'shuva*.)

29. Here are some examples of the statements which appear in these *Poskim*.

. . . and the Gaon Bais Meir has also so written and his advice is correct, to persuade the Government that it obligate the husband to provide support for his wife and that he fulfill all of the other obligations he owes his wife, and then he will inevitably agree to give a *Get*. That is the advice of the Bais Meir. . . . (Chasam Sofer in the name of Bais Meir)

. . . when I first looked at this question I remembered that there is a difference in the *Din* of *Get Me'usah*, such that where we obligate the husband on *Mezonos*, and in order to satisfy that obligation he gives a *Get*, that is not called a *Get Me'usah*. . . . And, I remembered that this difference was agreed to and relied upon by the Mahara Ashkenzy. . . . And, he attributes the origin of this difference to the T'shuvos Hamabit, *z"l*. . . . And, these same words emerged from the holy mouth of the Tashbatz, *z"l*. . . . And, look also into the Maharam Galanti, *z"l*, in his book *Gedulas Mordechai* in which he cites the Mahabit, *z"l* . . . and he cites none who differ with the Mahabit, *z"l*, on this point. (Rav Pealim)

. . . And these words came from the holy mouth of the Tashbatz, *z"l*, you may derive from the Tashbatz the rule in our case, that the obligation imposed by the secular courts for her support was consistent with *Din* . . . and it is hoped, that the [10,000 francs] will be sufficient for her, in view of her young age and her needs for the remainder of her life. . . . (Mahara Ashkenazy)

30. The text of the proposed Israeli *Get* law recites in pertinent part as follows: "If cause exists for the issuance of the injunction, the Rabbinical Court (*Bais Din*) may obligate the husband to pay for support, including the imposition of greater support for the wife's benefit, in an amount to be specified, *over and above* any entitlement of support by virtue of *Halacha* or existing agreement." (Translated from the Hebrew; emphasis added.)

31. These two distinguished Rabbis issued the *T'shuvos* in September 1992 upon which the critics of the new law premise their positions.

32. Presumably, Rabbi Morgenstern is referring to a situation where the wife is found to be a "*Moredes*," a rebellious wife, who forfeits any entitlement to *Mezonos*. However, the point is of little or no significance. Those familiar with *Botei Din* or *Get* proceedings in New York know that the issuance of a *P'sak* in a *Get* dispute declaring the wife a *Moredes* is rare especially among women who seek *Gittin*, since

those who are so accused generally have defenses to such accusations. Similarly, there is no merit to the implication by Rabbi Morgenstern that regardless of whether the wife is found to be a *Moredes*, if she leaves the marital home there is an automatic forfeiture of the right to *Mezonos*. In this regard see Ramo, *Even Ha'Ezer, Siman 70*, Paragraph 12; Ramo is predicated upon the Mordechai, *Kesuvos*, Paragraph 273 and Ritva, *Kesuvos*, 113a; *see also T'shuvos Sh'vus Yaacov, Even HaEzer*, Part I, *Siman* 113. (As made clear in the Ritva, Mordechai, Ramo, Sh'vus Yaacov and in other *Poskim*, if the wife appropriately explains her departure from the marital home, she does not forfeit her entitlement to *Mezonos*.) For a more comprehensive discussion of this point, see *Piskei Din Shel Botei HaDin Horaboniyim B'yisroel*, Vol. 15, 103–107 (5790). In any event, if for any reason a wife has actually forfeited her right to *Mezonos* and therefore, is in no position to effect an exchange of *Mezonos* for a *Get*, the *Bais Din* can and should refuse to be *Mesader* (arrange) the *Get*. And, as shown above, there would be no adverse consequence to the husband or possibility of *Get Me'usah*. *See Igros Moshe, Even HaEzer*, Part II, *Siman* 137, where Rav Feinstein, *zt"l*, does such an analysis and concludes that there was no forfeiture of *Mezonos* by the wife and hence no *Get Me'usah*.

33. In the second *P'sak* of Rav Elyashiv of May 1993 discussed below, certain additional arguments are made in this regard. But, those arguments are also contrary to the rulings of Rav Moshe Feinstein, *zt"l*, and the other *Poskim*, set forth above, which deal with precisely the same issues. It is not clear why the views of Rav Moshe Feinstein, *zt"l*, and all of these *Poskim*, were not followed or even cited.

34. As is shown hereinafter, Rav Elyashiv's understanding of the law, taken apparently from Agudah's request for a ruling, conformed precisely with Agudah's view of the new law.

35. In *Igros Moshe, Even HaEzer*, Vol. 4, *Siman* 106 (the *T'shuva* used as the Halachic basis for the 1983 Law), Rav Moshe Feinstein, *zt"l*, sets forth the categories of *Issuy* or compulsion, physical and monetary, that invalidate a *Get*. Regarding statutory or governmental *Issuy*, Rav Moshe, *zt"l*, states as follows: "*Where the government obligates the husband to transfer his property to his wife as a penalty for his refusal to give a* Get." This is the category into which Agudah has mistakenly sought to place the new law. Needless to say, the new law does not fit into any of the categories which Rav Moshe, *zt"l*, described as creating *Issuy* which invalidates a *Get*.

36. Among other things, there may be no effect whatever on the wife's future financial circumstances, and even if there is such an effect, the balance of the equities may be in favor of the husband.

37. *Margulies* v. *Margulies*, 42 A.D.2d 517 (1st Dept. 1973); *Rubin* v. *Rubin*, 348 N.Y.S.2d 61 (Fam. Ct. Bronx Co. 1973). To the same effect, *see Avitzur, supra*. But *see, Waxstein* v. *Waxstein*, 90 Misc.2d 784 (Sup. Ct. 1976), *aff'd* 57 A.D.2d 863 (1977); *Stern* v. *Stern*, 5 Fam.L.Rep. (BNA) 810 (Sup. Ct. 1979). The latter two cases predated *Avitzur, supra*, and appear to raise serious constitutional concerns, among other things.

38. Sections 2(4)–(6) of the Ontario Family Act.

39. Section 21.1 of the Canada Divorce Act.

40. It should be noted that although the Canadian *Get* laws do not appear to be *Mezonos* statutes, they do appear to exculpate a spouse for failing to remove barriers that are beyond his or her "control," *e.g.*, where the *Bais Din* or Rabbi refuses to arrange the *Get*. It has also been pointed out by Rabbi J. D. Bleich (*see Ohr HaMizrach* article referred in fn. 27, *supra*) that the Maharik's premise that all litigation in secular courts is uncertain, should also apply to the Canadian Statutes since the statute is couched in discretionary terms, *e.g.*, " . . . the defence may be struck out." *See also*, fn. 45, *infra*. Certainly, Rav Feinstein's *"S'vora Gedolah"* seems applicable to virtually all *Agunahs* nowadays. *See Igros Moshe, Even HaEzer*, Vol. 3, *Siman* 44. In any event, the statements made herein concerning the Canadian *Get* Laws are meant to be descriptive and are intended only to show the differences in structure and language between the New York and Canadian statutes. There is no intention to suggest that the Canadian statutes are Halachically infirm or need to be amended. The Rabbis in Canada who arrange *Gittin* are highly competent and it is for them to make such judgments. (For a description of certain *Get* laws that existed throughout Germany more than 150 years ago and the dispute among the German *Poskim* on whether they required amendment, *see T'shuvos Zaycher Simcha Siman* 197.)

41. If (i) equitable distribution (including the 1992 Amendments) was not enacted to compel *Gittin* and (ii) in making an additional distribution, the court does so to compensate the *Agunah* based on the equities, the *Get* should be valid, although the husband gave it to avoid the additional allocation. The equitable distribution statute should therefore operate no differently than, for example, the custody statutes. Those statutes were not enacted to compel *Gittin*; nor do courts use custody awards to compel *Gittin*. Accordingly, if a husband gives a *Get* to obtain a wife's consent to more advantageous custody terms, the *Get* is not a *Get Me'usah*. And, the bartering of custody rights for a *Get* is commonplace, and has not been held to invalidate a *Get*. For a more detailed discussion of these points, *see* the January 1993 *T'shuva* of Rav Yechezkel Roth, *Shlita*. It is noted, however, that Rav Roth differentiates between custody and equitable distribution and holds in the latter case that the *Get* is a *Get Me'usah*. But, his conclusion is predicated solely upon Agudah's interpretation that the Equitable Distribution Law mandates courts to compel *Gittin* and that it was enacted solely for that purpose.

42. That is why certain persons have raised questions about its constitutionality. See Governor's Memorandum of Approval, McKinney's 1983 Session Laws of New York, pp. 2818–2819.

43. Such legislation is fully in accord with the constitutional principles recently enunciated in *Board of Education of Kiryas Joel Village School District* v. *Grumet, et al*, 114 S.Ct. 2481; 62 USLW 4665 (1994).

44. This legislation has been widely reported in the Israeli press, *e.g.*, July 27, 1994 edition of *HaModiya*, August 23, 1994 edition of *The Jerusalem Post*.

45. Halachically, a threat by a wife to sue in the secular courts should not create the compulsion of *"issuy."* In fact, when a marriage deteriorates threats are often

exchanged between husband and wife. It's inherent in the process. If every threat made by a wife were disabling, no kosher *Get* could ever be given. *See* in this regard *Pischei T'shuva, Even Ha'ezer* 134, 11. For a *Get* to be rendered invalid because of *"issuy,"* the person who makes the threat should be capable of actually carrying it out with certainty. *See, e.g., T'shuvos Maharik,* 185, which is premised on *Maase D'Pardeisa, Bava Basra,* 40b; *see* also *Me'iri, Gittin* 88b. This appears to be the reason why Rav Elyashiv accorded no weight to Mr. Lewin's interpretation and saw no uncertainty in the ability of a wife to prevail. But, with all respect, the outcome of litigation is virtually always uncertain. As the Maharik, *supra,* points out, a threat to sue in the secular courts *is of no moment whatsoever,* because many have threatened and sued and not succeeded. The Maharik's conclusion is especially true here, where the matrimonial court acts as a court of equity and has broad discretion when it considers all of the equities under a statute which directs the court only "where appropriate" to "consider" the "effect" of a "barrier to remarriage."

46. Rav Elyashiv never advocated repeal; only Rav Auerbach had initially called for repeal.

47. Agudah has never offered an explanation as to why it chose to act in mid-1992 after having been silent for *eight years* during which time (i) the new law reposed in the New York State legislature prior to enactment, (ii) Justice Rigler issued his landmark decision, and (iii) Canada operated under statutes which should have been more problematical for Agudah than our own. Neither has Agudah reconciled its silence on the proposed Israeli *Get* legislation with its continuing opposition to the 1992 Amendments. Moreover, Agudah has published only one article on the new law which appeared in its house organ, *The Jewish Observer* (September 1993). It contained no legal or Halachic analysis, merely set forth Agudah's position in bottom-line, conclusory terms and failed to respond to the many points raised in this and other publications.

48. This was made clear at a meeting, at which Agudah was present, on January 31, 1993, in the offices of Assemblyman Sheldon Silver.

49. Some critics of the new law have questioned its usefulness. They contend that all it does is to compel a recalcitrant husband to appear before a *Bais Din.* However, these critics overlook entirely the maintenance aspects of the new law. As shown above, maintenance orders can be an effective tool against a recalcitrant husband or wife, since such orders can require maintenance to be paid until barriers to remarriage are removed. However, even assuming, *arguendo,* these critics are correct, those familiar with the Agunah problem understand the importance of compelling appearances before a *Bais Din. See, e.g. Avitzur, supra,* at fn. 18. In that case, which was litigated to the highest court in New York State, the issue was whether a civil court could enforce a provision in a *Kesuvah* requiring a husband to appear before a *Bais Din.* In other words, it is no small matter in the ultimate resolution of the *Agunah* problem to provide a mechanism to compel appearances before a *Bais Din* by a recalcitrant husband or wife. Indeed, the various pre-nuptial agreements that are being advanced as a possible solution to the *Agunah* problem contemplate that result, but pre-nuptial agreements work only for those who sign

them. The advantage of the new law is that it applies whether or not a pre-nuptial agreement was entered into at the time of marriage.

50. The new law has been endorsed by the *Botei Din* that are Mesader most of the *Gittin* in New York. For example, both the Igud Horabonim and the RCA and its *Rosh Beth Din* have supported the law. The *Menahel* of the Agudas Horabonim has similarly been supportive of the law.

The Draconian position taken by certain persons that the mere existence of the new law renders presumptively invalid all *Gittin* given in this state since August 1992, is plainly wrong, goes far beyond the views of Rav Auerbach, Rav Elyashiv and all other recognized *Poskim* and is without any sound Halachic basis. *See, e.g., Me'iri, Gittin* 88B; *T'shuvos Maharik, Siman* 185; *T'shuvos Zaycher Simcha, Siman* 197; *T'shuvos Shoel U'mayshiv, Mahadura Tinyona,* Vol. 1, 28 and 29; *T'shuvos Mahari Asad,* Vol. 3, 132. *T'shuvos B'air Yitzchok, Even Ha'Ezer, Siman* 10, *Anaf* 8; *Igros Moshe, Even Ha'ezer,* Vol. 3, *Siman* 44. Insofar as its message is concerned, that position is perhaps the saddest commentary to the plight of the modern-day *Agunah.* In generations past, our Torah giants labored to find a basis to free *Agunos* to remarry. Persons who assert such Draconian positions seek to re-impose *Agunah* status upon thousands of women who have already succeeded in obtaining *Gittin* through competent *Botei Din.*

VI

Orthodox and Conservative Positions

15
A Modern Orthodox Perspective

Shlomo Riskin

Brief History to the Present Day

Thus far we have traced the halakhic history of the *moredet* in an attempt to understand the development of Jewish law and the forces behind its evolution, dealing particularly with the issue of a woman who tries to free herself from a marriage she finds intolerable. Despite the Biblical statement that the husband must initiate the divorce, we have seen that the Babylonian Talmud in the frame of broad powers provides for coercion by the Jewish court until the husband agrees to grant a divorce to a wife who finds him distasteful. The Jerusalem Talmud allows for a special stipulation to be written into the marriage contract in order to ensure the wife this protection. The Geonim went further, and insisted that she even receive the entire sum of the alimony provided for in her marriage contract.

The early Sages of North Africa, Spain, and France, although differing in regard to her monetary compensation, upheld the right of a woman to initiate an action towards a court-imposed divorce if she so desired. In the twelfth century of the common era, the tide was dramatically turned by Rabbenu Tam, who by his interpretation influenced the overwhelming majority of subsequent halakhic decisors to deny the possibility of coercing the husband to grant his wife a divorce "merely" because she subjectively found him intolerable. With only rare exceptions, this has been the accepted halakhic opinion to the present day.

It is easy to understand why the legal position of Rabbenu Tam was accepted without significant controversy by many subsequent generations. The small, cohesive Jewish communities, generally bound together by familial ties, isolated from the surrounding Gentile society by external anti-Semitism and internal religious strength, existed primarily against a backdrop of a culture that insisted upon the permanence of the marital bond and the stability of family life. Such a society would hardly rally serious opposition to a halakhah which effectively denied the woman the right to initiate divorce proceedings.

In contemporary times, however, the situation has changed radically. Our freedom of social intercourse between Jewish and Gentile society, and the consequent assimilation and intermarriage, have reached staggering proportions. A vindictive husband, or one who is unconcerned with the requirements of Jewish law, can not only deny his wife a religious divorce if he so chooses, but can also—once he has obtained a secular divorce—remarry before a justice of the peace. Thereby he forces his halakhically concerned wife to languish as an *agunah* (lit., "chained," i.e., to a husband with whom she could not formerly live) and now, due to his reluctance to arrange for a *get*, is in an inextricable situation. In most instances he can even arrange a kind of religious ceremony for his second marriage (since most Reform rabbis do not require a halakhically validated divorce), while his first wife can only depend upon an impotent Jewish court which—even if it chose to coerce the husband to divorce her—is powerless in these days to impose its law upon a recalcitrant husband who refuses to accept its authority. As a result, many Jewish women are being forced either to live out their years as *agunot*, unable to remarry within the framework of Jewish law, or to pay staggering sums of money to a husband using his halakhic power of divorce as blackmail. All too often these women choose to marry and have children with their second husbands without having secured a Jewish divorce from their first, thereby committing adultery and giving birth to children considered halakhically illegitimate. Indeed, the very situation which caused the Geonim to enact their legislation on behalf of the wife seeking a divorce—"Jewish women were becoming dependent upon the Gentiles . . . and were satisfied with a . . . divorce not in accordance with Jewish law, from which ruin emanates"—certainly applies today. We have previously seen how the halakhic system is designed to respond to such agonizing human dilemmas. What can the halakhic system do today, especially when the combination of an American legal system, a secular climate, and the relative ease with which an individual can move great distances from his original community, makes it virtually impossible for a religious court to impose its will upon an intransigent husband? Let us summarize the various attempts which have been made in recent times to alleviate this intolerable situation.

In the early part of this century, when civil divorce was making incursions into the broad religious spectrum in France, a council of rabbis was convened to introduce a system of conditional marriage. It was their suggestion that at the time of the marriage, the bride and groom stipulate that if their marriage was terminated through civil divorce, their Jewish marriage would then be nullified retroactively, obviating the necessity for the husband to grant a religious divorce. The halakhic precedent for such a stipulation was a decision of Rabbi Israel of Brunn (1400–1480), who concluded that a man whose brother is an apostate may stipulate at the time of his marriage that if he should die childless, his marriage will be nullified retroactively, thereby protecting his wife from being forever "tied" to a brother-in-law who will most likely refuse to release her via *halitzah* from levirate marriage. So we see that the concept of conditional marriage has a valid halakhic basis.

Rabbi Yitzhak Elhanan Spektor of Kovno, Rabbi Yehudah Lubestski of Paris, and virtually all of the European luminaries of that time objected to the proposal that the council put forth. Their major argument against it was that the sexual relationship between husband and wife expresses a complete and total commitment, and it automatically rescinds any stipulation agreed upon at the time of the marriage. In the face of such serious opposition, the proposal was rejected. The rabbinic authorities similarly rejected any possibility of the Jewish court's being allowed to nullify a religious marriage retroactively, despite the Talmudic argument that "Everyone who marries, does so by consent of the rabbinic authorities; the rabbinic authorities have the right to retroactively nullify a marriage." They saw this right as being dependent upon a *unified* Jewish court, and limited to the period universally accepted as the sealing of the Talmud (ca. 500 C.E.).

In 1967 Rabbi Eliezer Berkovits similarly attempted to resolve this problem by means of a conditional marriage. His proposal differs from the proposal of the French council in that the stipulation involves the Jewish court as well as the secular one: The husband stipulates at the time of his marriage that if he does not acquiesce to the rabbinic court's demand to grant his wife a religious divorce, the marriage will be nullified retroactively. However, the same rabbinic opposition which befell the French plan similarly faced the Berkovits proposal.

In 1954 Professor Saul Lieberman of the Jewish Theological Seminary added a new clause to the marriage contract used by the Conservative movement. In it, the husband agreed to be bound by all decisions of the Rabbinical Assembly Beth Din in the event of a marital difficulty; he would thus be halakhically bound to grant a religious divorce if the Beth Din so ordained. In effect, Lieberman added an addendum very similar to the *ketubah* stipulation cited earlier in the Jerusalem Talmud. As far as the impotence of the rabbinic court in America is concerned, the new stipulation provides that, in the event of the husband's refusal to adhere to its ruling, "We authorize the Beth Din to impose such terms of compensation as it may see fit for failure to respond to its summons or to carry out its decisions." Lieberman hoped that such a monetary stipulation could be enforced in the secular courts as well, and would therefore give renewed strength to the marriage contract and renewed power to the wife.

The Orthodox rabbinical world reacted negatively to the Lieberman proposal. They argued on halakhic grounds that any agreement to pay an indeterminate sum of money is an *asmakhta*, and that such a vague understanding is not binding in Jewish law. Moreover, on legal grounds, they argued that the *ketubah*, the marriage contract, which is always read as an integral part of the Jewish marriage ceremony, is a *religious* document, and therefore the First Amendment to the Constitution of the United States precludes any power of the secular court to enforce it.

Nevertheless, the New York Court of Appeals decision in *Avitzur* v. *Avitzur*, declared by a 4–3 majority, that this *ketubah* is valid and enforceable. The case involved Susan and Araz Avitzur, whose marriage in May 1966 utilized the aforementioned "Conservative" *ketubah*. They obtained a civil divorce in 1978, but although Susan summoned Araz to appear before a Beth Din and grant her a religious *get* in accordance with his initial agreement, he refused to do so.

Araz argued that the *ketubah*, as a religious document, was inadmissible as a legal contract in a civil court. The Appellate Division of the New York Supreme Court accepted Araz's contention, declaring the *ketubah* a liturgical agreement without standing in civil court (*Avitzur* v. *Avitzur*, no. 41550 [31d Dept. April 8, 1982]), only to be reversed in Susan's favor by the New York Court of Appeals. That court decided that the provisions of the *ketubah* requiring the parties to enter into arbitration were merely an application of the neutral principles of contract law, entitled to the same legal status as any antenuptial agreement. Furthermore, whenever an antenuptial agreement is signed binding the parties to enter into arbitration in accordance with their accepted traditions—such as a particular Beth Din—the agreement is enforceable by the secular courts.

The Present Situation in Israel

As we explained above, Jewish law mandates that even in those instances where the husband can be compelled to give his wife a divorce, he must still formally present the bill of divorcement willingly. Unfortunately, therefore, there are a significant number of instances in Israel where recalcitrant husbands have chosen to spend years in jail rather than give their wives a *get*. However, the Israeli Rabbinical Courts have generally been reluctant to compel a husband to give his wife a divorce merely because she claims "he is repulsive to me," without her presentation of objective reasons why she finds him so. In some instances they have utilized compulsion, but only where they have some objective confirmation (*amatla*) for the wife's claim of repulsion.

Thus, in general, the Israeli Rabbinical Courts have been reluctant to take advantage of the early authorities who permit compulsion when a woman claims that she finds her husband repulsive. This despite the fact that Rabbi Chaim Palaggi, a noted Talmudic authority of mid-nineteenth century Izmir, at the conclusion of his Responsa, *Ha-Hayyim Veha-Shalom*, notes that if a couple is separated for eighteen months and there appears no chance of reconciliation, the Rabbinical Court must force the husband to grant his wife a *get*. Rabbi Eliezer Waldenberg, in his *Ziz Eliezer*, argues that even with a slight hint or taint of confirmation, "the Court must compel the husband to grant his wife a divorce if she claims that he is distasteful to her." Rabbi Yitzhak Halevy Herzog, a former chief rabbi of Israel, likewise maintains that it is proper for the Rabbinical Court to exact compulsion "for the sake of enabling Jewish women" to be able to remarry. The renowned Hazon Ish, in his commentaries on *Even Ha-Ezer*, suggests in a specific instance that it is possible to rely on those authorities who allow compulsion when a woman finds her husband is repulsive. And Rabbi Ovadiah Yosef cites the decision of the former Chief Rabbi of Jerusalem, Rabbi Zvi Pesach Frank, that since in Yemen the decisions of Maimonides were authoritative, it is permissible to coerce a *get* when a woman who was originally from Yemen claims that she finds her husband repulsive. Hence, אית דין ולית דיין, *it din ve-let dayyan*, the law exists, but the judges are often wanting.

A Proposed Solution

It would seem to me that a proposal based on the Lieberman addendum, but taking into account the rabbinic and legal issues involved, may well point to a solution to the problem, both in the Diaspora and in Israel.

The bride and groom could agree in a special prenuptial document that if a religious court subsequently decided that the woman was being prevented from remarrying by an arbitrary decision of the husband, he would be forced to pay a specified sum of money to his wife each day that he withholds a religious divorce. Since the sum is specified, the problem of *asmakhta* is avoided. Since we are dealing with a prenuptial agreement, which is not technically part of the actual religious ceremony, such a document would be enforceable within the secular courts. And since there already exists an accepted form of prenuptial agreement known as *tenayim*, which is generally signed immediately preceding the marriage ceremony, it is logical to make this stipulation an addendum to the *tenayim*. An ancient custom thus gains crucial relevance, and provides a framework for the final arbitration agreement from the very start. The following text would be the suggested one to use:

Final Articles of Engagement

May good fortune sprout forth and ascend to the greatest heights even as a well-watered garden. These are the words of the covenant and the provisions which were spoken and stipulated between the two parties at the time of the nuptials on the ____ day of the month of _____ in the year ____ in the city of _____; to wit:

Between _____ and his son, the groom _____, the party of the first part; and _____ and his daughter, the bride, _____, the party of the second part.

Firstly, _____ wedded and married _____ by means of a wedding ring and caused her to be brought under a nuptial canopy in accordance with the law of Moses and Israel, and she accepted the wedding ring from him.

_____ provided his son with dignified clothing for the Sabbath, festivals, and weekdays in a proper manner and in accordance with his status, and presented his son with marriage gifts in accordance with his status.

_____ provided his daughter, the bride, with dignified clothing for the Sabbath, festivals, and weekdays, clothing, kerchiefs, marriage gifts and furnished bed, all in accordance with his status.

Henceforth, the aforementioned couple will comport themselves with love and affection and will neither alienate nor conceal nor lock away, neither he from her nor she from him, any property whatever, but they shall both equally exercise jurisdiction over their property.

The aforementioned groom, _____, will work, honor, support, and maintain the bride in accordance with universal custom so long as she shares his board, and at any time that she does not share his board, may it be for any reason whatsoever, the groom obligated himself that he will thereupon immediately give his wife the sum of 200 dollars to spend for food, clothing, and domicile and will give her a like sum every single day throughout the period during which she does not share his board from the time a judgment is issued by a Beth Din declaring that she is prevented from marrying in accordance with the law of Moses and Israel because of him [i.e., because of the husband's feasance or nonfeasance]. And from this day and forevermore it is the prerogative of the aforementioned bride either to share her husband's board or to receive from him the aforementioned sum to spend for food, clothing, and domicile in accordance with her desire. If, Heaven forfend, there be any dispute between them, whether with regard to payment of maintenance, whether with regard to any marital matter, or whether with regard to custody and support of their issue, they will then present their suit before an established Beth Din composed of competent judges in their city or community, and if there is no established Beth Din composed of three qualified judges, one judge designated by each party and a third judge chosen by the two judges designated by the parties, within fourteen days after the application of either of the parties. Any quarrel or controversy shall be settled in accordance with their decree, and the award of said Beth Din may be entered as a judgment in a court of competent jurisdiction.

After a settlement is reached and the wife _____ returns to her husband's home, she shall return any balance of the funds received from her husband for purposes of maintenance, clothing, and domicile which remain in her possession as well as her clothing and jewelry, to their original site.

All of the foregoing in the presence of us, the undersigned witnesses through conveyance of a *sudar* (kerchief) and in the most efficacious manner, not in the manner of an *asmakhta* and not in the manner of a mere documentary form. We have accepted conveyance in the form of a vessel halakhically fit for purposes of conveyance from each of the aforementioned parties on behalf of the other party with regard to all which is written and stated, and Everything is Valid and Confirmed.

_____ (witness)
_____ (witness)

And we also have affixed our signatures in order that our signatures may attest even as a hundred competent and trustworthy witnesses to all which is written and stated above.

_____ (Groom)
_____ (Bride)

Hence we have seen how Jewish law has endeavored to protect the rights of the woman and to provide her with the means of disengaging herself from an intolerable marriage with personal and financial dignity. The Geonim of Babylonia and the earlier authorities of Ashkenaz and Sefarad agreed, especially in a climate of assimilation and apostasy, to the necessity of enforcing a divorce when the wife claims that she finds her husband distasteful. In our own times there is certainly sufficient reason to invoke halakhic precedent and provide our women with the same legal recourse. The sad truth is that many women are remarrying and even bearing children with their second husband without having received a religious divorce because of their first husband's intransigence. The sad truth is that many other women are being doomed to loneliness and isolation because they will not rebel against rabbinic authority. The sad truth is that the entire structure of Jewish law is being charged with rigidity and insensitivity because of its seeming inability to find an acceptable solution to the plight of these women. Indeed, whenever a solution has been offered, legal objections have caused it to be set aside. And yet Amemar found a solution; the rabbis of the Jerusalem Talmud found a solution; Maimonides found a solution; the sages of our generation dare do no less. The legal precedent exists; the courageous legalists must make their voices heard and their position accepted. "May the Almighty grant courage to His nation; may the Almighty bless His people with peace."

16

Conservative Judaism and the *Agunah*

Sidney H. Schwarz

Throughout its history, Conservative Judaism has preached a complement of tradition and change as the only responsible and authentic method of adapting Judaism to a new and changing environment. The movement's popularity can, in many ways, be attributed to American Jewry's perception of Conservatism as an approach to Judaism that is neither cavalier toward the inherited traditions of the Jewish people nor naive about the exigencies of modern American life. Yet striking a balance between tradition and change always proved more difficult in practice than in theory, for those leaders of the movement charged with the task. Examining the historical record invites the question: how creative was the tension between tradition and change, and contrariwise, to what degree did it breed paralysis?

The halakhic problem of the *agunah* provides an interesting case study of Conservative Judaism's attempt to modernize an aspect of Jewish law that was seen by many to be the source of a severe inequity. According to halakhah, a woman without a *get* (a Jewish bill of divorcement) cannot remarry. Since a *get* may only be granted by the husband, if he refuses to issue such a document, abandons his wife, or disappears leaving no proof of his death, his wife remains his wife, unable to remarry. She becomes an *agunah*. While this problem was not new for rabbinical authorities, it was exacerbated in the American setting where rabbis no longer had the kind of coercive authority over a recalcitrant husband that rabbis in Europe once had. Thus a remedy for the plight of the *agunah* was sought by Conservative authorities.

The issue was first raised in the Rabbinical Assembly (RA) in 1930 by Louis Epstein. Epstein was an acknowledged expert in the Jewish laws of marriage and divorce, having published a number of books on the topic. As a rabbi whose loyalties leaned unquestionably in the direction of the RA's right wing, he also was in a good political position to broach the subject of halakhic revision. The source of the problem, Epstein indicated, was that Jewish marriage law was based upon the conception of the husband's right to purchase or release a woman from the marriage union. Because the court had no power, save for coercion, over the husband, the halakhah invited the unjust situation of the woman who could never again remarry while the husband was under no such sanction. Epstein suggested that the husband authorize the court at the time of marriage to provide for the mechanism whereby the wife could initiate divorce proceedings without him, should circumstances require.[1]

To gain maximum support for such a bold initiative, Epstein spent the next five years soliciting the opinion of Orthodox rabbis throughout the world. Most of the rabbis ignored him. Others expressed the opinion that while having no theoretical objections to the solution, implementation could only be sanctioned by some official Sanhedrin of rabbis. Conservative rabbis and the RA did not qualify as such. Epstein in turn offered the RA a revised proposal which had the husband authorize an agent to deliver a *get* to the wife in such cases as he could not or would not do it himself. Such a procedure would again be triggered by a *beit din*, a Jewish court, when it deemed advisable.[2] The RA, emboldened by Epstein's impressive citation of halakhic precedent and use of traditional methods of interpretation, voted to have a subcommittee work to implement the proposal while simultaneously publishing a pamphlet asserting the need and right of the RA to take action in this regard.

There was general elation among the members of the RA over this action. It was felt that this was an example of the kind of halakhic modernization that the Conservative rabbinate was meant to handle. Little prepared them for the kind of onslaught that the Orthodox rabbinate launched through the Yiddish press. The source of the campaign of vilification was the *Agudat Harabbanim*, an ultraorthodox union of rabbis. Their attacks did not contain any criticism of the halakhic points which the RA expected. Instead it sought to discredit the entire endeavor of the Seminary and its alumni.

The statement of the *Agudah* read in part:

This splinter assembly of rabbis [RA]—men without learning, who cannot even recognize the *aleph-bet* [Hebrew alphabet], much less understand the application of Talmudic principles—appoint themselves guardians of Israel though they are distant from Jewish practice and haven't the least religious inclination.[3]

Nor did the *Agudah* stop with this statement. They mobilized rabbinic opinion the world over so that few rabbis, even if they agreed with the RA plan, dared to declare themselves in favor. A South African Jewish paper wondered how a halakhic problem that could not be solved by generations of European rabbis could suddenly find resolution at the hands of a group of American rabbis. The paper answered its own question by saying,

the "Conservative" rabbis . . . do not hold themselves bound by the strict laws of the *shulhan arukh*. They therefore feel at liberty to propose plans which are not in accordance with the Jewish law.

Needless to say, it concluded, Orthodox rabbis could not accept such a solution.[4]

Not all reviews were so harsh. Much of the Anglo-Jewish press was very laudatory and, in turn, the laity expressed their approval to their rabbis. Members of the RA met with editors of two leading Yiddish dailies, the *Morning Journal* and the *Day*, and had reasoned replies published to the harsh Orthodox attack.

But despite the outward display of resolve and pledges not to bend under the Orthodox attack, the confidence of the RA was severely shaken. Their only hope for effectiveness in their attempts to modernize Judaism in a traditional way was to preserve their legitimacy in the eyes of the traditional Jewish public. Since these Jews took their cues from the Orthodox rabbinate, whom they recognized as the protectors of Torah values, the failure of the RA to win Orthodox support in their first *halakhic* venture was an irreparable blow to their prestige.

Louis Epstein recognized that his proposed solution was failing subject to political and psychological factors beyond his control. He wrote to Boaz Cohen, secretary of the RA Law Committee and a member of the Seminary faculty, in 1935, saying,

I do not think that the *halacha* of the case is going to decide whether our proposal [will] be accepted or not. If we yield it will not be for *halachic* reasons but because of weakness of our organization and movement.[5]

In another letter, Epstein observed that many of the RA men depended upon the *Agudat Harabbanim* for supporting their positions in their congregations. If this insecurity plagues the rabbis in areas where there is widespread lay support for an innovation such as the *agunah* case, he said, then there is little hope that Conservative Judaism will ever be more than a theological vision.[6]

Even as the RA published assertive replies to the *Agudah* in the press, they turned to Louis Ginzberg for support. Ginzberg alone, among the Seminary circle, had the kind of prestige in the Jewish world that was immune from the *Agudah* assault. His reputation as a halakhic expert was sufficient to, not only bolster the RA planned solution but, additionally, cast aspersions on the motives and basis for the Orthodox attack.

The RA did not get from Ginzberg what they expected. At first, they found it hard to get him to cooperate at all. Ginzberg was apparently insulted that he wasn't consulted prior to the plan's presentation in 1935.[7] A special midyear convention in 1937 at which Ginzberg was to read his paper on the *agunah* issue was canceled. When Ginzberg finally read his opinion at the 1937 RA convention, it fell far short of resounding approval for the Epstein plan. Ginzberg asserted that any change in halakhah required prior agreement from all sectors of world Jewry. While this might have seemed to be an admirable attempt to insure the unity of *klal yisrael*, it also effectively gave Orthodox Judaism veto power over any change in Jewish practice contemplated by the RA. The RA law committee concluded that a different forum was needed to promulgate so wide-ranging a change in halakhah, and thus tabled the issue indefinitely.[8]

Ironically, during World War II, Louis Ginzberg, who refused to support the Epstein plan a few years earlier, issued a statement to rabbis and chaplains that provided a solution to the anticipated large number of *agunot* that would be created by the war. It empowered the *beit din* of the RA to execute a *get* in the absence of the husband three years after the demobilization of the army when there was no hope of the husband's return. It also required a declaration by civil courts that the marriage was legally dissolved.

After the war this emergency provision was allowed to lapse, and the RA was again left with no workable solution to the *agunah* problem. The RA, no doubt, hoped that the *agunah* issue, which had been a source of frustration and embarrassment, would go away. However, the very publicity that this issue attracted assured its continued attention by groups who favored the equalization of status for women. The National Women's League of the United Synagogue, not usually wont to take on the authorities of Conservative Judaism in controversial matters, particularly in halakhah, petitioned the RA for action on the *agunah* issue in 1950. Their resolution read in part,

Whereas Jewish law and tradition have always sought justice, humane concern for the rights of all people and adjustment to problems as they arise in Jewish life . . . [we] call upon the Rabbinical Assembly to equalize the status of women in divorce with that of the men so that no longer shall women be deprived of the protection of the civil laws of the land in which they live or be penalized by the lack of equal rights in the matter of the *get*.[9]

The RA received a similar petition from the International Council of Jewish Women.[10]

In 1952 a special RA convention was held in Atlantic City which reviewed the solution set forth by David Aronson a year earlier at the RA convention.[11] This plan extended the powers of the *beit din* in cases when it failed in its moral and social suasion to have the husband issue a *get*. Recognizing the fact that *kiddushin* occurs under the authority of the *beit din*, Aronson felt that the *beit din* should be empowered to dissolve the marriage when circumstances so warrant. In such cases the *beit din* would issue a document (*shtar p'tur*) to the women which would allow her to remarry. The "Atlantic City plan" could not gain the approval of the convention. There were those who felt that this was an extension of the powers of a *beit din* to dissolve a marriage that went beyond halakhic guidelines. At the same time the Seminary administration voiced its opinion that the matter was too important for the RA to act upon alone. As a result, a Joint Law Conference between the RA and the Seminary was established which then had the sole authority to rule on matters of marriage and divorce.[12]

The major contribution of the Joint Law Conference was a clause inserted into the *ketubah* in 1953 which read:

And both together agreed that if this marriage shall ever be dissolved under civil law, then either husband or wife may invoke the authority of the beth-din of the Rabbinical Assembly and the Jewish Theological Seminary or its duly authorized representatives, to decide what action by either spouse is then appropriate under Jewish matrimonial law; and if either spouse shall fail to honor the demand of the other or to carry out the decision of the beth-din or its representatives, then the other spouse may invoke any and all remedies available in civil law and equity to enforce compliance with the beth-din's decision and the solemn obligation.[13]

This amendment to the traditional *ketubah* was the only innovation of the Conservative movement consciously labeled as a *taqqanah*, an addition to the corpus of halakhah. Although first conceived by Max Arzt, the addition came to be known as the "Lieberman clause" after Saul Lieberman who framed the Aramaic formula and was himself the reigning halakhic expert of Conservative Judaism. The new addition to the *ketubah* was an effort to reinvest the *beit din* with authority it once had in the premodern world. Under threat of a lawsuit, the *beit din* hoped to "persuade" a husband to issue a *get* according to halakhic requirements. Though no one knew whether such a clause would hold up in court, it was felt that the implied threat would be sufficient to impel compliance.

Still this *taqqanah* did not put to rest the *agunah* issue. No remedy was provided for anyone who got married without the Lieberman *ketubah*. Furthermore not all rabbis adopted the new *ketubah*. In 1967, thirteen years after its introduction, only 65% of RA members used it. Some objected to the employment of civil courts for enforcement while others felt that the *taqqanah* was a break with the Orthodox standard. More liberal members refused to use the *ketubah* because they felt it to be a mere palliative to the larger issue of the inequality of women.[14]

Those who complained about the inaction of both the RA, and the Joint Law Conference, pointed to the danger that Jews would simply ignore the halakhic procedures because they were so cumbersome and potentially unfair to women. In fact many already had circumvented the Conservative movement. Reform rabbis did not require a woman to have a *get* to remarry, and half of all Conservative rabbis would refer a couple to a Reform colleague when the absence of a *get* presented a problem. Thirty percent of the Conservative rabbinate did not even do that. They were prepared, under certain circumstances, to do a wedding themselves, without the required *get*.[15] With both civil and religious remedies available to a woman without a *get*, the Conservative movement was hardly besieged with *agunah* cases.

Only one case actually ever came to the Conservative Joint *beit din*. In 1961, Mrs. K was referred to the RA-JTS body because her husband had disappeared in a plane crash in Canada and his body was never found. After all the theoretical discussion that had taken place on solutions for the *agunah*, the members of the Seminary faculty serving on the *beit din* indicated that they were not prepared to break ranks with the Orthodox *halakhic* standard by permitting an *agunah* to remarry. The case was placed in the laps of Rabbi Jules Harlow and Rabbi Max Routtenberg, secretary and chairman of the Committee on Jewish Law and Standards of the RA, respectively, who in turn, convened a *beit din* among the RA which allowed Mrs. K to remarry.[16] After years of forbidding the RA to take independent action in the area, the Joint *beit din* could not resolve the one case that came before it. The Joint partnership came under intense criticism from the RA, and it effectively ceased being a functioning body.

With the RA now operating on its own, an acceptable theoretical solution was finally reached in 1968. Rabbi Edward Gershfield, a Talmud professor at the Jewish Theological Seminary, developed a clause for insertion into the *ketubah* which made the marriage conditional upon the husband's granting of a *get* within six months of a civil divorce. If this condition was not met, the *beit din* could annul the marriage. Many halakhic authorities had doubts about the permissibility of conditional marriages, but the new proposal was unanimously passed by the Committee on Jewish Law and Standards in 1968, thus becoming RA policy.[17]

Although the issue had become moot for many, the 1968 decision was a victory if only because it put the *agunah* issue to rest, once and for all. The spectacle of the movement struggling with an issue which in forty years produced only one actual case testifies to the symbolic importance the issue had acquired. As the *agunah* issue brought to the RA a stigma of timidity, first in the face of Orthodoxy and later in its relationship with the Jewish Theological Seminary, this resolution was at least a psychological victory for the RA.

Many of the internal dynamics of Conservative Judaism become clear upon the examination of the *agunah* issue. Of paramount importance to Conservative authorities was the acquisition of religious legitimacy in the eyes of American Jewry. Appearing on the American scene after Reform and Orthodoxy had established themselves, Conservative Judaism was challenged to find its own foothold. From the arrival of Solomon Schechter in 1902, the Seminary tried to make clear in every way that it was not sympathetic to Reform Jewish endeavors. At the same time, Schechter and the successive leaders of Conservative Judaism hoped to wrest from Orthodoxy the mantle as the true heirs to traditional Judaism. Loyalty to halakhah became the yardstick for this claim.

There was however, an inherent conflict in the goals of Conservative Judaism. While claiming that halakhah had the capacity to change and adapt to new circumstances, Conservative Judaism was still vulnerable to any charge from the right wing of the religious spectrum that a proposed alteration of a law was nonhalakhic. Such an accusation would freeze Conservative authorities in their tracks. In the early part of the century, Orthodox leaders had enough of a following within the American Jewish public to prevent the RA from implementing Louis Epstein's *agunah* solution. After World War II, Conservatism had already succeeded in siezing the momentum as the fastest growing Jewish denomination and thus Orthodox leaders held less sway. Yet a new "veto" from the right emerged in the form of the Seminary itself. Rabbis in the field, facing the problems caused by outdated halakhot, were eager to move forward with the changes that Conservative Judaism seemed to promise. But when the Seminary faculty and administration invoked their loyalty to halakhah, the RA again found its hands tied. Only by severing the partnership of the Joint Law Conference could the RA achieve a solution to the *agunah* problem.

Throughout its history, many Conservative rabbis have voiced unhappiness over the movement's failure to take bold steps toward the adaptation of halakhah. This became one of the key issues which led the Reconstructionists to leave the Conservative movement and begin a rabbinical seminary and movement of their own. Many other Conservative rabbis, though unwilling to follow the lead of the Reconstructionists, still felt that the RA was not sufficiently assertive in declaring its independence from the Seminary and moving ahead into areas of Jewish law and practice that needed attention. The success or failure of the RA to pioneer halakhic change was as much a function of the psychological affects of what Marshall Sklare has called the schoolmen/practitioner dichotomy[18] as it was a matter of the relative strength of right, center, and left wings in the RA. The *agunah* issue illustrates the overwhelming influence the Seminary faculty had over rabbis in the field who felt themselves too inferior in halakhic learning to their teachers to openly rebuff the faculty's stated wishes. A similar interplay has emerged on the respective positions of the RA and the Seminary on women's ordination.

What has preserved the unity of the Conservative movement, despite the sometimes conflicting interests of the Seminary and the RA, has been the consensus that all sectors of the movement shared—the desire to preserve Conservative Judaism's legitimacy vis-à-vis the Jewish tradition. This required that every action be defensible along halakhic lines. Of course the safer path was the one that rejected innovation in favor of the standing traditional practice. But those areas of law that cried out for modification, such as the *agunah*, could not be ignored. They truly tested the mettle of Conservative Judaism's claim that it could remain halakhic even as it allowed for change. The intellectual justification for such activity was the legacy of Conservative scholarship itself, which maintained that halakhah had inherent capacities for change.

The historical evaluation of Conservative Judaism is a matter of perspective. Halakhah, like beauty, is in the eye of the beholder. To the Orthodox world, Conservatism long ago broke ranks with halakhic Judaism. (The term more often used today is "Torah-true Judaism," which probably testifies to the fact that Conservative Judaism has succeeded in portraying itself and, in turn, has been accepted by the American Jewish public as halakhic). From the Reform perspective, Conservatism tied itself too closely to halakhah, which prevented the movement from effecting the changes truly needed in American Judaism. To the Reconstructionists, who had been part of the Conservative process for many years, halakhah was more a matter of semantics than meticulous attention to the parameters of rabbinic interpretation. From this perspective the time between the recognition that a change was needed and the time it took to find an ingenious enough halakhic argument to permit the change was too long to make the endeavor worthwhile. Essentially, they decided to stop playing the game.

Conservative Judaism's success in capturing the large middle ground between Orthodoxy and Reform during the past century can largely be attributed to its ability to provide American Jewry with a religious option that was halakhic as well as modern. To the popular mind this was what was required to be authentically traditional. Ironically, the movement succeeded in doing this even as it argued about what was or was not halakhic. Conservative Judaism's potential for continued success will rest largely on its constituencies' willingness to accept more and more changes as halakhic and on its own ability to continue to tread the fine line between tradition and change.

NOTES

1. "A Solution to the Agunah Problem," *Proceedings of the Rabbinical Assembly (PRA)*, 1930, pp. 83–90.
2. "Adjustment of the Jewish Marriage Laws to Present-Day Conditions," *PRA*, 1935, pp. 230–35.
3. *Ha-Pardes* (Hebrew weekly), April, 1936, pp. 3–4.
4. *Zionist Record*, July 19, 1935.
5. Epstein to Cohen 10/16/35, Jewish Theological Seminary Archives, "Boaz Cohen" (box 2).
6. Epstein to Cohen 9/13/35, ibid.
7. Boaz Cohen to Ginzberg 7/1/35, ibid.
8. *PRA*, 1937, pp. 432–34.
9. *Proceedings of the 1950 Biennial Convention*, National Women's League, p. 135.
10. *Rabbinical Assembly Law Archives*, Vol. X, p. 271.
11. "Kedat Moshe Veyisrael," *PRA*, 1951, pp. 120–140.
12. *PRA*, 1952, pp. 49–53.
13. *A Rabbi's Manual*, ed. Jules Harlow (N.Y.: Rabbinical Assembly, 1965), pp. 37–38.
14. "Some Comments on the Hilchot Ishut Questionnaire," Aaron Blumenthal, November, 1967, *Rabbinical Assembly Law Archives*.
15. Ibid.
16. CJLS minutes 1/31/61, RALA; Max Routtenberg interview 6/23/80, New York.
17. "Tnai B'Kiddushin," *PRA*, 1968, pp. 229–241.
18. Marshall Sklare, *Conservative Judaism* (New York: Schocken, 1955, 1972), pp. 185–190.

VII

Solutions

17

Jewish Women's Rights: For the Love of Law

Blu Greenberg

I am sitting at a table near the large windows of the lobby of the Kings Hotel. The two women at the next table have that elegant look about them: They are smartly dressed, neatly coiffed and manicured in preparation for Shabbat. I imagine they are tourists from Boro Park or Forest Hills, old friends who haven't seen each other since the calamity. I have no intention of eavesdropping, but I hear the name Deborah—pronounced as my Deborah does—and it engages my interest. From then on it's open season for they don't speak in hushed tones and the tables are within earshot.

Deborah is the wicked daughter-in-law of the blond women—let's call her Rose—out of whose perfectly drawn mouth comes the most wretched tale. The couple married young—Deborah is 24 and already has three children—and now she wants out. Avi is totally crushed and quite helpless. Aggressive Deborah will stop at nothing. She is trying to turn the children against Avi and his parents. She's spent his hard-earned money (Avi is in their family business) on a beautiful house with expensive fixtures and a marble parquet entrance hall. Every day she shops. She came from a poor family and now has everything but it's never enough. Her mother is egging her on. The father is a quiet man but the daughter is like the mother, a *machashefa* (witch). It breaks Rose's heart, poor Avi, and those adorable little grandchildren with whom a relationship from here on will be far more difficult and will have a cloud over it.

I rise to leave, full of sympathy for poor helpless Avi and his sad mother, and full of anger at that mean Deborah for the unfairness and cruelty of it all. That is, until I hear the last exchange.

Friend: "So what will Avi do?" Rose: "Nothing. There's nothing he can do at this point, she'll never take him back. But just wait and see, he'll *drey* [jerk] her around a little before giving her a *get* [writ of divorce]."

So this is the enemy! Not just the blackmailing husband about whom we speak with loathing and against whom we organize demonstrations, employ sanctions, plead with rabbinic court authorities, seek help from civil judges, wield brute force—but Rose. Polished, refined Rose. Why?

Because the law allows it. The husband alone is empowered to release his wife from the marriage. If she wants a divorce and he doesn't, or if he wants to punish or blackmail her, he has the leverage to withhold the *get*. Even if the *beit din* (rabbinic court) mandates one, he can resort to all kinds of ruses to avoid compliance.

So the question is not why but why not? Why shouldn't a badly stung middle-aged woman take comfort in a legal measure that evens out the abuse her son has suffered? Why shouldn't an otherwise decent man use whatever the law allows to do battle with someone he feels has victimized him, someone he now passionately hates?

The fundamental flaw in the law of Jewish divorce is its underlying principle: that it is a man's absolute right, and therefore the *get* can be given only at his will. This permeates everything connected to traditional divorce. It is mirrored in the particulars of the law: it is refracted in the protections for women built into *halakha* such as the talmudic ruling "We coerce him until he says 'I want to [give her a *get*]'"; it explains why ameliorations of past generations are rendered unusable in later ones; it is manifested in the *heter mea rabbanim*, the provision for a husband's release in the event the wife refuses to accept the *get*; it serves as a rationale for contemporary Orthodox authorities—many with genuine angst—who dismiss possible solutions with a tidy "it's against the husband's will."

On the surface the problem seems to be an Orthodox one. Reform Judaism dropped the *get* requirement 150 years ago (though Reform has talked of a Jewish divorce ritual in recent years). The Conservative movement, which follows traditional Jewish laws of marriage and divorce, established a special *beit din* to solve cases of recalcitrance. This stifles the fantasies of would-be blackmailers, and it allows a way out for victims of the few diehard crazies. Reconstructionist Judaism issues a release document when no *get* is forthcoming.

But the problem potentially affects all Jews and it deals a blow to Jewish unity. As long as Jews of different denominations cannot marry each other by virtue of different definitions of Jewish divorce the entire community is diminished. And in Israel it can affect everyone since all marriage and divorce is governed by Orthodox *halakha*.

Years ago when I first began to examine inequity in Jewish divorce, I believed the problem could and should be solved with as little change as possible to *halakha*. No tinkering with basic principles. I argued. What difference if a husband has absolute right or if hierarchy remains on the books, as long as equity can be achieved in real life. Now that the women's movement has focused attention on the problem, I thought, all positive precedents in the tradition will be used to rescue these defenseless women. Maximum goodwill shall prevail. To me these seemed to be altogether reasonable expectations.

And indeed, over the course of the past two decades there has been some progress within Orthodoxy. The community has moved past apologetics and hand-wringing, through civil-court solutions and prenuptial agreements into an activist stage where outright political techniques are used.

Yet the problem remains and has, in fact, worsened with the rising divorce rate. Worldwide there are several thousand Jewish women anchored to absentee, intractable, punishing husbands. Beyond the usual trauma of divorce, these women suffer withered lives and lost years and diminished productivity. There are deep wells of bitterness in the women and emotional damage to the young pawns.

The problem remains despite the serious halakhic solutions advanced during these past two decades by such rabbinical legal scholars as Emanuel Rackman, Zeev Falk, Irwin Haut, Shlomo Riskin and the late Eliezer Berkovitz.

The problem remains despite years of dedicated work by organizations devoted solely to this issue: G.E.T., Agunah and Kayama in the United States; Israel Women's Network and the Organization to Help Agunot in Israel; Coalition of Jewish Women for the GET in Canada; and committees in Australia and England.

The problem remains despite increasing public awareness and a growing body of horror stories.

The problem remains despite a wider legitimation by the Orthodox rabbinate of the prenuptial agreement (as in the new Rabbinical Council of America-approved agreements) and a greater willingness on the part of some rabbinic court judges to instruct a man to give the *get*.

Moreover, the efforts to release a single *agunah* are time consuming, expensive, and humiliating. There is an incredible squandering of resources of supporters, rabbinic authorities, and religious court adjudicators. Even the new breakthrough in Israel, the training of women to be *toanot*, advocates for the wife in the all-male religious courts, is designed to help support and move a woman through a system that at its core is adversarial to her interests. We have created an elaborate structure to fight its own system.

Today I no longer believe it is sufficient to address the symptom without addressing the root cause. No one should any longer try to defend or justify something which is unethical in principle and corrupt in practice. Clearly the original intent of the law was otherwise. The *get* was a procedure of existential closure, an altogether necessary exercise in the dissolution of a marriage. That it was formulated in hierarchical fashion ("he creates the marriage and therefore he dissolves it") was a legitimate response to the structure of society, the law addressing the people "where they were." But through the hands of its faithful practitioners the law has become unethical — and in need of thorough repair.

What is needed therefore is not a piecemeal approach to the problem, nor crisis intervention after the fact, nor civil-court remedies, nor solutions based on an ambivalent coercion but rather a fundamental halakhic reinterpretation of the basic principle upon which the law is based. Until such time as that happens the problem will remain with us. Every hard-won gain in one century will be undone in the next to uphold the principle of a man's absolute right. Unless the law undergoes an elemental shift, 100 years from now we will count thousands more *agunot*, martyrs who will pay for their faithfulness to the law. If we continue to address the problem in the manner of times past — symptomatically, after the fact and one victim at a time — we may well conclude a century from now that we have put our eggs into the wrong basket.

I have always defended incremental steps and organic change in Jewish law and have critiqued anything that hints of radicalism. But I believe the time for halfway measures is past. Meetings with the leaders of the *beit din* and promises for commissions and special courts have proven to be nothing more than stonewalling.

The question then becomes how to achieve a basic change in the principle considered sacred by those who hold the interpretive keys while remaining faithful to *halakha*. Underlying that question is an assumption about *halakha* that it is both fixed and dynamic, revelatory yet open to human reinterpretation. In every generation Jewish religious leaders were able to amend *halakha* relying on techniques within the law itself — novel interpretations, outright promulgations, urgent measures, overriding principles. Where there was a rabbinic will there was often a halakhic way.

Given the abuse the law allows or engenders, given the numbers and extent of hardship, given the staying power of the problem, the task for the community in these times is to generate the appropriate rabbinic will — not simply to solve this or that woman's *tsuris* but to reinterpret the *halakha* to forever strike the principle of a man's leverage. Jews cannot rewrite Sinaitic or talmudic law any more than they can rewrite history, but they do have the power to interpret and reinterpret it.

Can laypeople change the mind-set of *poskim*, the interpreters of the law? Not easily. But it's not impossible either. It will take massive action, thorough planning, and ample funding. We should look at it as a fight to the finish—not against individuals, though it may at times appear that way, but against a wrong principle. And let no one say that this is not what God wants.

Some might interpret these words as being contrary to *halakha*. But that is not the case at all. I am not suggesting that women remarry without a halakhic *get* or even turn to a *beit din* outside of one's community. I am not suggesting that we sidestep the *poskim* or diminish the significance of halakhic authorities of our generation. Rather I am suggesting the laity apply extreme pressure—political, financial, and moral—on those who lack judicial courage, who fear to issue lenient rulings, many of them embedded in the sources. The hands of the current religious leaders must be strengthened to grapple with nothing less than the underlying and biased principle. The community has the responsibility to compel these lawmakers until *they* say "I want to." For these reasons pressure tactics should be carried out with full advance disclosure to the halakhists. That will not limit their effectiveness; it will convey a sense of cooperation. The goal is not to embarrass but to apply pressure that will help spur action.

What are some of the urgent measures that can be used to effect a change in rabbinic will? There are many, including political techniques from the secular women's movement. Last summer a group of women leaders from the World Union of Jewish Students was meeting in Jerusalem. They had just returned greatly disheartened from a fact-finding visit to a rabbinic court. Among their suggestions: a massive hunger strike of *agunot* (many of whom say they are already dead) and supporters to take place in strategic locations and continue until every *aguna* in the world is released and all potential abuse is eliminated; a cage set up in an appropriate public place in which *agunot* would lock themselves to symbolize their status; bringing together a highly motivated group of rabbinic leaders to strengthen each other in issuing rulings; engaging the cooperation of the media to keep the story alive with a revolting case history each week; airing this dirty linen in the civil press despite the shame and embarrassment it brings to our community; withholding financial support from institutions where the leaders aggressively uphold the principle of a man's absolute right and supporting those who find solutions within *halakha* to reinterpret the principle; placing this matter on the agenda of every Jewish youth and student organization, not only the source of future leadership but a subcommunity available for action; the pooling of funds—vast sums of which are now being negotiated for blackmail or paid to lawyers—into a central bank to coordinate a plan of action.

If these are suggestions that came out of an ad hoc meeting, just imagine what will emerge with careful planning and coordination.

There are those who will say "How dare one apply politics to religion, speak power to *halakha*, levy human pressure against a Divinely revealed system?" The answer is that it is an act of Divine will that human beings have the power to influence the outcome of the law. Surely it is far more offensive to God to preserve that which enables some to inflict cruelty on others than it is to take on the Divinely sanctioned human responsibility to reinterpret the law.

For too long these women have suffered. Often they have not even been allowed the dignity of making their shame and abuse public. Sometimes they've been made to feel as culprit rather than victim. But no less than any of us they are entitled to happiness, even the Deborahs among them. No less than any of us they have a right to get on with their lives. And all of us should get on with the business of celebrating Jewish life and loving Jewish law—not fighting it.

18

Grappling with Divorce and Jewish Law

Steven Feldman

Few matters in life are as complex and painful as divorce. The concerns may be even more complicated if one is an observant Jew, committed to obtaining a divorce that is recognized by *halacha* (Jewish law). Recently, a significant portion of the Jewish community—including scholars, lawyers, and feminists—has been grappling with the issue of halachic divorce. And, while the matter may seem obscure to those outside of traditional circles, for many observant women the issue of the *get*—the halachic bill of divorce—is of central importance.

Halacha views the giving of a *get* as indeed it views marriage itself, as a personal act between a man and a woman, with the courts or civil governments playing no role in effecting either the divorce or the marriage. This means that no government, court of law, or even rabbi can wed a couple; a halachic marriage takes place when the man places a ring on the woman's finger and declares his intention to marry her, and through their subsequent cohabitation. What it also means is that a married couple cannot be declared by any government, court of law, or rabbi to be halachically divorced. What is needed is for the husband to reverse the marriage procedure by having a *get* drawn up, giving it to his wife before two witnesses and declaring her to be divorced from him. The Biblical source for this method of divorce, and the justification for the man initiating the entire proceeding, is the statement in Deuteronomy: "*He* shall write *her* a writ of divorce and put it in her hand and send her on her way" (emphasis added).

Failure to obtain a proper Jewish divorce leads to severe consequences for the halachically observant woman. Because a woman is not permitted more than one spouse, should she wish to remarry without a *get* from her first husband she would be unable to do so, being considered still married. Any subsequent cohabitation with another man is deemed adulterous and any future offspring would be classified as *mamzerim,* or bastards (themselves forbidden to marry anyone except other *mamzerim*). The consequences are less severe for the husband. Should he remarry without granting his first wife a *get,* he will have violated the relatively late (medieval) rabbinic ban on polygamy, but, following Biblical precedent (which permits a man to have more than one wife), his second marriage is nonetheless binding and causes no deleterious effects for his subsequent offspring.

Recalcitrant Husbands

The dynamics of halachic divorce present many problems. Perhaps the most acute is the problem of a man who disappears (usually in war) without any witnesses available to testify to his death. In *halacha,* unlike common law, there is no presumption of death from absence. Such a man's wife is an *agunah* (literally, "anchored woman"), unable to remarry. The problem of *agunot* was at its most severe after the Holocaust, when even the most ultra-Orthodox rabbis went to extraordinary lengths (such as accepting the testimony of relatives or of non-Jews) to permit women to marry again after the war.

More common today is the problem of the recalcitrant spouse who either refuses to give or to accept a *get.* There are also instances of one spouse using the need for a *get* to extort huge sums of money from the other or to blackmail the other spouse with regard to child custody.

Although it is the husband who must initiate proceedings, the wife's consent is needed as well. A medieval *takkannah* — rabbinic decree — forbade the divorcing of a woman against her will, though here again the situation is more difficult for the woman than for the man. Whereas the woman can only try to exert pressure on a reluctant husband to give her a *get,* the man, if his wife refuses to accept a *get,* or if she becomes mentally incompetent to do so, or if she disappears, can petition one hundred rabbis to allow him to remarry. It is important to remember that in so doing the hundred rabbis in no way effectuate a divorce, nor do they annul the marriage — they merely exempt the husband from the rabbinic ban on polygamy. But they cannot do the same for a woman in similar circumstances.

At any rate, people familiar with the issue say that it is the man who is recalcitrant in three-quarters of the cases. Overall, it has been estimated that there are 15,000 Jewish women in New York State alone who are civilly divorced but who are unable to obtain a *get*.

Legislative Solutions

It was out of a desire to thwart such recalcitrant spouses that a law was introduced in the New York Legislature last year. Popularly known as "the *get* bill," the law, signed by Governor Mario Cuomo last fall, states that anyone seeking a civil divorce must remove all barriers to the remarriage of his or her spouse. Though there is no explicit reference to Jewish or any other religious divorce procedure, the bill was clearly meant to help those people who have had difficulty obtaining a *get*. Most of the lobbying for the bill came from Orthodox rabbis and Orthodox rabbinical organizations. And, interestingly, much of the opposition was provided by the American Jewish Congress and the Reform movement's Union of American Hebrew Congregations, who felt the bill to be an issue of separation of church and state. The law is now being appealed.

Whether the *get* bill will actually do much good is open to question. Lawyer and Orthodox rabbi Irwin Haut, the author of *Divorce in Jewish Law and Life* (Sepher-Hermon Press), points out that the law only affects the plaintiff—the person seeking the civil divorce. That is, if someone asks for a civil divorce, he or she cannot at the same time prevent the other party from remarrying by opting out of a religious divorce. "But usually the party seeking the divorce is not the one who is refusing the *get*," Haut says. "The bill may be questionable constitutionally anyway (on church/state grounds). It would clearly be unconstitutional if it tried to force the defendant to give a *get* [when] he doesn't want a divorce or a *get*."

There are attempts to pass similar legislation in Connecticut, New Jersey, California, Maryland, and possibly Illinois in the near future. There are no serious efforts underway in Massachusetts as of yet. Rabbi Meyer Horowitz, Director of the New England Chassidic Center and son of the Bostoner Rebbe (who serves on the Presidium of Agudath Israel, one of the Orthodox groups that lobbied for the *get* bill in New York), would like to see Massachusetts pass a comparable law. "All we're saying in the bill is if one partner feels deprived of their right to remarry, the courts will be cognizant of that fact," he says. "Just like courts recognize religious marriage, it should work the other way, too (regarding religious divorce)."

Others who favor the bill think that it does not address the main issue. Blu Greenberg, author of *On Women and Judaism: The View from Tradition*

(Jewish Publication Society), who has long been wrestling with questions of sexual inequality in *halacha* from an Orthodox viewpoint, says of the bill, "It's just an interim solution. I welcomed it as such. It's a move past the hand-wringing stage. But it doesn't solve the problem for women outside of New York. We don't have to take our halachic imbalances to civil courts. We need better halachic solutions." She has suggested in cases of blackmail or with an *agunah* that the woman be empowered to authorize and deliver a *get*. "I'm not in favor of changing *halachot,* but when there is a real hardship, then we have to reformulate the notion of a man taking a woman in marriage."

Pre-Nuptial Agreements

There is clearly more sensitivity now than there was in the past to the plight of women experiencing difficulty in obtaining a religious divorce. New efforts are underway to insure that in many cases the woman need not end up in the civil courts to pressure her husband for a *get*. Of this new awareness, Arlene Agus, a founding member of the Jewish feminist group *Ezrat Nashim* and currently the Director of External Affairs at Yeshiva University's Cardozo Law School, says, "It has motivated Jewish courts to look over their more progressive shoulder."

Among Orthodox rabbis, there is growing favor toward the use of pre-nuptial agreements, in which both parties would agree to participate in a *get* procedure should either of them seek a civil divorce. Marc Stern, Assistant Director of the American Jewish Congress' Legal Department, who worked against New York's *get* bill partly because, "This rush to legislation will deflect from dealing with the problem within the Jewish community," says he favors the use of pre-nuptial agreements. "There the parties consent; with the *get* bill, the state coerces."

The Conservative movement began to address the issue 30 years ago when it introduced a modification to the traditional *ketubah* (the document that a man gives his wife at their wedding which stipulates the monetary support he will give her during their marriage or in the event of their divorce). The modification stated that both parties would accept as binding the decision of a Conservative *Beth Din* (rabbinic court) in questions relating to any future divorce. The enforceability of such a clause in civil courts was recently upheld by the New York Court of Appeals in *Avitzur v. Avitzur.* But that particular case is still not settled. "You can win in court and not get a *get,"* points out Rabbi Edward Gershfield, a Conservative rabbi and faculty member at the Jewish Theological Seminary who deals with divorce cases. "Mrs. Avitzur still doesn't have a *get."*

Rabbi Gershfield, too, thinks it misguided to turn to civil courts in these matters. "It's an internal Jewish problem. The place to solve rabbinical problems is with rabbis," he says. He is also critical of those whom he considers to be using the issue. "It's a women's liberation problem that has been fanned. Jewish law is not full of oppression or craziness as many people would have it. The problem of an *agunah* is serious, but it should not be looked upon as a male versus female problem."

For the two other branches of American Judaism, the *get* problem raises different issues. "Rather than trying to find a Jewish legal loophole or a secular legal loophole, it has to be faced directly. The traditional *get* is regressive, repressive, and unethical. It clearly has to be changed," says Rebecca Alpert, Dean of Students at the Reconstructionist Rabbinical College. Reconstructionist rabbis have made available to women the option of initiating Jewish divorce proceedings. They have also revised the text of the *get* to make it more egalitarian. Rabbi Joy Levitt, who has a Reconstructionist congregation in Montclair, N.J., says, "Some Reconstructionists don't think a Jewish divorce is necessary, but I require it because it's no longer unequal." Similarly, she doesn't see the need for pre-nuptial agreements because nothing prevents either party from giving a *get*.

For Reform Jews, questions regarding a *get* do not even come up. "Historically, Reform Judaism did away with Jewish divorce, deeming it a civil procedure," explains Rabbi Sanford Seltzer, the Brookline, Mass., based Director of Research for the Union of American Hebrew Congregations. Some Reform rabbis, however, have been calling for a reinstitution of a *get* procedure, while other favor some other type of divorce ritual. "Those rabbis feel that since the synagogue is the place for weddings, it should also be the place for the divorce," Rabbi Seltzer says. He too opposes efforts such as a *get* bill.

Grassroots Efforts

The problems associated with obtaining a *get* have stimulated more than rabbinic attempts to improve the situation. At the community level, people have been organizing to correct inequities and to try to head off bitter battles over a *get*. One prominent grassroots group is Getting Equitable Treatment (G.E.T.), which began in the fall of 1979 among some members of the Young Israel of Flatbush. Gloria Greenman, the founder and first president, recalls how the group came to be founded. "We were commiserating over a friend's daughter (who had been unable to obtain a *get*), and I just said, 'Let's stop talking, let's do something.' "

The main thrust of the group was and still is to have a couple go to a *Beth Din* for adjudication of their divorce. G.E.T. has 400 paid members, and while most are Orthodox, Greenman emphasizes that the group serves all Jews, from the nonreligious to the very Orthodox. "We don't think of ourselves as an Orthodox organization. We want people to have a *get* that will be accepted universally. That means it has to be an Orthodox *get.*"

Leila Karlin, the Executive Director of G.E.T., says a "good percentage" of the cases they handle have been settled. For those cases where the talking process has failed to lead to a *get,* the organization is prepared to exert pressure on the recalcitrant spouse. Such pressure includes, in the case of a man, barring him from synagogue honors and functions and economic pressure. G.E.T. is also prepared to publish the name of the uncooperative party in the Anglo-Jewish press, though it has never had to go that far.

Greenman sees positive changes taking place. "Four years ago, my rabbi came to my house and said, 'Forget about changing the *halacha.*' But we've had an indirect effect. The rabbis have felt the need more than ever before to do something." She adds, "It's snowballing, there's activity. Four years ago you wouldn't have called."

The near future should see further discussion and change in the field of Jewish divorce. Many of the important changes will no doubt come at the grassroots, community level. Perhaps even more important in the long run will be changes brought about within *halacha* regarding marriages and divorces. As Blu Greenberg put it, "The issue is to solve the problems of *halacha* not in the civil courts but under the canopy of *halacha.*"

19
Getting a *Get*

Honey Rackman

Margaret's Orthodox upbringing had made her respectful of rabbis. She was a regular at Sabbath services. She quite naturally regarded her rabbi as a father figure, despite the fact that he was at most a few years older than she. And though she considered herself a very private person, it seemed natural to take her personal problems to the rabbi. She was also confident, as she sat in his study pouring out her misery, that he would be able to solve them.

His answer was not what she expected. "If you want the *get* [a Jewish bill of divorce], you'll have to pay him," he said.

She had retained an expensive lawyer; it had been a hard-fought divorce. But she had won. Was she now going to be required to forfeit her victories in civil court in exchange for the precious *get*?

And where was the anguished outcry she had expected from her rabbi over her husband's unconscionable demands?

Margaret did, in fact, ransom her *get* by relinquishing everything the court had awarded her. She is supporting herself and her three daughters on a teacher's salary with no help from her affluent husband. She cannot afford the lifestyle she once enjoyed (which her husband continues to enjoy), but she is at least free of the intolerable harassment she suffered during her marriage, and she is also free to remarry and have children if she wishes.

The civil divorce freed her from the harassment. But the *get* gave her the freedom to remarry and have children.

Unlike other women, observant Jewish women like Margaret are not free to remarry with only a civil divorce. The bonds of Jewish marriages must be undone by the formal act of the husband having a *get* (plural, *gittin*) written for his wife, which she must then accept if she wants to be freed from the marriage. An entire tractate of the Talmud—Gittin (Divorces)—is devoted to this subject and the minutiae of its enforcement and ramifications.

Without a *get,* a Jewish wife is considered an *ayshet ish* (a married woman). Should she disregard this religious law and take a second husband without a *get* from the first husband, children from the second marriage will be *mamzerim* (illegitimate). This pariah designation carries a far greater stigma than simple bastardy, a term that applies to children born out of wedlock. In the eyes of Jewish law the latter are considered legitimate if the woman is unmarried. *Mamzerim,* on the other hand, are illegitimate. Rabbi Irving Greenberg, president of CLAL, the National Jewish Center for Learning and Leadership, has estimated that as many as 15,000 *mamzerim* are born each year in the United States.

A *mamzer* is forever forbidden to marry a legitimate Jew. "A *mamzer* shall not enter the congregation of the Lord" (Deuteronomy 23:3). Should a *mamzer* marry a non-*mamzer* despite the prohibition, the *mamzer* passes on the trait of *mamzerut* to all offspring since "*mamzerim* are forbidden and forbidden for all time, whether they are males or females."[1] The rule is that in the case of a prohibited union, the child follows the status of the "defective" parent.[2]

The punishment for the sins of the parents is inflicted on all succeeding generations. The only escape for the descendants occurs if a male *mamzer* marries a gentile and has a child with her. Since the child carries the lineage of the mother, the child is gentile rather than a *mamzer,* and if the child is then converted to Judaism, he or she would acquire the status of a legitimate proselyte. The fact that the father was a *mamzer* would be irrelevant.[3] For women there can be no such release from stigmatizing their descendants.

A woman whose husband refuses to give her a *get* is called an *agunah,* a chained woman. This classification also applies to a woman whose husband has disappeared, or become insane (and therefore is incapable of giving a *get*) or even if he has died without proof of death (Jewish divorce law does not recognize presumptive evidence of death). An *agunah* must accept her fate—a life of bitter despair, unable to remarry.

But the case of a woman whose husband deliberately and wrongfully refuses to give her a *get* is especially egregious, not only because it is by far the most common kind of *agunah,* but also because it involves deliberate malice.

Even though at the time of her divorce, a woman may have no plan to remarry, she naturally wants that option and the possibility of having children. The *get* then becomes a critical bargaining chip in divorce negotiations. Since it is only the husband who is empowered to give it,[4] he has tremendous leverage.

The ultimate source of the Jewish law of marriage and divorce is, of course, biblical:

"A man takes a wife and lives with her. She fails to please him because he finds something obnoxious about her and he writes her a bill of divorcement, hands it to her and sends her away from his house. When she leaves his house, she may go and be another man's wife" (Deuteronomy 24:1–2).

The talmudic law of divorce is an extrapolation from this verse. One could fill as many volumes as there are books of the Talmud (20, and they are massive) with tearful sagas of Jewish women waiting for *gittin* from tormenting husbands who dangle the *get* on a string of preposterous demands, as a cat might toy with a mouse before devouring it.

Is there no answer?

One solution lies in the creative development of *halacha* (Jewish religious law). As long ago as the 11th century, Rabbenu Gershom of Mainz recognized that a law giving a husband the unilateral right to divorce his wife, for reasons serious or cavalier, left women prey to arbitrary abandonment. Rabbenu Gershom came to their rescue:

"When he [Rabbenu Gershom] saw how the generation was abusive of Jewish daughters insofar as divorcing them under compulsion, he enacted a *takkanah* [a directive with the force of law] that the rights of women be equal to those of men, and just as a man divorces only from his own will, so too, a woman might henceforth be divorced only willingly."[5]

Rabbenu Gershom's *takanah* protected women from divorce against their will. Later, Rabbenu Gershom outlawed polygamy as well (known as the *cherem d'Rabbenu Gershom*), although it was permitted in the Bible. These *takanot* were based on ethical considerations—the abuse of Jewish women to which Torah law has always responded. Rabbenu Gershom's *takanot* did not, however, address the problem of the husband who refuses to give his wife a *get,* but they do reflect the kind of legislation permissible within the bounds of *halacha.*

The same kinds of ethical and moral considerations are involved when a husband wrongly refuses to give his wife a *get.*

Some prominent Orthodox rabbis have proposed halachic solutions to the problem. But they have met with formidable opposition from the Orthodox establishment.

Rabbi Emanuel Rackman, chancellor of Bar-Ilan University in Israel, has called for a "demythologizing" of *halacha:*

> By demythologizing, what do we mean? Some Orthodox rabbis say that Jewish law never changes; that it is fixed, immutable. They know this isn't true, but perhaps they say it because they feel that this in itself creates a value: that people should not get used to the idea that Jewish law can be changed. Changes are often requested by people whose motivation is simply selfish. They want to justify what they want to do . . . .
>   Rabbi Joseph B. Soloveitchik suggests that instead of saying *halacha* does not change, we should perhaps speak in terms of innovation in *halacha,* or of creativity in an immutable *halacha.*[6]

According to Rackman, social considerations may properly be given weight in the interpretation of *halacha,* such considerations, Rackman says, obviously weighed heavily with Rabbenu Gershom in formulating his *takanot:*

"There are three factors that play a part in all legal development: One is logic, the second is the sense of justice, and the third concerns the needs of society. All three elements play a part in Jewish law that there's no escaping. This is true of all legal systems and of the *halacha* as well."[7]

Some rabbinic groups would like us to believe that halachic solutions to *get* blackmail are unavailable; a pretense that flies in the face of extensive talmudic research done by several eminent scholars besides Rackman, such as Justice Menachem Alon of Israel's Supreme Court, author of *HaMishpat Ha'Ivri,* "Jewish law" (1973) and Rabbi Eliezer Berkovits, author of *T'nai B'Nisuin U'Get,* "stipulative marriage and divorce contracts" (1967).

The essence of the recommendations in these legal analyses is to restore the annulment process used in the days when there was a centralized rabbinic authority. The annulment process fell into disuse when Jews were dispersed and it was feared that *batei din* (religious courts, singular, *bet din*) in different cities would not recognize or be aware of one another's rulings, especially rulings in distant jurisdictions. Drawing on volumes of texts and supporting *responsa,* modern Orthodox authorities like Berkovits, Alon, and Rackman urge the reintroduction of the annulment process under the aegis of Israel's chief rabbinate.

The late Rabbi Moshe Feinstein issued such an annulment in a case of fraud. In this precedent-setting decision, he reasoned that the aggrieved wife would not have entered into the marriage had she been apprised of certain facts about her husband which he had concealed prior to their marriage.[8] In reaching his decision, Rabbi Feinstein cited authorities that supported his ruling and rejected those whose interpretation of law differed from his.[9]

Although this halachic precedent was handed down in 1961, and despite the venerated position of the rabbi who decided it, no attempt has been made in religious courts to use it in cases where a husband wrongfully refuses his wife a *get*. Summarizing the tension between the need for and the resistance to change, Rackman states:

> It is with regard to divorce law that there is presently the greatest need for halachic creativity. Those who clamor for change make it appear that the *halacha* is unfair to women. Those who resist change rest their case on numerous maxims which make one dread any tampering with the sanctity of the marital status. Neither group does justice to the *halacha*. The former ignore the overwhelming evidence to be found in thousands of talmudic folios which deal with the obligations of a husband to a wife. The latter freeze the *halacha* against further development by ignoring the dialectic which is the very essence of the halachic process.[10]

In a more recent study entitled *Divorce in Jewish Law and Life,* attorney and rabbi Irwin H. Haut fortifies the ranks of those seeking to cure *get* blackmail with halachic surgery. Haut's is a comprehensive and convincing analysis affirming the viability of Jewish law to end the *agunah* tragedy through traditional exegesis and/or *takanot*. In short, Rabbi Haut has examined the abused body of Jewish divorce law, and his diagnosis is that the patient is curable if only the qualified doctors would administer the medicine at their disposal.

Despite the attention *get* blackmail has been given in the Jewish media and the waste of young women spending their childbearing years in ugly and often vicious conflict with recalcitrant husbands, the Orthodox establishment has not responded. Ostrich-like, some Orthodox rabbis have even suggested that there is no problem. They maintain that they are dealing satisfactorily with the individual cases that come before them. With their best handwringing gesture, they gently shoo from their presence "feminist" troublemakers, with the condescending assurances that they too are deeply troubled and suffer sleepless nights but cannot change the law.

Rabbis are not stampeding to utilize even the limited arsenal that is available to them in the battle for a *get*. Recalcitrant husbands are not being denied honors in synagogues, and in some cases they are even asked to give classes in Jewish law.

The New York Board of Rabbis, which has Orthodox, Conservative, Reform, and Reconstructionist members, has overcome the inertia with a resolution urging sanctions against any divorced person who refuses to cooperate with the giving or receiving of a *get*. The board also unanimously agreed to encourage the use of prenuptial agreements in which the husband agrees that he would give his wife a *get* in accordance with a ruling of a *bet din*. The Board of Rabbis also urged their constituents to dissolve a marriage by obtaining a *get* whenever there has been a civil divorce. Unfortunately, the resolution has no binding force on its members, and there is no mechanism to monitor compliance with its terms.

With Orthodox rabbinic acceptance of halachic reform seemingly light years away, poultices are being applied to the potential sufferers of *get* wounds. One such palliative is the prenuptial agreement mentioned above, in which both partners in the marriage agree to abide by the ruling of a *bet din*. One agreement reads as follows:

"We, the undersigned, agree that if after we wed we, God forbid, separate, then each of us shall obey the order of a designated *bet din* regarding the giving or accepting of a *get.*"

Conservative rabbis have incorporated such qualifying addenda into their standard *ketubah* (marriage contract). Although the use of such agreements was officially sanctioned years ago by the Orthodox establishment, to date there has been no uniform agreement among Orthodox authorities on the wording of such agreements, nor are they in widespread use.

In any event, the solution is only partial, for several reasons. Some couples find the inclusion of such language, contemplating divorce at the time of marriage, offensive. In addition, protracted and expensive litigation, in civil as well as in religious courts, may be necessary to enforce these agreements.

Bet din procedures are unfortunately labyrinthine, to say the least. The following series of letters reveal, by way of example, part of a seven-year *get* battle waged by a young mother of two who attempted to support her family and maintain a semblance of normal life while under litigious siege from her lawyer-husband (because these were sent to me privately, I have deleted all identifying names):

April 17, 1985
Dear Mr. − −:
The Jewish Ecclesiastical Court of − − has again received a request from your wife, − − to summon you for an appearance before the *Bet Din*, regarding a claim against you.

You realize, of course, that according to Jewish law it is incumbent upon you to respond to this second *hazmanah* [summons].

Please contact our office to arrange for the *Din Torah* [hearing] on a day and at a time convenient to you.

April 25, 1985

Dear Mr. − −:

Although we have written to you previously that it is the policy of the − − Rabbinic Council not to proceed with a *get* until after a Civil Decree has been issued, your case has to be an exception to the general rule because of its unusual circumstances.

If you refuse to proceed with a *get* at this time, please consider this letter as the third and final *hazmanah* for a *Din Torah* as requested by your wife.

Therefore, disregard all previous correspondence on the issue and contact our office to arrange for such an appearance.

July 25, 1985

Dear Mr. − −:

The − − Court has again received a request from your wife, − −, to summon you for an appearance before the *Bet Din*. You realize, of course, that according to Jewish Law it is incumbent upon you to respond to this second [sic] *hazmanah*.

Please contact our office to arrange for the *Din Torah* on a day and at a time convenient to you.

July 29, 1985

Dear Mr. − −:

After receiving your phone call I have decided that since I am leaving the − − office next month, I can no longer be involved with the *Din Torah* that your wife requested.

Furthermore, since the case is still pending in civil court, the *Bet Din* is not in a position to intervene at the present time. Therefore, please discount the recent *hazmanah* sent to you.

In the future, you may contact Rabbi − −, chairman of our *Halacha* Commission, for any action on the *get*.

With best wishes for the upcoming year, I remain

Sincerely yours,

This correspondence is not unusual and reflects the often flippant treatment women receive before the *batei din*. The total absence of structure or consistency leaves the petitioner with the feeling that she is, indeed, Alice in Wonderland.

After three *hazmanot* have been issued, a *seruv* (contempt citation which means, literally, "refusal") is supposed to be issued stating that the spouse summoned has refused to come before the *bet din*. While a *seruv* carries no penalties whatsoever, it has a certain moral force. But it is rarely issued. Some *batei din* simply state, as does the Rabbinical Council of America, "We don't issue them."

In the absence of satisfactory Orthodox rabbinical response to the problem, several lay organizations have been formed to combat *get* abuses and to aid victims of *get* blackmail.

The best known is G.E.T., an acronym for Getting Equitable Treatment. As is often the case, its formation was prompted by a particular incident.

A young man who was being divorced by the daughter of a well-to-do family decided he could obtain a fatter settlement by refusing his wife a *get* than by pleading the merits of his case in civil court. The girl's parents grew frantic as it became apparent that the rabbinic solutions they had hoped for were chimeras. Except for covert suggestions that the parents hire some mafioso types to make their son-in-law "an offer he can't refuse" (from which the beleaguered mother recoiled even under siege), none of the rabbis before whom they pleaded their case could suggest anything but payment. The family finally settled on a six-digit figure as the price for their daughter's freedom.

As anger mounted among the family's friends, all agreed that something must be done. The result was that Gloria Greenman, a retired teacher who was a friend of the family, channeled the community's outrage into the establishment of G.E.T.[11]

G.E.T. attempts to use community pressure to fight *get* abuses. G.E.T. caseworkers, volunteers from all professions, attempt to encourage divorcing couples to go to a *bet din* for the writing of the bill of divorcement. Where there is resistance, the G.E.T. caseworker begins with subtle urging, proceeding to more radical measures if resistance stiffens. A strategy committee weighs other available options if obstinacy continues. Dr. Norman Tokayer, current president of G.E.T., admits that the group does not always get their *get*, but it is not for lack of trying. Unfortunately, the pressure G.E.T. can apply is limited.

In one widely known case, however, G.E.T. organizers went so far as to picket the offending husband. The announcement from the pulpit on a Shabbat raised eyebrows. The rabbi urged his congregation to join a picket line in front of a store owned by the family of a recalcitrant husband to force the husband to give his wife a *get* as decreed by a legitimate *bet din*.

There was enthusiastic support from some and outrage from others. The G.E.T. organization issued a community brief, substantiating its view that such action was justified halachically and explaining why community action was a "good" rather than an "evil." Most were won over, but not all.

Permits for the picketing were obtained, and people who usually spend their Sundays playing tennis or watching football carried signs that read: "Give a *Get*" and "Free Your Wife." They chanted similar sentiments as bewildered shoppers bypassed the store because they agreed with the chants, or were astonished at the pickets, or both. Although the picketing was successful, it was a humiliating experience for everyone, including the community itself. But it was the only way to secure a young woman's freedom after more than five years of tortuous battles before *batei din*.

Legal action in civil courts may also be effective in some cases. In the landmark case of *Perl v. Perl,* the wife claimed that she had agreed to give up virtually all marital property in order to obtain a *get* from her husband. The property settlement agreement specifically provided that it was conditioned on the husband's granting the wife a *get.* The husband gave the *get* and the ex-wife then dishonored post-dated checks and promissory notes given to him in the settlement. The ex-husband sued to enforce the settlement agreement. The ex-wife defended herself on the ground that the agreement had been obtained by coercion and under duress and was therefore unenforceable because, as the court stated:

> The husband, knowing that his wife was of the Orthodox Jewish faith and could never remarry or bear children without a *get,* and aware that only he, under Jewish law, could permit such an instrument to issue, used this knowledge to crush the wife's resistance to his extortionate financial demands and that she, because of her desperation to be free to remarry, bear children and live a normal life, simply capitulated.

The court ruled that if the wife could prove these claims, it would not enforce the settlement agreement. The trial, the court said, was to "focus upon the diminished capacity of the alleged victim-wife brought about by the husband's stance and the objective unfairness of the bargain."

The court concluded: "Where either spouse has invoked the power of the state to effect a civil dissolution of a marriage, an oppressive misuse of the religious veto power by one of the spouses subjects the economic bargain which follows between them to review and potential revision."

This ruling sends a signal to lawyers who would counsel their male clients to withhold a *get* for extortionate demands. Not only is such behavior unethical, it may prove counterproductive if courts continue to overturn inequitable financial settlements obtained as a ransom for a *get*.

Moreover, New York state passed legislation in 1983 that requires parties suing for a civil divorce to sign statements saying they have taken or will take steps to remove any barrier to remarriage. But this law only helps if the husband sues or countersues for divorce; if only the wife sues, it has no effect on the husband. In approving the legislation, Governor Mario Cuomo noted that "the requirement of a *get* is used by unscrupulous spouses who avail themselves of our civil courts and simultaneously use their denial of a *get* vindictively or as a form of economic coercion."

But this is only a partial solution. It is distressing to think that Jews must apply to the civil courts for relief on issues of *halacha*. A proper solution should come from the Orthodox rabbinate. Whether the rabbinate will offer one remains doubtful.

Conservative Judaism's Approach

"Jewish law should be used and seen as it always has been, concerned with the well-being of both the man and the woman," says Rabbi Morton Leifman, vice president of the Jewish Theological Seminary (JTS) and past coordinator of the *bet din* (religious court) for the Rabbinical Assembly and JTS.

"Almost 35 years ago, the Rabbinical Assembly and the JTS established a joint *bet din*. At that time, Rabbi Saul Lieberman advocated an addition to the *ketubah* which was to be signed at the point of marriage. It is a civil contract wherein both spouses agree that if there were a civil dissolution of the marriage, and one spouse requested that the other appear before a *bet din,* they both would do so, and would abide by its decision. Since it is a civil contract, it holds civil consequences, and often my office pursued recalcitrant spouses and tried to adjudicate, threatening a civil case. That seemed to work, and even just getting a letter from our office was sometimes enough to pressure a spouse into appearing before the *bet din*. People respond to stationery that says 'National *Bet Din.*' "

But many will not sign a prenuptial agreement, and so the other alternative, according to Leifman, is *hafka'at kiddushin*, an annulment. "The actual practice comes from the Talmud. They reasoned this way: People who marry do so with the consent and authority of the court. Since the court granted it, the court can withdraw it. We prefer, of course, a clean break, a *get*. We try very, very hard to convince the man to cooperate. We don't annul a marriage lightly. Marriage is not simply a civil agreement—it involves two people, the tradition, and God. If, after months of trying, we can't convince the husband to relent, we gather a special court together and listen to the woman, and if it's clear that we have tried for months to get the *get,* then we grant a *hafka'at kiddushin*."

"There are cases where a man will try to blackmail his wife before giving her the *get,*" says Leifman. "And, while we try hard to convince the husband to cooperate, we will not allow a woman to be blackmailed. Again, the *halacha* is concerned with the well-being of both the man and the woman."

While most of the divorce cases with which he came in contact were tragic, or at least sad, Leifman does have amusing stories. "My files are fascinating! Once, a man came to me and said 'I want to give my ex-wife a *get.*' I spoke with the ex-wife, and yes, she was willing to accept a *get* since they had already been divorced in civil court. I was curious. 'Why the hurry to give her a *get?* She's not planning to remarry.' It turned out that he was about to remarry a Catholic woman. Being a Catholic, she wanted to be married in church, but when he met with the priest, the priest asked, 'Were you ever married before?' 'I was,' the man told him, 'but we're divorced now.' The priest then asked him if he had given his ex-wife a *get.* When the man admitted that he hadn't, the priest said, 'You have responsibilities to your Jewish wife still. Go fulfill them, and then come back.' So he went at once to get the *get.*"

"Most of the cases are tragic, but we have had tremendous successes," says Leifman. "Now, if we can't succeed through fear and trembling, we will do the annulment."

Notes

1. Babylonian Talmud (B.T.) tractate Yevamot 8:3.
2. B.T. Kiddushin 66b.
3. B.T. Kiddushin 67a, Rashi; Maimonides Yad Hachazakah, Issurei Bi'ah 15:3.
4. B.T. Gittin 33a.
5. S. Eidelberg, "Teshuvot Rabbenu Gershom Meor Hagolah," pp. 19–21.
6. Dr. Emanuel Rackman, "Jewish Values in Bioethics," in *Jewish Values in Bioethics,* edited by Rabbi Levi Meier (New York: Human Sciences Press, 1986), pp. 150–159.
7. Ibid., p. 153.
8. Iggerot Moshe, *Even Ha'ezer,* 1961.
9. Emanuel Rackman, *One Man's Judaism,* 1970, p. 242.
10. Ibid. p. 222, 223.
11. G.E.T. is located in Brooklyn, N.Y.; telephone (718) 871-3407. Other such organizations include Agunah, Inc., which does not deal with individual cases, but attempts to arouse public opinion to force the hand of the Orthodox rabbinate to find a halachic solution; Kayama, an outreach group that educates the unaware as to the need for a *get;* and the Israel Women's Network, in concert with an organization called Mitzvah, which attempts to confront the Israeli rabbinic establishment on several legal issues involving women, focusing mainly on the inequities in the Jewish divorce laws.

20

The Struggle of the *Agunot*

Francine Klagsbrun

This is the Year of the *Agunah*. An *agunah* (literally, a chained woman) is a woman trapped in an unwanted marriage because she cannot obtain a *get,* or Jewish divorce, from her husband. Why? In earlier days, the main source of the problem was men who deserted their wives or men lost in wars but not definitively known to be dead. Recently, the cause has become more sinister. A man may withhold a *get* in order to extort great sums of money. (In one case I know of, middle-aged parents used up their own savings to help pay their daughter's estranged husband $50,000 for his *get.*) He may use the *get* as a weapon to gain custody of his children. (In another case, a woman in an abusive marriage, fearing for her children's safety, has remained an *agunah* for years rather than give in to her husband's custody demands.) Or he may simply want to punish his wife, to exact revenge, to make her beg.

How is a man able to do these things? In Jewish law, the power to dissolve a marriage lies in the hands of the husband, who must grant his wife a *get* of his own will. Although a wife must consent to a divorce, she has no right to issue a *get.* Nor does a civil divorce satisfy Jewish law. Without a *get,* a woman may not remarry; if she does, the union is considered adulterous and children born of it are seen as *mamzerim,* bastards, forbidden to marry other Jews. Children of a man who remarries without a *get,* however, are legitimate.

Reform Judaism has ignored these laws and not required a *get* at all. Conservative Judaism has worked around them by establishing a central *beit din,* a rabbinic court, with the power to annul a marriage when a husband is recalcitrant. But for the Orthodox, there has been no ignoring and no getting around. The problem of the *get* has created almost a thousand *agunot* in the United States and an estimated 16,000 in Israel, where religious law alone regulates marriage and divorce.

For years now activist Orthodox women have organized and struggled to remedy the abuses of Jewish divorce law, and I'm ashamed to say they have organized and struggled alone. Many of us outside Orthodoxy — and even those of us deeply dedicated to feminist goals — have nodded our heads sympathetically, occasionally dipped into our purses to help out, but essentially stayed uninvolved. We saw this as their problem; we had plenty of our own.

We were wrong. The more I read and hear about the *agunah* situation, the more I am convinced that this is not "their" problem, it is ours; not an Orthodox issue, an all-denominational one; not a women's matter, a community one. For the problem of the *get* can affect anyone, from the Conservative woman who marries an Orthodox man to the parent whose daughter weds an Israeli. More important, when Jewish women suffer, the entire community needs to heed their pain.

Within the last year, Orthodox women's groups, working with Jewish women's organizations of varying religious viewpoints and from countries around the world, have created the International Coalition for *Agunah* Rights (ICAR), and they have proclaimed this year — through 1994 — the Year of the *Agunah*. They are calling on all of us to pay attention to the tragedy of the *agunah,* and help.

What can we do?

We can learn to understand the issues. A major issue has been the reluctance of rabbinic authorities in the United States or Israel to enact legislation that could alleviate the situation for women. The excuse they use is that because a divorce must be granted freely, they may not create rules that might smack of coercion. (Never mind that in the twelfth century Maimonides ruled that a recalcitrant husband may be flogged until he says "I am willing." Today's rabbis have taken the narrowest approach to interpreting the law.)

But the continued pressures of *agunah* supporters have begun to make inroads. In Israel, the chief rabbis have said that a committee of women's representatives and rabbis who deal with divorce cases will discuss ways to help *agunot*. And at their last convention, the Rabbinical Council of America, the central body of Orthodox rabbis, accepted a resolution requiring couples to sign a prenuptial agreement designed to forestall *get* blackmail in the event of divorce. The council had adopted a similar resolution in the past and then withdrawn it as too coercive. So the pressure needs to be kept up, with backing from the whole community, to make this resolution stick—word-of-mouth pressure, financial support for *agunah* activists pressure, and as much press and publicity pressure as possible.

We can put the *agunah* and related problems on our personal and communal agendas. For example, individuals, foundations, and agencies that fund Orthodox *yeshivot* should insist that these institutions train their rabbis in contemporary (not only talmudic) marriage and family matters. As things stand now, rabbinic law courts, composed of three rabbis, are the only recourse many women have when a husband withholds a *get*. They are also the chief arbitrators of property and custody settlements between disputing partners. Yet few of these rabbis have any training in dealing with marital problems, and fewer still are inclined to stand up for a woman against her husband. In fact, under the present system, litigants themselves pay the *beit din* fees, and because husbands usually have more money than their wives, they also have undue influence on the judges. The institutions that train rabbis should also be held responsible for undoing such inequalities and standardizing their courts so that all follow the same—ethical—procedures.

Finally, we can urge rabbinic leaders of all denominations to address not only the problem of the *agunah,* but the very basic anti-women, anti-family Jewish divorce laws. Surely with serious thought and determined purpose, our rabbis can find a halachic means to revamp those laws and establish that in Judaism, marriage is a true partnership between wife and husband.

Dreaming? Maybe. But this is the Year of the *Agunah,* a time to set things right.

Appendix
Sources for Help

No guarantee is made of the accuracy of these addresses and phone numbers as these sources may become outdated. Always remember that Orthodox Jews will not answer the phone on the Sabbath from sunset Friday to sunset Saturday and on major Jewish holidays. Please be considerate of people's privacy and call only during business hours. Contact your local rabbi or rabbinical board for more information.

Organizations

Agunah, Inc.
Contacts: Susan Aranoff, Rivka Haut, and Susan Alter
463 East 19th Street
Brooklyn, NY 11226
(718) 859-4760

American-Israeli Civil Liberties Union
New York City
   Contact your local American Civil Liberties Union or law school library.

American Jewish Congress
New England Region
Contact: Sheila Decter
126 High Street
Boston, MA 02110
(617) 457–8888

Amit
817 Broadway
New York, NY 10003
(212) 477–4720

Coalition of Jewish Women for the GET
7 Irving Place
Dollard des Ormeaux
Quebec H9A 1Y4 Canada
(514) 342–5931

Emunah Women of America
370 7th Avenue
New York, NY 10003
(212) 947–5454

G.E.T., Getting Equitable Treatment, Inc.
Contact: Ruth Englard
Founder, Gloria Greenman
President, Stanley Goodman
POB 300 131
1012 Avenue I
Brooklyn, NY 11230–0003
(718) 435–1310

Hadassah
50 West 58th Street
New York, NY 10019
(212) 355–7900

International Coalition for Agunah Rights (ICAR)
Contact: Dr. Deborah Eiferman (She might be helpful with other names of
other organizations that are sensitive to the *get* issue as well as other
contact people.)
240 East 27th Street
New York, NY 10021
(718) 435–1310

Israel Women's Network
Contact: Alice Shalvi, Founder
c/o New Israel Fund
1330 Center Street
Newton Center, MA 02159
or
Israel Women's Network
7 Gihon Street
Jerusalem, Israel 93547
02–713–033

The IWN has helped address the needs of some 1,000 Israeli women who are unable to obtain a divorce. In 1992, lecturers supported by IWN also conducted workshops about rape and sexual harassment on Israeli army bases around the country.

Jewish Marriage Council
Contact: Jeffrey Blumenfeld
23 Ravenshurst Avenue
London, England
081 203–6311

Na'Amat
15 East 26th Street
New York, NY 10021
(212) 779–3932

Organization to Help Agunot and Those Denied Divorce
POB 3095
Tel Aviv, Israel 61316
03–391–164

For *national* Orthodox, Conservative, and Reconstructionist organizations, check the latest issue of the *American Jewish Yearbook*. The back of the book contains the most up-to-date addresses and phone numbers of these groups. In addition, a local Orthodox rabbi, council of rabbis, or synagogue association will usually direct you to the right person.

Individuals

Rabbi Dr. Moshe Chigier
Hotel Ramat Tamir
Box 23081
Jerusalem, Israel 91230
 Dr. Chigier is an expert on the Israeli *agunah* and Israeli divorce law.

Irwin Haut, Esq.
Morris, Duffy, Alonso, and Marulli
170 Broadway, Suite 700
New York, NY 10038

Marvin E. Jacobs, Esq.
Weil, Gotshal, & Manges
767 Fifth Avenue
New York, New York 10153
(212) 310–8473
Fax (212) 310–8007
 Mr. Jacobs is also a rabbi and an adjunct professor of law at New York
Law School.

Dr. Jack Nusan Porter
The Spencer Institute
8 Burnside Road
Newton, MA 02161
(617) 965–8388
 Readers interested in the *agunah* issue may write or call Dr. Porter at the
above address.

Rabbi Shlomo Porter
Baltimore, MD
(410) 764–6083
 Rabbi Porter (my brother, by the way) has connections to others if he
cannot mediate the problem himself.

John T. Syrtash, Esq.
4100 Yonge Street
Suite 330
Toronto, Canada
(416) 221–4100
 Mr. Syrtash was instrumental in getting the Canadian GET Law passed.

Rabbi Michel Twerski
Temple Beth Jehudah
2700 N. 54th Street
Milwaukee, WI 53210

Chaim Dovid Zwiebel
Director of Government Affairs
 and General Counsel
Agudath Israel of America
84 William Street
New York, NY 10038
(212) 797-9000

Rabbinical Courts

Local rabbinical courts often adjudicate cases. Many chasidic groups have their own rabbinic court (e.g., Lubavitch and Satmar). There are such courts (called a *beit din*) in every major city. Seek out the local Orthodox rabbi or contact the local Orthodox rabbinical court. For example, Rabbi Leib Landesman is the *rosh beit din* of the Kollel Horabonim Beit Din in Monsey, New York, just north of New York City, and Rabbi Herschel Kurzrock is head of the *beth din* of Chelsea in New York City.

Other *Battei Din* include:

Beth Din of Long Island
132 Southern Parkway
Plainview, NY 11803
(516) 938-5766

Beth Din of Agudath Harabonim of America
235 East Broadway
New York, NY 10002
(212) 964-6337

Beth Din of America (R.C.A.)
305 Seventh Avenue, 12th Floor Avenue
New York, NY 10001
(212) 807-7889

Beth Din of Beth Joseph
1427 49th Street

Brooklyn, NY 11219
(718) 436-5146

Beth Din of Elizabeth
c/o Jewish Educational Center
330 Elmora Avenue
Elizabeth, NJ 07208
(908) 355-4704

Beth Din of Rabbinical Alliance
3 West 16th Street
New York, NY 10011
(212) 242-6420

Beth Din of Vaad Harabonim of Flatbush
1575 Coney Island Avenue
Brooklyn, NY 11230
(718) 951-6161

Beth Din of Vaad Harabonim of Queens
90-45 Myrtle Avenue
Glendale, NY 11385
(718) 847-9206

Rabbinical Court of Kollel Horabonim
P.O. Box 144
Spring Valley, NY 10977
(914) 352-4714

Glossary

Agunah (pl., agunot) Lit. "a chained woman." The much rarer male *agunah* is called an *agun*. *Igun* is a word that denotes the state of being an *agun* (or *agunah*). Described as a woman who cannot remarry because her husband has disappeared due to accident, war, or abduction or is senile, because there is no proof of his death, or because he has refused to grant her a *get*.

Amatla A reasonable explanation for a claim.

Asmakhta A vague contract; unspecified contract. Contracts must be specific in Jewish law in order to be valid. Vague understandings, such as indeterminate sums of money, are usually not binding in Jewish law.

Asur Forbidden by Jewish Law.

Bet din (pl., battei din) A court of Jewish law either in America or Israel; sometimes called a rabbinic court. They vary tremendously in experience, efficiency, and sensitivity. Israeli religious courts have the power and backing of the state; American religious courts rely more on persuasion and community support.

Chuppah Wedding canopy; also a metaphor for marital union.

Dayan A Jewish judge.

Dinei Mishpacha Family law.

Eirusin A marital status, conferring on the parties all the commitments and obligations of marriage with the exception of the right of cohabitation.

241

Gedolim   Council of Rabbis; lit. "the great ones."

Get (pl., gittin)   A divorce. Also, divorce proceedings.

G.E.T.   Get Equal Treatment, a Brooklyn, New York, organization established in 1980 to help *agunot*. There are a growing number of similar groups throughout the world.

Gittin   Divorces; a book in the Talmud dealing with divorce.

Halacha   Orthodox Jewish law based on masoretic texts.

Halitzah   Lit. "removal of the shoe." An ancient ceremony that releases a childless widow from the obligation to marry the brother of her deceased husband.

Herem   Excommunication, as in the "herem of Rabbeinu Gershom." Applied against any man who divorces his wife against her will, or who enters into a bigamous marriage or who breaks other serious Jewish laws that endanger the Jewish community, such as the case of Baruch Spinoza.

Ketubah (pl., ketubbot)   The marriage contract presented to the bride by the groom in which the husband's obligations are spelled out. It is a valid contract in secular law too, with damages paid if the contract is broken or if fraud or misrepresentation is present.

Kiddushin   Lit. "consecration." Betrothal. The legal act of marriage that may be carried out in one of three ways: by the groom's presentation of an object of value to the bride, by formal written agreement, or by cohabitation.

Kinyan   A formal act of acquisition.

Knas   A fine; damages.

Kohen (pl., kohanim or cohanim)   Of priestly stock; a descendant of Aaron, brother of Moses. Certain restrictions apply to the marriage, divorce, and remarriage of Kohanim that do not apply to others, either Israelites or Levites.

Mamzer (fem., mamzeret; pl., mamzerim)   The act or process of becoming a *mamzer,* is *mamzerut.* A bastard; an offspring of an adulterous union. The term has a very specific meaning; it is not simply a child born from extramarital sex or out of wedlock. It refers to the offspring of an adulterous union between an *agunah* and another man, between a *married* woman and a single or married man, or incest. There is a great stigma attached to such an offspring. However, an illegitimate child—for example, the offspring of a single woman and a single man—is not a *mamzer* and does not carry the same stigma as in Western societies. In other words, being born out of wedlock is not by itself a stigma, but a child by a *married* woman is stigmatized heavily. In general, the onus on the woman is much greater than on the man in terms of sexual infidelity and cognate affairs.

Ma'us alay Lit. "he is repulsive to me." A women's claim that her husband is repulsive to her, which, according to some authorities, is sufficient cause for her to be granted a divorce. Ugliness, impotence, criminality, and spousal abuse could be grounds for *ma'us alay*.

Mikveh Ritual bath.

Mishnah The definitive collection of Jewish law, prepared and edited by Rabbi Yehudah HaNasi, in approximately 220 C.E. Rabbis of the mishnaic period are known as *Tannaim*.

Mitzvah A righteous deed.

Moredet A rebellious wife is considered to be a *moredet* if she knowingly violates Torah law or conventional morality or if she refuses to engage in sexual relations with her husband. She may have, according to *ma'us alay,* strong reasons for such refusal. The label *moredet* is often used in Israeli courts to deny or delay a divorce to a woman.

Nisuin The final status of a marriage; the granting of cohabitation rights through the use of *chuppah* (a wedding canopy) or *yichud* (being alone together for the purpose of marriage). Also called "conditional marriage"; a marriage unconsummated.

Nizrach Helpless.

Pilpul Religious argument; contentious and complex intellectual debate.

Pitzuim Damages, as in a voided contract.

Psakim (sing., *psak*) Rabbinical decisions; *poskim* are respected scholars who interpret the law and make decisions.

Rabbanim Rabbis.

Responsa Oral decisions, which are later written down, of a rabbinical response to a person's question in interpreting or understanding the law.

Seruv Contempt citation served by religious court.

Shul A synagogue.

Shtar A formal written document.

Shtar Piturin A document that declares the woman free to remarry.

Shulhan Arukh Lit. "prepared table." The authoritative code of Jewish law, compiled in the sixteenth century by Rabbi Joseph Caro.

Taharah Ritual of preparing the body of a dead person.

Takkanah (pl., *takkanot*) An authoritative legislative decree, enacted by duly constituted rabbinic authorities. The last great *takkanah,* by Rabbeinu Gershom in the year 1000 C.E., outlawed bigamy among Jews, especially among Ashkenazic Jews. A *takkanah* may be needed to resolve the *agunah* problem.

Talmud The oral, as opposed to the written, law, transmitted at Mount Sinai and onward. The Talmud consists of the Mishnah and the Gemara.

The Gemara was completed at about 500 C.E. The rabbis of the Gemara, who flourished between 220 C.E. and 500 C.E., are called *Amoraim*.

Tenayim   A prenuptial agreement generally signed immediately preceding the marriage ceremony. There is a need to add an addendum to this agreement to protect the *agunah*.

T'nai   A conditional clause in a *ketubah*.

To'en (pl., *to'anim*)   An advocate for the wife in the all-male religious courts; someone who counsels or acts as a consultant to the female litigant in the trial system.

Zabla   A type of *beit din* (religious court) in which each litigant selects one *dayan* (judge) and those two *dayanim* choose a third. It is an acronym for the Hebrew phrase *zeh borer lo echad*. It is used on an ad hoc basis only.

For Further Reading

As in any topic that goes back 1,000 years or more in Jewish history, there are layers and layers of sources, depending on one's knowledge of Hebrew and Judaica. There are bibliographies in Hebrew on the *agunah* that should be consulted. See any major research library like Brandeis, Yeshiva, Harvard, and the University of California–Berkeley, or Jewish libraries and archives such as the Magnes Museum in San Francisco, the American Jewish Archives in Cincinnati, Ohio, and the American Jewish Historical Society on the campus of Brandeis University in Waltham, Massachusetts, outside Boston.

Agnon, Shmuel Yosef. *Twenty-One Stories*. Ed. Nahum N. Glatzer. New York: Schocken Books, 1970.
　　See his short story "Agunot."
Amram, David Werner. *The Jewish Law of Divorce in the Bible and Talmud*. 2d. ed. New York: Sepher-Hermon, 1968.
　　Amram wrote in the 1890s and early 1900s, so he is a pioneer in this field.
Berkovits, Eliezer. *T'nai be'Nisuin U-ve'get* (Conditional Clause in Marriage and Divorce Agreements) (in Hebrew). Jerusalem: Mossad Harav Kook, 1968.

A classic work. Berkovits is a pioneer in many fields of modern
Orthodox theology. He was a professor at the Chicago Theological
Seminary before moving to Jerusalem.

Bleich, J. David. "Modern-Day Agunot: A Proposed Remedy." *Jewish Law
Annual* (1981): 167–187.

—— "A Suggested Ante-Nuptial Agreement: A Proposal in the Wake of
Avitzur." Journal of Halachah and Contemporary Society 7 (Spring
1984): 25–41.

These are pioneering articles in modern Orthodox circles.

Breitowitz, Irving (Yitzhok). *Between Civil and Religious Law: The
Plight of the Agunah in American Society*. (Westport, CT: Greenwood
Press, 1993).

A crucial book in the literature, richly detailed and researched, it is a
great scholarly achievement and an important contribution to legal
studies, both religious and secular.

Chigier, Moshe. *Husband and Wife in Israeli Law*. Jerusalem: Harry
Fischel Institute for Research in Talmud & Jurisprudence, 1985.

A classic work that contains primary sources on Israeli courts and
commentaries, *poskim* of *shakh (Shulkhan Aruch)*, law reports, and
court cases. Chigier, ordained by Rav Kook of Israel, is a qualified
rabbi and barrister who served for many years as legal advisor to the
Rabbinical Courts in Israel.

Encyclopaedia Judaica. Jerusalem: Keter, 1972.

Has excellent sections on Jewish marriage, divorce, and related problems.

Epstein, Louis. *Hatza'ah L'maan Takanat Agunot* (A Suggestion to Avoid
Agunot) (in Hebrew). New York, 1930.

——. *The Jewish Marriage Contract*. New York: Jewish Theological Seminary, 1927; Arno Press, 1973.

——. *Li-she'elath ha-agunah* (The Agunah Question). New York, 1940.

——. *Marriage Laws in the Bible and the Talmud*. Cambridge, MA:
Harvard University Press, 1924; Oxford University Press, 1944.

Epstein was an important and courageous pioneer in Conservative
Jewish circles. He was a Boston rabbi.

Falk, Ze'ev. *Divorce Action by the Wife in the Middle Ages*. Jerusalem:
Hebrew University Press, 1973.

—— .*Jewish Matrimonial Law in the Middle Ages*. London: Oxford University Press, 1966.

Falk is an Orthodox Jew and a professor at the Hebrew University
in Jerusalem.

Feldblum, Meyer S. *Talmudic Law and Literature*. New York: Yeshiva
University Press, 1969.

A noted halachic authority, Feldblum often raised the *agunah* question at meetings of the RCA, Rabbinical Council of America in the late 1970s.

Geffen, Rela M., ed. *Celebration and Renewal: Rites of Passage in Judaism.* Philadelphia: Jewish Publication Society, 1993.
> See especially the essay by Irwin Haut, pp. 151–166 (reprinted in this sourcebook). Geffen is a well-known sociologist of Jewry from Gratz College in Philadelphia.

Grade, Chaim. *The Agunah.* New York: Menorah Publishing Company and Twayne Publishers, 1974.
> This famous Yiddish writer handles the *agunah* issue from the perspective of a wife whose husband is missing, not recalcitrant. His is the world of Vilna between the two World Wars. Merl Tswilling is a woman alone for fifteen years because her husband failed to return from World War I. The rabbis of Vilna refuse to give her permission to remarry. The description Grade provides of pre-Holocaust Vilna gives us an understanding of religious conflicts within the Jewish community even today. A very interesting tale. Grade had intimate knowledge of Eastern European Jewry and their culture.

Greenberg, Blu. *On Women and Judaism: A View from Tradition.* Philadelphia: Jewish Publication Society, 1981.
> An important pioneer in adapting *halacha* to modern "feminist" ideas, this is an important source for reconciling feminism with Jewish observance. See her chapter "Jewish Attitudes Toward Divorce," pp. 125–145.

Haut, Irwin H., *Divorce in Jewish Law and Life.* New York: Sepher-Hermon, 1983.
> Another pioneer in this field, Haut is a well-known New York lawyer and an ordained rabbi. This book has a short but good bibliography on legal articles on the enforcement of Jewish divorce in secular courts and in Israel, on the *ketubah*, and the *agunah*. He is the husband of Rivkah Haut, a founder of Agunah, Inc.

Index of Conservative Responsa. 1992. See pp. 38–41 on the *agunah* and annulment.

Jewish Law: Bibliography of Sources and Scholarship. 1989.
> This work contains a very useful and complete bibliography (in English) on family law and cognate issues. What is so useful is that it gives the place where the books were reviewed as well as published. It is highly recommended. See especially pp. 102–129.

Kahan, Isak Farkas. *Sefer ha-agunot.* Jerusalem, 1954–1955.

Kahana, K. *The Theory of Marriage in Jewish Law.* Leiden: Brill, 1966.

Kasher, M. "In the Matter of T'nai B'Nisuin" (in Hebrew). *Noam* 12:338.

Krich, Rochelle Majer. *Till Death Do Us Part*. New York: Avon Books, 1992.
    The first mass-market paperback mystery novel to deal with the *agunah* in a sensitive and deeply knowledgeable way, it will become a classic literary source on the subject in the future. Krich is an Orthodox Jewish woman from Los Angeles. Other Orthodox Jewish heroines in literature include those in books by Faye Kellerman (*The Ritual Bath*, for example, another murder mystery), Rebecca Goldstein, and Dvorah Baron.

Lamm, Norman. "Recent Additions to the Ketubah: A Halakhic Critique." *Tradition* 2:1 (Fall 1959): 93–119.
    Pioneering work by the president of Yeshiva University.

Lehman, Marcus. *Ithamar*. New York, 1981.
    Reprint of early literary work (a novel) on the *agunah*. Lehman (1831–1890) was a prolific writer of historical romances and juvenile literature. Originally written in German, his books have been translated into English and distributed by the Lubavicher Hasidim. See, for example, *Five Novelettes* ("Busenai," "Meor Hagolah," "Unpaid Ransom," "The Adopted Princess," and "Out of the Depths"). Translated by Dr. Nissan Mindel (Brooklyn, NY: Merkos Linyonei Chinuch, 1964). "*Meor Hagolah*" deals with the life of Rabbenu Gershom, the renowned talmudist and physician who won the admiration and confidence of the rulers of Constantinople.

Meiselman, Moshe. *Jewish Woman in Jewish Law*. New York: KTAV and Yeshiva University Press, 1978.
    An important book with a useful bibliography that has excellent sources in biblical commentaries, Targum, midrashim, Talmud and commentaries, Codes and commentaries, responsa, halachic articles, and a general English bibliography on the Jewish woman in Jewish law. Meiselman is widely read in Orthodox circles.

Porter, Jack Nusan. "Sexuality and Judaism." *The Reconstructionist* 44:10 (February, 1979).

——. *The Sociology of American Jews: A Critical Anthology*. 2d. rev. ed. Washington: University Press of America, 1980.

——. *The Sociology of Jewry: A Curriculum Guide*. Washington: American Sociological Association, 1993.

Rabinowitz, Jacob J. *Jewish Law: Its Influence on the Development of Legal Institutions*. New York: Bloch Publishing, 1956.

Riskin, Shlomo. *Women and Jewish Divorce: The Rebellious Wife, the Agunah, and the Rights of Women to Initiate Divorce in Jewish Law, a Halakhic Solution*. Hoboken, NJ: KTAV, 1989.

An important book with a useful bibliography by the Chief Rabbi of Efrat, Israel, and founding Orthodox rabbi of the Lincoln Square Synagogue of Manhattan. His conclusions are interesting and his book contains important leads on various issues regarding the rights of women to initiate divorce in Jewish law.

Schereschewsky, Benzion. *Dinei Mishpacha (Family Law)*. 2d. ed. (in Hebrew). Jerusalem: Rubin Mass, 1967, 1974.

An excellent source.

Schwarz, Sidney H. "Conservative Judaism and the Agunah." *Conservative Judaism* 36:1 (1982): 37–44. Reprinted in this sourcebook.

Singer, Isaac Bashevis. *The Collected Stories of Isaac Bashevis Singer*. New York: Farrar, Straus, and Giroux, 1982.

See especially the story "Taibele and Her Demon," pp. 131–139. The "demon" is her lover in the guise of a human body, a friend from the *shtetl*. Her husband deserted her and later died in an epidemic. At least that's what the "demon" tells Taibele. She's an *agunah* but a sexually fulfilled one. Interesting tale. Recently adapted into a play and shown in Newton, Massachusetts.

Tykocinski, Chaim. *Takanot Hagaonim* (The Gaonic Decrees) (in Hebrew) Jerusalem: Yeshiva University Press, 1959.

Tykocinski lived from 1862 to 1942. This book deals with the laws of the *geonim*.

Weiss-Rosmarin, Trude. "The Agony of the Agunah." *Conservative Judaism* 20:1 (1965).

Pioneering essay that brought attention to the *agunot's* plight written by an influential and important early Jewish feminist and former editor of *The Jewish Spectator*.

Contributors

Shmuel Yosef (Shai) Agnon (1888–1970) shared the Nobel Prize for Literature in 1966 with Nelly Sachs. He was a leading figure of twentieth-century Hebrew literature. His works include *The Bridal Canopy* (1922, 1937), *A Guest for the Night* (1968), *Temol Shilsholm* (1947), and the posthumously published *Shira* (1971), which is considered by many to be his most important work.

Susan Alter is a member of the New York City Council and a director of Agunah, Inc., of New York.

Susan Aranoff is a member of the executive committee of the UJA/Federation Women's Campaign and a director of Agunah, Inc., of New York.

Labish Becker is director of Torah Projects for Agudath Israel of America in New York City.

Moshe Chigier is a scholar and expert on Israeli jurisprudence living in Jerusalem, where he was ordained rabbi by Chief Rabbi Kook and other *geonim*. He holds M.A., M. Jur., and D. Litt. degrees.

Steven Feldman is a former editor of *Genesis 2* in Boston.

Glenn Frankel is a reporter for the *Washington Post*.

Blu Greenberg is the well-known Orthodox Jewish feminist writer and the author of *On Women and Judaism: A View from Tradition* and *How to Run a Traditional Jewish Household*.

Netty C. Gross is a freelance writer and journalist from Jerusalem.

Irwin Haut is a lawyer and rabbi living in New York and the author of *Divorce in Jewish Law and Life*.

Rivka Haut is a coeditor of the anthology *Daughters of the King: Women and the Synagogue* and a director of Agunah, Inc., of New York.

Peter Hellman is a freelance writer living in New York.

Marvin Jacob, a New York attorney, is a partner in the firm of Weil, Gotshal & Manges, Esqs., an adjunct professor of law at New York Law School, and chairman of the Commission on Law and Legislation of the Orthodox Union.

Francine Klagsbrun, a writer and a columnist for *Moment* magazine, has written or edited seventeen books for both adults and young people, including *Free to Be . . . You and Me* and *Voices of Wisdom: Jewish Ideals and Ethics for Everyday Living*.

Rochelle Majer Krich is a Los Angeles–based mystery writer and the author of *Till Death Do Us Part* and *Fair Game*.

Lucette Lagnado is editor of the *Forward* of New York.

Leib Landesman is the *rosh beit din* of the Kollel Horabonim Beit Din in Monsey, New York.

Moshe Meiselman is a Jewish scholar and the author of *Jewish Woman in Jewish Law*.

Honey Rackman is a writer for *Moment* magazine.

Shlomo Riskin is the chief rabbi of Efrat, Israel, founding rabbi of the Lincoln Square Synagogue in Manhattan, and the author of *Women and Jewish Divorce*.

Sidney H. Schwarz was rabbi of Congregation Beth Israel in Media, Pennsylvania.

Sharon Shenhav is director of legal services, Na'amat, in Jerusalem.

Isaac Bashevis Singer (1904–1991) won the Nobel Prize for Literature in 1978. His works include *The Family Moskat* (1950), *The Manor* (1967), *Enemies: A Love Story* (1972), and *The Collected Stories of Isaac Bashevis Singer* (1982).

Chaim Dovid Zwiebel is the general counsel and director of governmental affairs of Agudath Israel of America.

Acknowledgments

I gratefully acknowledge with thanks the following publishers and writers for allowing me to reprint their essays and articles:

"Of Human Bondage" by Lucette Lagnado, *The Village Voice* (July 14, 1992). Copyright © 1992 *The Village Voice*. Reprinted by permission of the author and *The Village Voice*.

"Playing Hard to *Get*" by Peter Hellman, *New York* magazine (January 25, 1993). Copyright © 1993 *New York* magazine. Reprinted by permission of the author.

"The Rabbinical Ties That Bind" by Glenn Frankel, *The Washington Post* (March 11, 1989). Copyright © 1989 The Washington Post. Reprinted with permission.

"The Agunah: An Ancient Problem in Modern Dress" by Sharon Shenhav, *Women's League Outlook* (Conservative Judaism) 64: 4 (Summer 1994): 18–19, 29. Copyright © 1994 *Women's League Outlook*. Reprinted by permission of *Women's League Outlook*.

"A Horror Story—Ours" by Netty C. Gross, *The Jerusalem Report* (June 17, 1993). Copyright © 1993 *The Jerusalem Report*. Reprinted by permission of *The Jerusalem Report*.

" 'The Altar Weeps': Divorce in Jewish Law" by Irwin H. Haut, in *Celebration and Renewal: Rites of Passage in Judaism*, ed. Rela M. Geffen, pp.

151–166, published by the Jewish Publication Society. Copyright © 1993 Jewish Publication Society. Used by permission of the publisher.

From *Jewish Woman in Jewish Law*, pp. 103–115, by Moshe Meiselman. Copyright © 1978 KTAV Publishing House. Used by permission of the publisher.

From *Husband and Wife in Israeli Law*, pp. 256–281, by Moshe Chigier. Copyright © 1985 Moshe Chigier. Published by the Harry Fischel Institute, Jerusalem. Reprinted by permission of the author.

"Taibele and Her Demon" from THE COLLECTED STORIES OF ISAAC BASHEVIS SINGER. Copyright © 1963, 1964, 1982 by Isaac Bashevis Singer. Reprinted by permission of Farrar, Straus & Giroux, Inc., and Jonathan Cape Ltd.

From TWENTY-ONE STORIES by S. Y. Agnon, edited by Nahum N. Glatzer. Copyright © 1970 by Schocken Books, Inc. Reprinted by permission of Schocken Books, published by Pantheon Books, Inc., a division of Random House, Inc.

From TILL DEATH DO US PART (pp. 1–12) by Rochelle Majer Krich. Copyright © 1992 by Rochelle Majer Krich. Reprinted by permission of Avon Books.

"Agunot: Is the System Working," by Susan Aranoff, Rivka Haut, and Susan Alter, and Leib Landesman. *The Jewish Homemaker* (October 1992). Copyright © 1992 The Committee for the Furtherance of Torah Observance. Reprinted by permission of *The Jewish Homemaker*.

"Tragedy Compounded: The *Agunah* Problem and New York's Controversial New '*Get* Law,' " by Chaim Dovid Zwiebel, *The Jewish Observer* (September 1993). Copyright © 1993 Agudath Israel of America. Reprinted with permission from *The Jewish Observer*, published by Agudath Israel of America, 84 William Street, New York, NY 10038.

"The *Agunah* Problem and the So-Called New York State *Get* Law: A Legal and Halachic Analysis," by Marvin E. Jacob, October 1994. Copyright © 1994 Marvin E. Jacob. Reprinted by permission of the author.

From *Women and Jewish Divorce*, pp. 134–142, by Shlomo Riskin. Copyright © 1989 KTAV Publishing House. Reprinted by permission of the publisher.

"Conservative Judaism and the *Agunah*," by Sidney H. Schwarz, *Conservative Judaism* 36:1 (Fall 1982):37–44. Copyright © 1982 The Rabbinical Assembly. Reprinted by permission of The Rabbinical Assembly.

"For the Love of Law," by Blu Greenberg, *Hadassah Magazine* (May 1993): 18–21. Copyright © 1993 *Hadassah Magazine*. Reprinted by permission of the publisher.

"Grappling with Divorce and Jewish Law," by Steven Feldman, *Genesis 2* (April 1984):15. Copyright © 1984. Reprinted by permission of the publisher.

"Getting a Get," by Honey Rackman, *Moment* (May 1988): 38–41, 58–59. Copyright © 1988 *Moment*. Reprinted by permission of the publisher.

"The Struggle of the Agunot," by Francine Klagsbrun, *Moment* (December 1993): 26–27. Copyright © 1993 *Moment*. Reprinted by permission of the publisher.

The Glossary is adapted from the one in *Divorce in Jewish Law and Life*, pp. 145–146, by Irwin H. Haut (New York: Sepher-Hermon Press, 1983). Used by permission of the publisher.

Index

About the Editor

Dr. Jack Nusan Porter is a native Milwaukeean who graduated from the University of Wisconsin–Milwaukee with degrees in sociology and Hebrew and later received his Ph.D. in sociology from Northwestern University. He was the founder and first editor of the *Journal of the History of Sociology*, a former research fellow at Harvard University, and former assistant professor of social science at Boston University. He is the author or editor of twenty-five books and monographs and over three hundred articles and reviews. His books include *The Sociology of American Jews, Confronting History and Holocaust, Jews and the Cults, The Sociology of Jewry: A Curriculum Guide*, and *Jewish Radicalism*. He lives in Newton Highlands, Massachusetts, with his wife, Miriam Almuly Porter, and their two teenagers, Gabe and Danielle.